# Mark's Gospel

Mark's 'biography' of Jesus is the earliest of the four Gospels and influenced them all. The distinctive feature of this biography is the quality of 'good news' which presupposes a world dominated by the forces of evil.

John Painter shows how the rhetorical and dramatic shaping of the book emphasise the conflict of good and evil at many levels: between Jesus and the Jewish authorities; Jesus and the Roman authorities; and the conflict of values within the disciples themselves. These matters of content are integral to this original approach to Mark's theodicy, while the stylistic issue raises the question of Mark's intended readership.

John Painter's succinct yet thorough treatment of Mark's Gospel opens up not only these rhetorical issues but the social context of the Gospel, which Painter argues to be that of the Pauline mission to the nations.

**John Painter** is foundation Professor of Theology at St Mark's National Theological Centre, Charles Sturt University. He has taught New Testament Studies in England, South Africa and Australia and is a member of *Studorium Novi Testamenti Societas*. His publications include *The Quest for the Messiah* (second edition 1993) and *Theology as Hermeneutics* (1987).

New Testament Readings
Edited by John Court
*University of Kent at Canterbury*

**JOHN'S GOSPEL**
*Mark W. G. Stibbe*

**EPHESIANS**
*Martin Kitchen*

**2 THESSALONIANS**
*Maarten J. J. Menken*

**MARK'S GOSPEL**
*John Painter*

*Forthcoming books in the series:*

**MATTHEW'S GOSPEL**
*David J. Graham*

**ACTS**
*Loveday Alexander*

**GALATIANS**
*Philip Esler*

**JAMES**
*Richard Bauckman*

**THE GOSPEL OF THOMAS**
*Richard Valantasis*

**READING THE NEW TESTAMENT**
*John Court*

# Mark's Gospel

## Worlds in conflict

John Painter

London and New York

First published 1997
by Routledge
11 New Fetter Lane, London EC4P 4EE

Simultaneously published in the USA and Canada
by Routledge
29 West 35th Street, New York, NY 10001



Typeset in Baskerville by
Florencetype Ltd, Stoodleigh, Devon
Printed and bound in Great Britain by
Mackays of Chatham PLC, Chatham, Kent



*British Library Cataloguing in Publication Data*
A catalogue record for this book is available from the British Library

*Library of Congress Cataloguing in Publication Data*
Painter, John
Mark's Gospel / John Painter.
p. cm. – (New Testament readings)
Includes bibliographical references and index
1. Bible. N.T. Mark – Criticism, interpretation, etc. I. Title.
II. Series.
BS2585.2.P26 1996
226.3′06–dc20

96–9727
CIP

ISBN 0–415–11364–4 (hbk)
ISBN 0–415–11365–2 (pbk)

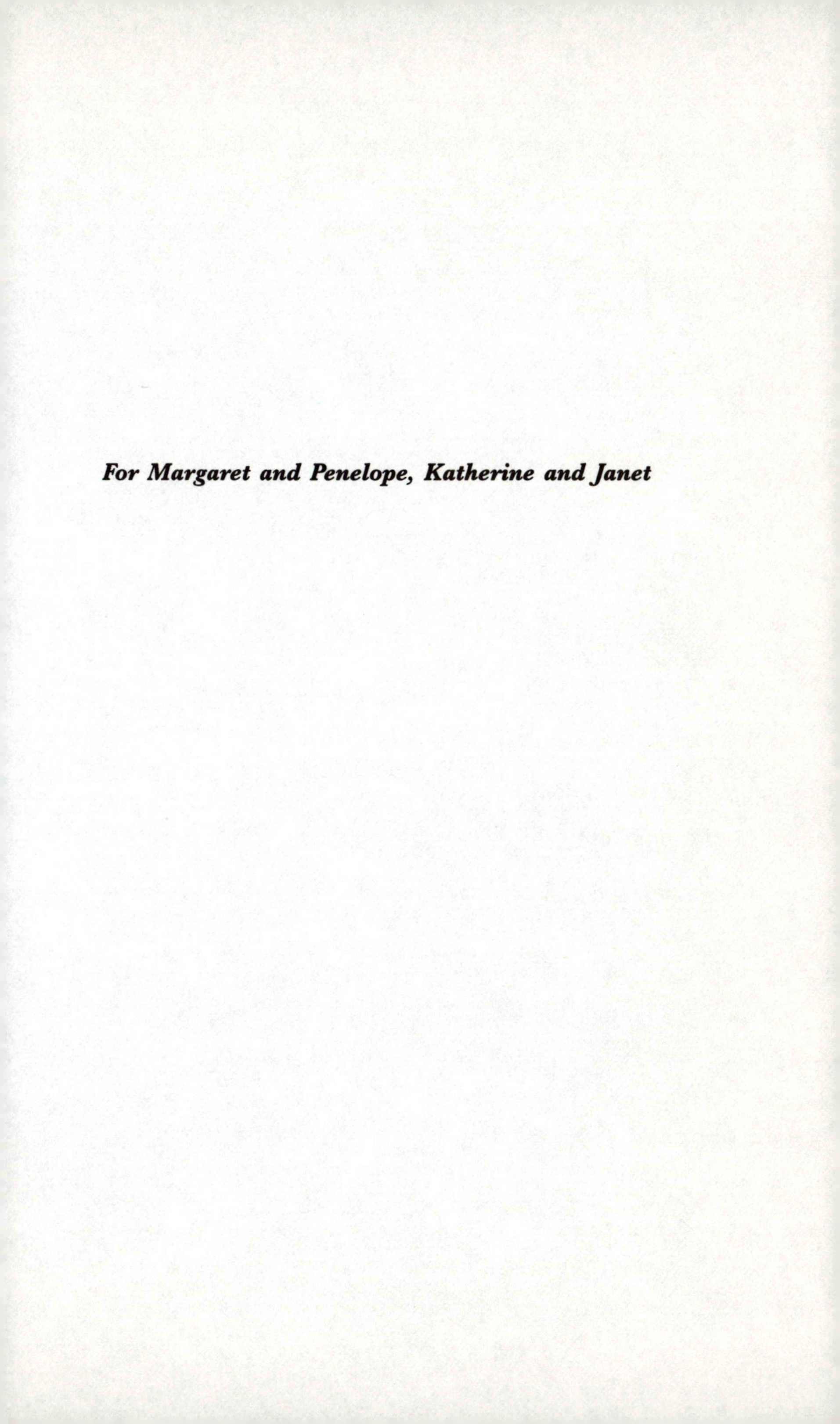

***For Margaret and Penelope, Katherine and Janet***

# Contents

# An Outline of Mark

In this analysis, upon which the commentary is based, changes in time, place and *dramatis personae* are given due weight in discerning the structure of the Gospel. Attention is also given to the arrangement of rhetorically shaped stories into collections which shape the plot of the story. At one point in the analysis, the structure determined by a change of place (5.1–20) interrupts the analysis of the structure based on a collection of rhetorically shaped stories (4.35—5.43). In this case the change of place indicates a significant change in the orientation of Jesus' mission which proves to be a foreshadowing of the mission to the regions beyond Galilee in 7.24—8.10.

While this commentary has been written to be read as a whole, this outline provides page references to each rhetorical unit of Mark, thus enabling the reader to find quickly the discussion of any passage. The outline is also a better guide to the structure of Mark and the relative importance of the units of tradition than the Chapter divisions of the Table of Contents which have been introduced to make this book conform to the pattern of the series in which it appears. **Note:** Those sections beginning with 'And ...' are signified by + left of the numbered section. Other sections are indicated by *.

# Acknowledgements

The manuscript for Mark was written in four months of long service leave at the beginning of 1996. Writing in what was, for me, such a short time was made possible by years of teaching the Gospels and work done on another book, on James the brother of Jesus in history and tradition, over the past couple of years. The first draft of Mark was written away from libraries, with only the Greek text of the New Testament as reference. Naturally I was drawing on all that I had read on Mark in order to teach the Gospels over the years. Consequently, I am grateful to the Universities that have given me the opportunity to teach and to the students who have interacted with the teaching. Sadly, none of my graduate students has worked on Mark, so that the stimulation has come from thinking through the way Mark is to be understood for undergraduate students. Only when the manuscript was complete did I turn to recent literature that I thought should be taken into account. When this was done I found that my manuscript was little changed. Of course this does not mean that I have not learned from many other studies of Mark. It means that I had already assimilated what was helpful to my approach. In keeping with the series there are no footnotes. Nevertheless, the bibliography makes clear that the work is built on a tradition of scholarship and readers who wish to test what they read in this volume will find reference there to works that broaden the perspective on Mark, and which provide support for both the views taken here and alternative views on various issues. I have enjoyed writing Mark and thank the editor, John Court, for asking me to take on this task. It is one I have wanted to do for some time, but without his invitation might never have got around to it. The editorial staff of Routledge, Richard Stoneman, Ruth Schafer and Shankari Sanmuganathan, have my grateful thanks for their superefficient and sympathetic dealing with all the needs of an author. Thanks also to my wife Gillian for sharing the task of proofreading.

John Painter
Minnesota, November 1996

# Abbreviations

| | |
|---|---|
| BCE | Before the Common Era |
| CE | Common Era |
| LXX | Septuagint |
| NT | New Testament |
| OT | Old Testament |
| *ABD* | *Anchor Bible Dictionary* |
| *JBL* | *Journal of Biblical Literature* |
| JSNTMS | Journal for the Study of the New Testament Monograph Series |
| *NovT* | *Novum Testamentum* |
| *NTS* | *New Testament Studies* |
| SBLDS | Society of Biblical Literature Dissertation Series |
| SNovT | Supplement series of *Novum Testamentum* |
| SNTSMS | Studiorum Novi Testamenti Societas Monograph Series |
| WBC | Word Biblical Commentary |
| *ZNW* | *Zeitschrift für die neutestamentaliche Wissenschaft und die Kunde der ältern Kirche* |

# Introduction

Sensitive readers, who want to hear more than their own ideas echoing back from the text, know that they need to attend to the signals within the text that can keep the reader on course. These signals are especially important for the reader of Mark, who is separated from the teller of the story and the subject of the story by almost two millennia of radical changes in the perception of reality and commitment to values. Reading Mark jolts us into the awareness of an understanding of the world that is in conflict with our own.

## MARK AMONGST THE GOSPELS

Each of the Gospels tells the story of Jesus in its own way. This is both an advantage and a problem. Four Gospels enrich the depth of our perception of Jesus but cause problems with conflicting presentations. Modern critical scholarship is more conscious of conflicts than was the early church but, from the second century, there have been attempts, such as Tatian's *Diatessaron*, to harmonise the Gospels. Although the four Gospels are read in the churches today, most readers tend to conflate them in their minds. Yet each Gospel has its own story to tell, its own contribution to make to our understanding of Jesus.

From the end of the second century the order of the Gospels was discussed. Clement of Alexandria said that the Gospels with the genealogies were earlier than those without. The view soon emerged that Mark summarised Matthew (thus Augustine in his *Harmony of the Gospels*). Only in the nineteenth century did the deficiencies of this view become apparent. Augustine had recognised that there was a literary relationship between the first three Gospels. He argued that Luke and Mark were both dependent on Matthew. At first he accepted the canonical order, but later came to see that if the composition of the three Gospels was to be explained on the basis of Matthew, Mark must also have used Luke.

From the late eighteenth century the first three Gospels (Matthew, Mark and Luke) have been known as the Synoptic Gospels because, when their accounts are laid side by side, they can be seen to tell the same story in more or less the same order and words. There are also differences and it is the combination of similarities and differences that constitutes the Synoptic problem.

In the nineteenth century comparative study of the Synoptics led to the recognition that, almost without exception, where the three Gospels cover the same material, either Matthew or Luke supports Mark. This observation led to the conclusion that Mark best preserves the common source used independently by each of the three evangelists. This gave way to the view that Mark was the common source and thus the first Gospel. It seemed to follow that it presented a relatively undeveloped and straightforward account of the ministry of Jesus, a view seemingly supported by the relatively simple language used by Mark and the unsophisticated literary style of the book.

Today it is generally conceded that Mark was the first of the Gospels and that it was used, in different ways, by Matthew and Luke. In doing so they modified the Markan material to suit their own purposes. Matthew used about 90 per cent of Mark and Luke about 50 per cent. Only about thirty verses of Mark do not appear in some form in either Matthew or Luke. Nevertheless, Mark has survived and continues to be read and valued because it presents a distinctive and powerful account of the mission and message of Jesus.

Mark used traditions, oral and written, in composing his Gospel. Some scholars think it possible to separate neatly tradition used by Mark from Markan interpretation and editorial additions. The aim of that enterprise, which is known as 'redaction criticism', is to show how Mark utilises tradition, bringing to light more clearly the precise interpretation of Mark. Over the years a number of criteria have been developed in the attempt to identify tradition and distinguish it from Markan interpretation.

First, there was the distinction between the individual narratives (*pericopae*) and the linking framework, leading to the conclusion that Mark was responsible for these frameworks. This position is undermined by the recognition that Mark made use of collections of stories and is further complicated because Mark has modified traditional material and might have constructed individual *pericopae.* Then there was the recognition of summary statements, which are generally taken to be Markan constructions. It is likely, however, that some summaries are traditional.

It is commonly thought that sandwich structures or intercalations are Markan redaction or arrangement of traditions. Even this criterion is problematical because such a wide range of material is covered under this category and some of the clearest examples of the category look suspiciously like pre-Markan connections. See 2.1–12; 3.1–6, 20–35; 5.21–43; 6.6–30; 11.12–25; 14.53–72; 15.6–32 (all biblical references are to Mark unless otherwise stated). The problem is that 2.1–12 and 3.1–6 can be understood as traditional *objection* stories rather than as 'a story within a story' and 3.20–35 depends on identifying 'those with him [Jesus]' in 3.20 as his family, although the family has not been mentioned to this point in the Gospel. It is more likely a reference to the disciples (see 3.13–19).

There is no doubt that 5.21–35 is a good example of intercalation, but the reasons for the connection suggest a pre-Markan arrangement, perhaps from the oral period. The woman had been afflicted for twelve years and the little girl raised from death by Jesus was twelve years old. Connection by catchwords is characteristic of oral tradition. Both stories are good examples of restored life.

That some of the intercalations are Markan arrangements is almost certain. Mark's story of the mission of the twelve presupposes a gap between the sending out and return of the twelve to allow time for their mission. Something (the account of the death of John) had to be put in that gap (see 6.7–30). Between the cursing and withering of the fig tree Mark had placed the cleansing of the temple, not only to fill a necessary gap but because the cleansing of the temple is the interpretative clue to the cursing and withering of the fig tree (11.12–26). But intercalation was not peculiar to Mark and some of these arrangements were probably traditional.

## EVIDENCE OF AUTHORSHIP

Like the other Gospels, Mark is anonymous. The title of the Gospel, though quite early, is an addition appearing in longer and shorter forms ('Gospel according to Mark' and 'According to Mark'). In a fragment preserved by Eusebius, the fourth-century bishop of Caesarea and church historian Papias, bishop of Hierapolis in the mid-second century, wrote:

> And the *Elder* used to say this, 'Mark became Peter's interpreter and wrote accurately all that he remembered, not, indeed, in order, of all the things said or done by the Lord. For he had not heard the Lord, nor had he followed him, but later on, as I said, followed Peter, who used to give teaching as necessity demanded but not making, as it were, an arrangement of the Lord's *oracles*, so that Mark did nothing wrong in thus writing down single points as he remembered them. For to one thing he gave attention, to leave out nothing of what he had heard and to make no false statements in them.
>
> (Eusebius, *History*, 3.39.15)

According to Eusebius, Papias attributed this and other traditions to the *Elder* John, whom he distinguished from the apostle. The Mark spoken of by Papias is John Mark, the cousin of Barnabas, companion of Paul and Barnabas on their first missionary journey and later, according to tradition, a companion of Peter. According to Acts the Last Supper was held at the home of the parents of Mark and there the early Jerusalem church used to meet. Papias provides no clues as to the order of the composition of the Gospels. Papias makes three points. He identifies Mark as author of the Gospel and he associates him with Peter. The link with Peter is made the basis of the claim for the reliability of Mark.

Some scholars continue to defend the Petrine connection with Mark but it has no widespread support today. The Papias tradition is the only basis for this and its credibility is put in question by what Papias said of Matthew:

> Matthew collected the *oracles* in the Hebrew language and each person interpreted them as best he could.
>
> (Eusebius, *History*, 3.39.16)

Scholars today are convinced that Matthew was written in Greek, not in Hebrew or Aramaic. There is no good reason for connecting the second Gospel to Peter. Matthew appears to be the Petrine Gospel and a good case can be made for identifying Mark more closely with Paul.

The titles of the Gospels are earlier than the Papias tradition and give grounds for associating the Gospel with Mark quite independent of the Petrine tradition which is used apologetically to validate Mark. On the assumption that Peter stands behind Mark, apparent irregularities are explained in terms of the purpose of Mark. The Papias fragment shows that Mark's failure to provide an ordered account of the *sayings* (oracles) of Jesus was perceived as a problem in the light of Matthew. Such is the focus on the passion of Jesus that Mark came to be characterised as a passion narrative with an introduction, inviting comparison with the Pauline passion gospel. While Mark and Paul knew and valued the sayings of Jesus, their purposes in writing concentrated attention on the *death* of Jesus.

## MARK AND PAUL

Paul was at pains to demonstrate his independence from Jerusalem (Galatians 1.11–12) but his 'gospel' is not what we mean by 'gospel tradition'. Paul's gospel, which is the 'drift' of what Paul preached, can be summarised in terms of the justification of the sinner, apart from the works of the law, by God's grace through faith in Jesus Christ. Paul did not get this gospel from the Jerusalem church. Indeed, this gospel brought him into serious conflict with the Jerusalem church. This does not mean that Paul had no interest in the gospel tradition. Indeed, there is a case for connecting Mark with Paul (Acts 12.12, 25; 13.5, 13; 15.36–41). While there is evidence of a rift between Mark and Paul, there is also evidence that suggests a later reconciliation (Philemon 24; Colossians 4.10).

Although Paul wrote letters not a Gospel, he used and appeals to the Jesus tradition on various issues such as marriage and divorce, the Last Supper, the death, burial and resurrection of Jesus (1 Corinthians 7.10; 11.23–26; 15.3–11). On such matters Paul and the Jerusalem church were in complete agreement (1 Corinthians 15.11). But concerning Paul's gospel there was serious contention. Perhaps we can say the same concerning Mark's Gospel. The defence of that Gospel by Papias reflects an awareness of its questionable status.

Not only is there a concentration on the passion of Jesus (the cross) in Mark (see 1 Corinthians 1.17–18, 23), there is also a critique of the law more in keeping with Paul than Peter. The use of 'gospel' language and the equation of the gospel preached by Jesus (1.14–15) with 'the word' (4.33) are also features common to Paul (see 1 Corinthians 1.18). The Jesus of Mark not only does not keep the sabbath, he declares all foods to be clean (7.19), thus invalidating food and purity laws which were essential to the Jewish way of life.

Each of the four Gospels represents a different faction within early Christianity. Although Matthew and Luke used Mark, they did so by reinterpreting Mark. Matthew is a major modification of the Markan perspective through the interpretation of the Markan material and the introduction of new material, largely teaching of Jesus.

B.H. Streeter recognised that the final form of Matthew, with the well-known Petrine text (16.18), is the Petrine Gospel. It reinterprets Mark and a more extreme Judaising position represented by M (tradition peculiar to Matthew), emanating from the faction of James the brother of Jesus which restricted mission to the Jews. Matthew, under the influence of Petrine tradition (Q), broadened the Christian Jewish mission to include the nations, demanding circumcision and the keeping of the law (Matthew 28.19–20) but without observing the tradition of the elders (15.1–20). The Jesus of Matthew represents a reformed Judaism in which the demands of the law are intensified by Jesus (Matthew 5.17–48) who is seen as the one who has authority to reinterpret the law. This represents the position of the Jerusalem church as it developed after the Jewish war. Both Mark and Paul struggled with this at an earlier stage of development.

Mark presents a Jesus who provides a basis for the law-free mission to the nations, whose first public act after calling his disciples occurs on the sabbath (1.21). Although this exorcism of an unclean spirit occurred in a synagogue on the sabbath, there is no controversy at this point. An implied growth in opposition to Jesus for his failure to keep the sabbath is found in 3.2, where the opponents of Jesus watched him to see if he would heal on the sabbath.

After summary material Mark provides an account of the healing of a leper (1.40–45). The means of healing the leper used by Jesus in response to the man's request was to stretch out his hand, to *touch* the man and to say, 'I will, be cleansed'. In the first two detailed healing stories two purity issues are dealt with (see also 7.1–23, especially 7.19), and the first also raised the question of sabbath observance, although the narrative of Mark passes over this at this point. Sabbath controversy is raised later (2.23–28; 3.1–6). The issues of purity and sabbath observance were crucial boundary markers for Jewish self-definition. These were challenged by the Markan Jesus at the beginning of his ministry.

## PLACE AND DATE

Tradition associates Mark with Peter in Rome. While a Roman destination is possible, there is no positive indication that this was the case. The concentration of Mark on the passion of Jesus and the call of the disciples to follow Jesus, bearing a cross, is thought to fit the situation of Rome in the time of Nero's persecution or the consciousness of it. Yet Mark 13 makes sense in a Palestinian context, immediately before, during, or soon after the Jewish war (66–73 CE). Thus it would be unwise to tie Mark to a Roman context. Mark 13 makes the Jewish war a more specific and likely context for Mark, which was probably written in the turmoil leading up to the war or in the throes of the war itself.

## THE APPROACH OF THIS STUDY

It might be possible sometimes to isolate pre-Markan tradition. It is likely that the evangelist drew on a wide fund of material including collections of stories and sayings. Because Mark was the first Gospel, the task of separating tradition from redaction is quite uncertain. It seems best, therefore, to concentrate on those aspects of compositional technique that apply whether or not Mark was working straightforwardly with tradition. A case can be made for approaching the Gospel from the perspective of the selection and arrangement of the material, whatever its origin. At this point redaction criticism operates in a way similar to narrative criticism, which pays attention to what is in the text, how it is arranged and the overall effect produced by the text. Repetitions and resumptions are important, as is the use of characteristic Markan language spread throughout the Gospel.

Recognition of these characteristics brings to light the diversity of early Christianity. Each of the Gospels gives expression to its own distinctive view of Jesus and in so doing provides a 'mission statement' for a 'faction' or 'sect' in early Christianity. Although almost all of Mark was used by Matthew and Luke, the distinctive perspective of Mark remains. Where, in the history of early Christianity, does the distinctive language and perspective on Jesus place Mark? This study shares with redaction criticism the concern to understand Mark in its historical context. Mark is recognised as a document aimed at persuading its readers and needs to be understood in terms of the rhetoric of its day. (See 'What is a Gospel?' below, p. 10).

Mark's use of the noun 'gospel' appears at the very beginning of his book and has a concentration not found in the other Gospels, being absent altogether from Luke and John. Mark's focus on exorcisms is altogether absent from John, and only present in Matthew and Luke when dependent on Mark. The same is true of the theme of the suffering Son of Man. This alerts us to the distinctive and overarching Markan christology. Other overarching themes concern the 'disciples' and the secrecy motif which run through the Gospel. The geographical basis for the structure of Mark's plan raises the question of what is meant by the focus on Galilee at the beginning of Jesus' ministry. While it is followed by an excursion into dominantly Gentile territory before returning through Galilee on the way to Jerusalem, the Gospel concludes with a narrative redirecting the disciples back to Galilee from whence they began (16.7). Identification of these Markan characteristics should alert the reader to watch out for them in the text.

Some peculiar aspects of Mark's vocabulary are not *theologically* charged:

1 The use of 'and' (1, 078 times), especially opening sentences, paragraphs and *pericopae*. Eighty-nine of Mark's 105 rhetorical units set out in our 'Outline' of the Gospel begin with 'And . . .'.
2 The use of the historic present tense (the present tense when an aorist tense is expected) over 150 times compared with about twenty times in Matthew and only once in Luke.
3 'Immediately' forty-three times in Mark, eight times in Matthew, only three times in Luke and four times in John.
4 'Again' twenty-eight times in Mark, seventeen times in Matthew, three times in Luke and forty-three times in John.

Given that this vocabulary is spread throughout the Gospel we seem to have identifications of Markan characteristics. These few pieces of evidence are indicators of the rudimentary nature of the Markan *literary* style which must be set over against the overall dramatic effectiveness of the Gospel. Limited facility with syntax, grammar and vocabulary makes clear that Mark is not a work of 'high literature' and was capable of being read by those of moderate education.

The beginning and ending of the Gospel (1.1–20; 16.1–8) are sections of great importance, revealing its meaning and purpose. The beginning introduces the term 'gospel' as a key to the understanding of the book and key christological terms provide the reader with a privileged position. The story is quickly given an eschatological (concerning the end of the age) setting in which John (the Baptist) is portrayed as the forerunner of the day of the Lord and the place of Jesus is confirmed by the heavenly voice at his baptism. Nevertheless, the kingdom of God, which the Markan Jesus speaks of rather than the day of the Lord, does not arrive without a struggle, which is signalled immediately (1.12–13).

Given that Jesus' triumph over the demonic powers is presented as evidence of the dawning of the kingdom of God, the crucifixion of Jesus creates a serious plausibility problem. To deal with this Mark has attempted to make the death of Jesus a positive and central aspect of Jesus' ministry. The kingdom of God is manifest in humble service and nowhere more clearly than in the Son of Man, who gave his life a ransom for the many. Mark has played on the dramatic revelation and recognition of Jesus' kingship precisely at his crucifixion. While Mark wrote from the perspective of the resurrection, he has made no attempt to treat the crucifixion as a disaster reversed by the resurrection (as in Acts 2.22–24). Perhaps this is why the ending of Mark tends to play down the resurrection by not narrating resurrection appearances.

The scope of this commentary is the story of Jesus according to Mark. There are occasions when we will look at Matthew and Luke to clarify points of difficulty in the Markan text because they provide us with the earliest evidence of the way Mark was read. Because they had their own agendas they are not always useful for this purpose. Thus they will be used only where it seems likely that they can clarify a difficulty we have in reading Mark.

Modern study of the Gospels has shown that each has its own distinctive understanding, developing plot and emphasis which is only properly discerned by a continuous reading from beginning to end. A chronological and thematic development is evident in the way Mark has brought the individual narratives together. Indeed, it may be that Mark is the most dramatically effective of the Gospels. This conclusion is supported by the evident success of modern dramatic readings of Mark, such as the public performance of Mark by British actor Alec McCowen (see his *Personal Mark: An Actor's Proclamation of St Mark's Gospel*).

Those who wish to gain most from reading this study would do well to make time to read Mark from beginning to end in one sitting. If this can be done a number of times, so much the better.

No sensible reader would think of reading a modern book a few lines at a time. Yet this is the way most people read the Gospels. Mark is 'holy scripture'. It is also a book which can only be appreciated adequately when read as a story.

The following sections of the Introduction feature important aspects of the approach adopted in this study.

## WHAT IS A GOSPEL?

In the ancient world the opening words of a book often were taken to be its title. On this assumption Mark is 'The Gospel of Jesus Christ'. The phrase might mean, the gospel that was preached by Jesus Christ, or was preached about Jesus Christ. Certainly Jesus is portrayed as 'proclaiming the gospel of God' (1.14), which is a crystallisation of the gospel of the kingdom (of God):

> The time is fulfilled and the kingdom of God is at hand; repent and believe in the gospel.
>
> (1.15)

But Mark has less concentration on the content of the preaching or teaching of Jesus than the other Gospels. Further, in the apocalyptic discourse of Mark 13, Jesus asserts that 'the gospel must first be proclaimed to all the nations' (13.10) and elsewhere he refers to 'wherever the gospel is proclaimed in the whole world' (14.9). Mark implies that this proclamation was undertaken by messengers other than Jesus. What then did they proclaim? If the content of the proclamation of Jesus was the kingdom of God, the concentration of Mark is on the *activity* of Jesus as the Christ. Even when presenting summaries of the teaching of Jesus, Mark was more intent to show the effect of the teaching than its content (1.21–22). It is likely that Mark built on this ambiguity, taking account of Jesus' proclamation of the kingdom of God while maintaining the awareness that the content of the church's gospel was Jesus Christ himself.

Mark's narrative shares enough common features with Graeco-Roman biographies to justify identifying it as a popular biography. Its links with ancient Graeco-Roman biographical literature are seen in the use of the *chreiai* (cf. Plutarch in his *Lives* and *Moralia*). Use of these stories links Mark to the Graeco-Roman rhetorical tradition. An excellent introduction has been provided in a volume of *Semeia* entitled *Pronouncement Stories* edited by Robert Tannehill. His work builds on Rudolf Bultmann's *The History of the Synoptic Tradition.*

It differs from it in one important respect. Bultmann was concerned with the history of the tradition. Tannehill is concerned with the rhetorical effect of the *chreiai*, whether they came from pre-Markan tradition or were a consequence of Markan composition/redaction. His analysis of the Synoptic pronouncement stories overlaps ancient rhetorical analysis of the *chreiai.*

Tannehill has analysed the various pronouncement stories found in the Synoptic Gospels into six sub-types, 'correction', 'commendation', 'objection', 'quest', 'inquiry', 'description' and hybrids which are mixed types of stories. Of these only 'description stories' are absent from Mark and the common Synoptic 'quest stories' are scarcely found in the Graeco-Roman rhetorical tradition, where the 'correction story' is by far the most common. While Bultmann made some distinctions amongst those stories he called *apophthegmata*, Tannehill's analysis is more detailed and precise, providing a good basis for understanding the way these stories function rhetorically in the Gospel.

The stories have two parts, the setting and the response or pronouncement which forms the climax, generally near the end. The different types of story manifest differing tensions between the setting and the response. Some names feature the response (the saying)('correction' and 'commendation'), while the others ('objection', 'quest' and 'inquiry') describe the setting or context to which the saying responds. But the names are appropriate to the whole story because of the correlation between setting and response. Correction and commendation stories are often hybrids combining correction (of one character) and commendation (of another). Quest and inquiry stories are also combined with correction and commendation. A quester or inquirer is sometimes commended or corrected.

1 Correction stories. In these stories Jesus corrects an attitude, saying, action or practice. The setting provides the basis for Jesus' corrective response (1.35–38; 9.33–37, 38–40; 10.35–45; 11.15–17; 12.18–27; 13.1–2). There are also hybrid correction/commendation stories, 3.31–35; 10.13–16; 14.3–9.
2 Commendation stories. Most of these are hybrids in which the *commendation* of Jesus *corrects* the objection raised by someone else (3.31–35; 10.13–16; 12.41–44; 14.3–9).
3 Objection stories. In the setting the behaviour of Jesus or his disciples gives rise to an objection which is answered by Jesus (2.15–17, 18–22, 23–28; 3.1–6, 22–30; 6.1–6; 7.1–15; 8.31–33;

9.9–13; 10.23–27). Tannehill also notes a sub-category which he names 'testing inquiries', which overlap objection stories and inquiry stories (8.11–12; 10.2–9; 11.27–33; 12.13–17, 18–27, 35–37). In these the inquiry is not genuine but a trap aimed at laying bare the grounds for objection. There is also a good example of a quest/objection story, 2.1–12.

4 Quest stories. These are rare outside the Gospels. Peculiar to these stories is an interest in the quester who approaches Jesus with a concern important for life. There is normally an obstacle to be overcome if the quest is to succeed. Indication of the outcome of the quest, success or failure, is essential to quest stories, which can be combined with correction, commendation and objection stories (2.1–12; 7.24–30; 10.17–22, 28–31). Only the quest of 10.17–22 is unsuccessful and yet this is combined paradoxically with a kind of commendation.

5 Inquiry stories. These stories exist to elicit the answer which is all important. The fate of the inquirer is of no significance (4.10–20; 8.27–30; 11.20–25; 13.3–37). Reference has already been made to the testing inquiries.

The tension that is manifest between the setting and the response is evidence of 'worldviews' or values in conflict. Use of this term indicates that the values reflect differing groups (not simply individuals) with their worlds of discourse. The stories are important indications of the values over against which Mark challenged believers to struggle, and of those which he called on them to embrace. They are rhetorically charged instruments of persuasion, appealing to the emotions and the will rather than to the intellect alone. Drawing the reader to take sides in the conflict between the worlds of values, they open up an understanding of Mark's social world, especially as the Gospel weaves together individual *chreiai* into groups constructing plot development.

Biographies are not all the same. Mark is significantly shaped by aspects of the early Christian preaching, which has its roots in the proclamation of Jesus. Mark begins, 'The beginning of the Gospel of Jesus Christ [son of God]'. There has been a long discussion about whether the Gospels are a unique and separate genre. This is a complex question. The notion of uniqueness can only be relative when it comes to the matter of literary genre because all literary works find expression in writing, are written in languages in which other works have been written, written by authors, written for readers and so on. Consequently, to be meaningful, any talk of uniqueness must specify in what respect or respects a work is unique.

A genre is recognised when a group of writings is perceived to share a sufficient number of differences from other writings. In this way both authors and readers become aware that a work is philosophy, history or biography and so on. In the ancient world authors and readers were aware of the genre of the 'lives' (βίοι) and, as might be expected, the lives written concerned 'famous men', generally philosophers and politicians or rulers. In the Jewish context there were the 'lives of the prophets'. In general terms Mark fits into this genre. Mark also exhibits differences from the general characteristics built up from an awareness of all the works that fit this classification. But so would any individual 'life'. Authors of 'lives' did not replicate every characteristic of the genre. Rather, each 'life' conformed generally and was recognised as belonging to the 'lives', or biographies ('life' = βίος and 'writing' = γραφή).

Because individual characteristics of Mark were made basic to Matthew and Luke we recognise the emergence of a new sub-genre. Had Mark been the only work of this kind we would not talk of a sub-genre. Because Mark has decisively influenced the other Gospels, it set important precedents that were built on by them in such a way as to create a sub-genre which we may, on the precedent of Mark, call 'Gospel'.

The Markan biography signals its links with Jewish historiography by linking the story of Jesus to the outworking of the purposes of God in history. In this Mark and the other Gospels differ from early Rabbinic sources (*The Mishnah*) of the time which, Jacob Neusner argues, develop traditions to provide principles and interpretations of the law applicable in a changing world. But there is little interest in God's saving purposes in history or the lives of the rabbis who taught the principles and interpretations. The Qumran texts show an interest in the purposes of God being worked out in their own history, but there is no evidence of a figure comparable to Jesus in the texts, the teacher of righteousness at best being a shadowy figure whose role within the sect remains unclear.

For Mark, the appearance of Jesus was the culmination of the purposes of God in history, providing a basis for the early Christian conviction that Jesus came as the fulfilment of the Jewish scriptures. No one read the scriptures *precisely* in this way until they were applied to Jesus as the one who fulfilled them.

That way of reading is bound up with an apocalyptic 'world-view'. The use of this term draws attention to the fact that Mark's narrative world or story world significantly overlaps the narrative world expressed in a significant body of other texts which we designate 'apocalyptic'. The Markan story will not be understood unless the reader recognises that, in this story, it is understood that, although God created the world, the world lies in the power of (the) evil (one). Human lives lie in the grip of evil and human agencies are powerless to break free. Only God can break the power of evil, in his time and in his way and Mark has his own distinctive understanding of the outworking.

Mark tells the story of Jesus as 'good news' or 'gospel'. But this begins with the recognition that the world lies in the power of evil. Mark did not need to argue this case. For him and for his readers this was self-evident and put in question the reality, power and goodness of God. Mark wrote after the death of Jesus by crucifixion, betrayed by one of his followers through the intrigue of his opponents and at the hands of the greatest human power of the day, the power of Rome. Mark is an apologetic work. In a world dominated by evil Mark kindles belief in the goodness and power of God. The ministry of Jesus is portrayed in such a way as to provide evidence of this (see 3.22–30). To fail to see Jesus' work in liberating those oppressed by evil as the work of God was to blaspheme the Holy Spirit. But the case built upon Jesus' liberation of the oppressed was dealt a mortal blow by the crucifixion of Jesus. Mark integrated the death of Jesus into the good news of the dawning of the kingdom of God in and through him. Consequently, the proclamation of the gospel and the writing of his Gospel are works of *theodicy* in the face of prevailing evil, and this book has been written from this perspective.

Although Mark indicates that there were glimmerings of insight along the way, only when Jesus had been crucified does any human character *confess* that Jesus is son of God, and he was not one of the disciples but a Roman centurion (15.39). Even here the reader has the impression that the centurion said more than he knew, that his confession had an altogether more profound meaning for Mark, which the reader is in a position to grasp in the light of 1.1, 11, 34; 3.11; 9.7; 14.61–62. The Gospel ends with the instruction that was to be given to the disciples, telling them that the risen Jesus was going before them into Galilee (as he had told them, 14.29), and that there they would see him (16.7). Thus for the characters in the story the mystery of Jesus remained unresolved to the very end of the Gospel. In this way too, the reader, though better placed, is also called into the future where the faith expressed in *following* Jesus is promised greater fulfilment.

## MARK'S STORY OF JESUS

If Mark presents us with a unified understanding of Jesus, it does so only through a compilation of traditions collected by the author. Mark was no mere collector but a genuine author, who utilised traditions to lead readers to believe certain things about Jesus and to a commitment to follow him. When the story ends the disciples are called to follow Jesus, who goes before them to Galilee (16.7). The reality of discipleship (following Jesus) lies in the future for them and Mark leaves the outcome open. Because it is not reported it remains not only unfulfilled, but uncertain. What is more, it is indicated that the message was not passed on to them. Yet the existence of the text of Mark implies that the message was made known. What of the outcome for the disciples? More important are the implications for the reader.

Mark's story presupposes that the dominant powers controlling the world and human history are evil. The story of Jesus recounts the strategy and purpose of God to overcome the powers of evil, liberating those who will receive and enter the kingdom of God. This takes place in the ministry of Jesus, who assaults the powers of evil seeking to bring about a transformation of human consciousness. The story is the manifestation of a struggle between God and the powers of evil. The heavenly voice revealed Jesus to be the chief protagonist for the kingdom of God. Characters in the story are seen to represent one of these two sides. On the side of Jesus and the kingdom of God are the disciples. While they have made a decisive move, Mark shows that a transformation of their consciousness remains incomplete and their role is ambiguous. On the other side the Jewish authorities appear as the chief protagonists of Jesus, and they successfully plot to bring about his destruction.

Mark has carefully outlined the itinerary of Jesus' mission, which the reader needs to follow. The plot suggests that Jesus drew his main support from Galilee, although responses in the regions beyond dominantly Jewish territory provided anticipations of the universal Gentile mission. In the middle section there is a journey complex devoted to the teaching of the disciples. The main assault of Jesus took place in Jerusalem in the temple (Malachi 3.1–2). From that point onwards the powers of the Jewish authorities were concentrated on the destruction of Jesus (14.1–2). One of the disciples provided the means to bring this about (14.10–11). While this was a disastrous outcome, Mark portrays the crucifixion of Jesus as his triumph, as the means by which the powers of evil were broken and the transformation of human consciousness made possible.

The need for the transformation of human consciousness provides a basis for understanding what has been called the messianic secret in Mark. Even when Jesus is revealed he remains a mystery. Those who confessed their faith in him hardly knew what they said. Mark links this blindness with the failure to understand that Jesus' vocation was one of service and that his service involved giving his life, being crucified. Just how Mark thinks that the death of Jesus overcame the power of evil and transforms consciousness, at least of those who believe, is unclear. But it is clear that he thinks that it has the power to do so. In spite of the failure of the disciples within the narrative of the Gospel, the existence of the Gospel implies the success of Jesus' mission in his combat with evil and in transforming the believing understanding which finds expression in this Gospel. For the reader the conclusion is a call to follow where Jesus leads (16.7).

Galilee, not Jerusalem, is the place where, it is promised, 'you will see him'. At the level of the story this affirms the responsiveness of the piety of Galilee over against official temple and priestly Judaism represented by the high priest, the chief priests, the Jerusalem scribes and elders. But for Mark there was also a conflict between the response to Jesus represented by his Gospel and the Jerusalem church, the church that failed to respond to Jesus' challenge to follow him into Galilee, though that failure is partly excused by the silence of the women (16.8).

## MARK AND WORLDS IN CONFLICT

Mark presents a number of conflicts which reflect conflicting worldviews. The first is between Jesus, as the representative of the kingdom of God, and the devil. Mark presents this as the testing of God's son, the Messiah. If this element were seen in the tradition of the testing of Job, we might think of God testing Jesus. But even a cursory reading of Mark makes clear that the devil is opposed to

God and his Messiah. This perspective reflects an apocalyptic world-view in which:

1 This world is dominated by evil forces which normal human agencies are powerless to resist. Only the direct intervention of God in his power is able to overcome the power of evil. The context of this conflict is expressed in both spatial and temporal terms.
2 There is a gulf between this world and the realm of God, the world above. At the 'anointing' or baptism of God's son, the Messiah, the real action is initiated from above, when the heavens are opened to reveal the Spirit descending like a dove and abiding on God's son, who is so named by the heavenly voice (1.11; 9.7).
3 This world, dominated by the powers of evil, corresponds to this age. The coming of the kingdom of God is an expression of the coming age. Thus the ministry of Jesus is portrayed as the breaking in of the new age. Nevertheless, at the end of the ministry of Jesus, the kingdom of God had not come with power. Mark is a Gospel oriented to the future, to the eschatological judgement of the world, 13.24–26.

The conflict between the two worlds is a feature of Mark. After the testing of God's son by the devil, conflict re-emerges with the appearance in the synagogue at Capernaum of a man with an unclean spirit, which Jesus casts out, 1.21–28. This is followed by two summary accounts of Jesus' activity, which include summaries of the exorcisms 1.33–34, 39. More detailed accounts or discussions of exorcisms follow in 3.20–30; 5.1–20; 9.14–29, 38–41. See also the authorisation of the disciples to perform exorcisms in 3.15; 6.7. From these passages it becomes apparent that there is a correspondence between 'being beside himself' (a popular diagnosis of 'madness', 3.21), being under the influence of Beelzebul, the prince of demons (a theological diagnosis, 3.22), and having an unclean spirit (a priestly diagnosis, 3.30). The exorcism of demons is portrayed by Mark (and by Q) as the evidence that the kingdom of God has come, overpowering the forces of evil. Mark is an apocalyptic Gospel which features the account of the ministry of Jesus in terms of the conflict between the two kingdoms, the two worlds.

The conflict is portrayed also in human terms. The Jewish authorities from Jerusalem (2.6, 16, 24; 3.6, **22**; **7.1**; 8.11, **31**; **10.33–34**; **14.1–2**, **10–11**, **43**, **53–65**; **15.1**, **3**) are portrayed as the opponents of Jesus (bold type indicates the more important references). Committing the unforgivable sin, they charged Jesus with acting under the power of Beelzebul, confusing God with the devil. The chief priests, scribes and elders, the groups from which the Sanhedrin was constituted, appear as opponents of Jesus (11.27) and it is apparently this group (or the chief priests and scribes, or just the chief priests) that sought Jesus' arrest (12.12; 14.1, 10, 43, 53; 15.1).

In a world dominated by evil, it is only to be expected that the servants of God will suffer oppression and persecution, and in apocalyptic narratives the patterning of history is a characteristic feature. The pattern is repeated in the lives of the people of God in their confrontation with the powers of the evil world leading up to the end-time judgement of God. In the development of this view of history earlier scriptures are important. By the time of Mark the book of Daniel had become a paradigmatic apocalyptic text. In this apocalyptic interpretation of history the reuse and reinterpretation of scripture is an important feature. This serves to emphasise that, in spite of the apparent domination of evil in the world, the purpose of God is certain and will be fulfilled. The scribal nature of apocalyptic writing is important. Mark, like other writers of apocalyptic drama, reinterprets the earlier scriptures, especially Isaiah, Malachi, Daniel and Psalms, to show that history reaches its climax in the coming of Jesus.

One characteristic of this patterning of history was to write from the perspective of the past in such a way as to make what was actually the present, appear to be the imminent future, confirming predictions of the intervention of God in judgement. In this way past events appear to be confirmations of prophecy from the perspective of the reader. See especially Mark 13.

Norman Perrin (*The New Testament: An Introduction*, pp. 144–5) has shown that Mark follows a threefold pattern in which:

1 John (the Baptist) preaches (1.7) and is delivered up (1.14);
2 Jesus preaches (1.14) and is delivered up (9.31; 10.33);
3 The followers of Jesus preach and (future) must preach to all the nations (1.1; 13.10), and will be delivered up (13.9–13).

When this third act of the drama is completed the eschatological judgement of God will take place through the coming of Jesus as Son of Man (13.26). His coming is the judgement of God for the overthrow of evil and the establishment of the kingdom of God in power.

To some extent the sequencing suggests a pattern of conflict that has always been, but which reaches its climax in the final three acts. Thus, for Mark, while the conflict between the two worlds is not new, it reaches a new level of intensity and significance with the appearance of John.

The Gospel was written from the perspective of the completion of the first two acts. John had preached and been delivered up, and Jesus had preached and been delivered up. His resurrection is reported and at this point the narrative breaks off. It is as if the third stage was about to begin. What Jesus had done, and what had happened to him, must be repeated in the lives of the disciples. This is the point of the teaching on discipleship in 8.31–38. The confirmation of the purpose of God is to be found in the fact that, according to Mark, Jesus predicted his own fate (8.31–32; 9.30–32; 10.32–34) and this fate is expounded in terms of the purpose of his mission (10.45). Thus Jesus' fate was a fulfilment of prophecy. The prediction that the disciples will suffer the same fate also becomes a confirmation when this occurs to them, but now it is stressed that the end is near.

While the preaching of the gospel to the nations and the turmoil and suffering of the events of Mark 13 are expressed in future terms, many scholars today think this chapter reveals the situation in which Mark was written. The historical events reflected are those of the Jewish war and Mark is generally dated in the months leading up to the outbreak of the war, or in the midst of the war, or at latest, soon after the destruction of Jerusalem. Writing as if these events were future enables the author to use them as fulfilments of prophecy. Nevertheless, it is likely that Jesus predicted the destruction of the temple. All of the Gospels make the accusation that Jesus said he would destroy the temple an aspect of the charges brought against him leading to his death. The charge, in the form stated, was obviously false, but it probably reflects the reality that Jesus predicted the end of the temple.

Mark cannot have been written long after that event because the narrative assumes that the coming of the Son of Man in judgement was associated with it. The failure of this event to arrive helps us to date Mark. From this perspective Mark is seen as an attempt to proclaim the good news of God in a world dominated by evil. Mark's Gospel, good news, is a form of theodicy. While Mark lacks a full account of the creation of the world by God, 10.6, 'From the beginning of the creation male and female he made them', is enough to show full dependence on the Genesis account. Nevertheless, in a world created by God, the *mystery* of evil is given full weight. This is perhaps the most significant development in historical apocalypses such as Mark. In earlier Jewish historical writings all being and action were understood as expressions of the will of God, and if Israel suffered it was understood to be a consequence of disobedience to God. But there emerged in the Psalms and in Job an awareness of the individual righteous sufferer. From this point it was a short step to acknowledge that, in the mystery of God's purpose, Israel, the righteous nation, might also suffer. In the historical apocalypse this development is taken a step further. Without rejecting the mystery bound up with the purpose of God, the origin, nature and activity of evil is itself shrouded in mystery and there is no attempt to ground this mystery in God. Evil is seen to be antithetical to the purpose of God, and opposed to him and all who serve him. The faith of the apocalypse is that, in spite of the apparent dominating power of evil, God would triumph over it. Thus, in Mark, faith in God's deliverance through Jesus as the Christ finds expression in eschatological hope, Jesus the coming Son of Man.

The modern reader of Mark will be conscious of encountering an understanding of reality quite different from prevailing views today. It is not just that we are unaccustomed to attributing behaviour to demons. There is Mark's view that the world is dominated by the powers of evil. Mark challenges the modern reader to come to terms with the mystery of evil encountered in the world which the believer affirms is God's creation.

## READING THE GOSPELS AS LITERATURE AND THE TEXT OF MARK

Mark, like the New Testament generally, was written in Hellenistic Greek. To read Mark at all involves the historical recovery of the grammar, syntax and vocabulary of the Greek of Mark's time. If the reader turns to a modern translation, this only masks the historical work that others have done to make the text accessible.

Mark is about actual persons, John the Baptist, Jesus, Herod, Pilate; and institutions and groups like the temple, synagogues, chief priests, Pharisees, Sadducees. It presupposes that the readers know more than is apparent in the text; that scriptural allusions will be recognised as such. By using the scriptures and terms like 'Christ', 'Son of Man', 'Son of God', Mark implies that the reader has a basic understanding of what they meant in the first century. The modern reader needs to fill in the cultural and historical gaps if the text of Mark is to be meaningful.

Mark is the product of almost 2, 000 years of textual transmission. The first English-language translations were made from late manuscripts which conformed to a single textual tradition. In the last two centuries discoveries of a number of great codexes from the fourth and fifth centuries and even earlier papyri have transformed this. A critical reconstruction of the text using all textual evidence is generally accepted to be the most useful approach to the recovery of the original text of Mark. To all intents and purposes the text used as the basis of this study is that produced by the fourth edition of *The Greek New Testament*, which corresponds to the twenty-seventh edition of the Nestle–Aland text. This text is the product of the critical use of all available textual evidence and the methods developed in the long history of the study of the text.

For hundreds of years Mark was thought to begin with the words 'The beginning of the Gospel of Jesus Christ Son of God'. But the evidence for the inclusion of the words 'Son of God' at the beginning is doubtful and textual evidence makes clear that the original ending is 16.8. Two other 'endings' are known: the so-called longer (16.9–20) and shorter endings. These are not without variations of placement and wording. The variations themselves confirm their secondary nature. Thus *The Greek New Testament* gives the conclusion of Mark at 16.8 an 'A' rating. Once the other Gospels had produced accounts of the appearances of the risen Jesus, some scribes could not be content with Mark's stark ending. Some scholars feel that Mark would not have ended abruptly in the manner of 16.8, but no one defends the authenticity of the additional material. There is no evidence of a lost ending or that Mark was unfinished. It is only in the light of the other Gospels that Mark seems deficient at this point. Because Mark was first, such a comparison is unhelpful. Indeed, by judging Mark by the standards of the other Gospels, the distinctive character of Mark is obscured. Other textual variants concern only the precise wording of the text.

In the analysis upon which this commentary is based (see the Outline of Mark, p. ix), changes in time, place and *dramatis personae* are given due weight in discerning the structure of the Gospel.

Attention is also given to the arrangement of rhetorically shaped stories into collections which shape the plot of the story.

*Note*: Those sections beginning with 'And . . .' are signified by + left of the section heading. Other sections are indicated by *.

# Chapter 1

# The Prelude

## The Beginning of the Gospel, 1.1–13

The opening scenes are foundational, providing a context and perspective for the story. Through the narrative of the baptism, Jesus moves from anonymity to become the central figure of the story. The following narratives (in 1.12–20) illuminate the whole story *for the reader.* The summary account of the testing of Jesus signals a dimension that the reader must keep in mind. Similarly, the summary of Jesus' preaching does not indicate an audience because it does not represent a single act of preaching, but stands over the whole of Jesus' (Galilean) ministry. The call of the first four disciples is placed before the first event of Jesus' *public* ministry in the synagogue at Capernaum to make clear Jesus' authority and his manner of working with a group of disciples. The choosing and formal appointment of the twelve is narrated only in 3.13–19.

In spite of the foundational nature of 1.1–20, a case can be made for ending the Prelude after 1.13, because 1.14 involves a change of location from the desert and the Jordan to Galilee and a change of the *subject* of action, from John to Jesus. Jesus *had been* baptised and tested. Now, when John *was arrested, Jesus came preaching.* From here on Jesus is the central character of the story. Thus there are grounds for making 1.14 the beginning of the Galilean ministry of Jesus. Alternatively, because 1.14–15 shares the 'gospel' terminology with 1.1, it can be seen as an *inclusio*, bracketing 1.1–15. Given the changes of location and central characters it seems better to see 1.14–15 as a resumption, a restatement of the beginning of the Gospel. But 1.14–15, 16–20 also share with the Prelude the function of providing the reader with necessary insights to understand the ministry of Jesus. Notwithstanding that 1.14–20 continue to lay the foundation of the story, these sections are to be seen as the beginning of the Galilean ministry rather than as part of the Prelude.

## *JOHN AND JESUS, 1.1–11

Mark set the opening of his work concerning the coming of John (the Baptist) *in relation to Jesus* in the context of scripture and as the fulfilment of prophecy.

### *The beginning, 1.1

The opening words, known as the *Incipit*, provide the means by which ancient texts were known. Of the canonical Gospels, only Mark uses the term 'gospel' in a way that implies that the reader should understand it to be a Gospel and that this is a key term for understanding this book. By the end of the first century the early church, following this clue from Mark, had identified the fourfold Gospel according to Matthew, Mark, Luke and John. The titles probably date from the early second century and are the earliest evidence concerning the identity of the evangelists.

The word 'gospel' has as its basic meaning 'good news' and has a history of use in the LXX (Septuagint) in relation to the good news of the salvation of God. In Greek and Roman use it conveyed the good news of victory in battle. The early Christians used the term to convey *the* good news proclaimed concerning Jesus Christ. It was a favourite Pauline term. The noun is used by Mark and Paul and the deutero-Paulines and rarely elsewhere.

| | Mark | Matthew | Luke | Acts | Paul | Other | New Testament (NT) |
|---|---|---|---|---|---|---|---|
| 'gospel' (εὐαγγέλιον) | 7 [8] | 4 | 0 | 2 | 59 (-10) | 2 | 75 |
| 'to proclaim good news' | | | | | | | |
| εὐαγγελίζω | 0 | 1 | 10 | 15 | 20 (-2) | 7 | 53 |
| κηρύσσω | 12 [14] | 9 | 9 | 8 | 19 (-3) | 2 | 61 |

These statistics are consistent with the recognition of some connection between Mark and Paul.

The words 'the Gospel of Jesus Christ' are capable of being understood in two ways.

1 As the good news that has Jesus as its subject. This is supported by the evidence of the early Christian preaching within which Mark fits neatly.
2 As the good news Jesus himself preached. While Mark provides comparatively little detail here there is enough (see 1.14–15) to make this meaning possible. Because the reader is given no clues to aid in the choice between Jesus as preacher and Jesus as content of the Gospel, we may be right in thinking that the ambiguity was intentional.

Mark's use of 'Gospel' to epitomise his work suggests a recognisable genre of literature. Matthew and Luke used Mark, to greater and lesser extents following his outline, but neither is called a Gospel.

While Mark shows awareness of the messianic meaning of 'Christ', the opening of the Gospel reflects the Gentile use of 'Jesus Christ' as a double name. The textual evidence suggests that the words 'son of God' are a scribal addition. So appropriate are these words that it is not possible that they would have been omitted. Three significant uses show the centrality of this ascription. At Jesus' baptism the voice from heaven announced, 'You are my son' (1.11); then at the transfiguration the voice from heaven again announced for the benefit of Peter, James and John, 'This is my son' (9.7); finally, the climax of the revelation is expressed at the death of Jesus by the centurion who declared, 'Truly this man was [a] son of God' (15.39). It should not be overlooked that the demons also confessed Jesus as 'holy one of God' and 'son of God' (1.24; 3.11; 5.7). Thus, though 'son of God' in 1.1 is a scribal addition, the title is entirely appropriate.

While Mark's Gospel is a new development in Jewish and Greek literature, it broadly fits the category of the Jewish, Greek and Roman 'Lives' (βίοι). (On this see the discussion in the Introduction, 'What is a Gospel?', p. 10.) The early church recognised the genre, identifying two distinct categories in its new collection of scriptures, the first being Gospel.

In Mark there are no miraculous birth stories because the greatness of Jesus is revealed in his relation to God, which is made clear in the opening scenes. John, as Elijah returned, is the forerunner of Jesus, the eschatological representative of God (Malachi 3.1; [4.4–6]; Isaiah 40.3), who is revealed at his baptism by John.

***As it is written . . ., John came . . ., 1.2–8**

1 'As it is written . . .' The placement of the quotation at the beginning and the recognition that only here in the Gospel does the Markan narrator introduce a scripture quotation (most are on the lips of Jesus) make likely that this quotation is a key to the understanding of the Gospel. The narrator appeals to what is written in the prophet Isaiah, but in fact quotes a combination of Malachi 3.1 and Isaiah 40.3. Malachi 3.1 is dependent on Exodus 23.20 and Mark has modified his quotation concerning the forerunner of God to make it fit the appearance of John and his relationship to Jesus. The conflation of Malachi 3.1 with Isaiah 40.3 could be because Mark has drawn his quotation from a collection of early Christian *testimonia* in which the two texts occurred together. But, if there was such a collection, the reasons for conflating the two texts there might also explain Mark's arrangement. Both texts refer to the forerunner of God which Mark has understood in terms of John as the forerunner of Jesus. Mark has a tendency to conflate quoted texts (see Mark 1.11 and Isaiah 42.1 and Psalm 2.7; Mark 11.17 and Isaiah 56.7 and Jeremiah 7.11; Mark 13.24–26 and Isaiah 13.10; 34.4; Ezekiel 32.7–8; Joel 2.10, 31; 3.15; Daniel 7.13–14; Mark 14.62 and Daniel 7.13–14 and Psalm 110.1). Elsewhere only in Mark 11.17 is there a quotation formula and it is the quite general 'Is it not written . . .?' Consequently, the conflation of Mark 1.2 is more puzzling because Isaiah is named although Malachi is quoted first and provides the basis for understanding the role of John (see Malachi 3.1–4; 4.5–6; Mark 9.11–13) as Elijah who must come before the day of the Lord. The connection between the messenger of Malachi 3.1 and returning Elijah of 4.5–6 was certainly made by the rabbis and was apparently known to Mark also. While that is true, Isaiah 40.3 provides the appropriate introduction for the immediate scene, the appearance of John baptising and preaching in *the wilderness*. There he was preparing 'the way of the Lord' by his baptising and preaching. Reference here to 'the way of the Lord' is suggestive, but we should note that the reference is not simply to 'the way'. For example, in the parable of 'the soils' some seed fell beside 'the way' (4.4), that is, not beside the way of the Lord. The way is simply the road. Theology is not packaged into single words.

2 'John came . . .'. In Mark, as in Luke and John, the 'Baptist' is simply called 'John'. Only in Matthew (3.1) is he called 'John the

Baptist' and he is said to be preaching in the desert, whereas Mark says he came/appeared 'baptising and preaching in the desert'. Some texts insert the definite article and thus read as a variant of Matthew, 'John the Baptiser'. This is an assimilation to the text of Matthew, as is confirmed by the fact that some of the texts including the article omit 'and' after 'in the desert' while others include 'and'. But the 'and' only makes sense if Mark says that 'John appeared in the desert baptising and preaching'. The strongest textual evidence also supports this reading.

Josephus confirms the prophetic baptising role of John and his execution by Herod (*Antiquities*, 18.5.2). In the story of the death of John he is referred to as 'John the baptiser' by Herod (6.14) and Herodias (6.24). Here the present participle is used with the definite article emphasising the action of baptising (6.14). But when the daughter (perhaps Salome) repeats the words of her mother to Herod she uses the noun in requesting 'the head of John the Baptist', 6.25. Thus this story, known to Mark, confirms that the name 'the Baptist' was given to John because of his baptising activity. If anything this confirms the absence of these words at the beginning of Mark, supported by the weight of textual evidence.

The appearance of John signals the beginning of the Gospel. He does so in his role as the foretold forerunner. John is the beginning of the Gospel precisely in his relationship to Jesus. According to Acts, when Judas was to be replaced it was agreed that the qualifications for one of the twelve were to have been among the company of the disciples from the time of the baptism of John until the taking up of Jesus and including witness to his resurrection (Acts 1.21–22). Here also he is simply called 'John'. Mark begins with the baptism of John and concludes with the proclamation of the resurrection of Jesus.

All four Gospels use the text from Isaiah 40.3 appealing to the voice crying in the desert though Luke's use is more extensive and John's more abbreviated than Mark's. Only Mark uses the text from Malachi, and then without acknowledgement. Mark's purpose was to link John with the figure of the returning Elijah, an identification denied by the Baptist in John 1.21 but affirmed by Jesus in Mark 9.11–13. Matthew (17.10–13) recognises the identification of John with Elijah but does not use the quotation from Malachi. Mark thus portrays John as the eschatological messenger who announced the imminent approach of the great day of the Lord.

Whereas Matthew has John the Baptist (3.2), Jesus (4.17) and the early Christians (10.7; 24.14) all preach the same message, Mark distinguishes the message of John (1.4) from the message of Jesus (1.14–15) and implies that the message of the early Christians (1.1) was different from both of these. According to Mark, the early Christians proclaimed 'Jesus Christ'.

John's activity *in the desert* is reminiscent of Elijah, as is the description of his dress (Mark 1.6; 2 Kings 1.8). His diet of locusts and wild honey shows that he was not concerned with issues of purity but ate what was available in the desert. His words and action form a unity. He was preaching a baptism of repentance for the forgiveness of sins and was in the desert baptising those who responded to his message. Mark notes the popular response to John. A mass of people from the country regions of Judaea and Jerusalem came out to be baptised by John. The demand of repentance as a condition for baptism is emphasised by the note that those baptised were confessing their sins, confirming that the baptism was in preparation for the coming judgement (compare Matthew 3.7). In due course a new character will arrive. Unlike the masses he did not come from Jerusalem or the regions of Judaea but from Galilee.

Because the Jordan river (see 1.9) flows through desert regions the narrative is credible, but the reference to the desert location has two other functions. It associates John with Elijah and it is the location for 'the voice crying in the desert'. This text (Isaiah 40.3) had become important for various eschatological sects of the time, including the Jesus movement and the Qumran sect, not only because of the connection with Elijah but also as a new Exodus motif. The desert had become the *locale* for deliverance. Although, following the Jewish war of 66–73, Josephus shows no sympathy for eschatological deliverers, he notes the role of certain 'impostors', who were regarded as 'prophets' by the populace (*Antiquities*, 18.85–86; 19.162; 20.97–99; 20.167–172, 188; *War*, 2.258–263; 6.285–286) and offered 'signs of deliverance' as evidence of their role.

According to Mark, John did not perform any 'signs of deliverance' (compare John 10.41) but was rather a prophet of the end time, announcing the impending judgement of God and preparing those who responded to be ready for it. The tradition of Malachi 3.1 and Isaiah 40.3 presents John as the messenger, the voice announcing the impending judgement and the coming judge. In 1.4 his preaching is described in terms of a baptism of repentance for the forgiveness of sins, which is combined with the practice of baptism. In 1.7 another aspect of his preaching is elaborated. 'He comes after me who is stronger than me, the strap of whose sandals I am not worthy to stoop down to loosen. I baptise you with water, but he will baptise you with the holy Spirit.' This statement sets out the paradoxical relationship of John to Jesus.

Jesus is described as 'coming after' John, which is a synonym for 'following' in Mark (1.7, 17, 20; 8.33, 34). 'Following' is an essential component of discipleship. At the same time John affirms that the 'follower' is stronger or mightier. In this way the image of John coming first confirms his role as the forerunner, explicating the tradition of the day of the Lord in relation to Jesus. Matthew and Luke further elaborate the preaching of John, making use of a sayings tradition independent of Mark (Matthew 3.7–10, 12; Luke 3.7–9, 17 = Q). There John characterises the role of the coming one in terms of apocalyptic and cataclysmic judgement.

### +The baptism: Jesus came . . ., 1.9–11

John spoke of the baptism with the holy Spirit by the coming one. What happened was the baptism of the coming one by John. The new scene is set by reference to time, 'In those days', that is, while John was baptising in the desert; by reference to the coming of a new character – Jesus came from Nazareth of Galilee and was baptised in the Jordan by John. Given that no other background has been given for Jesus, the reader would conclude that, unlike the crowds, Jesus was from Galilee and was a native of Nazareth. This identifies Jesus in normal social terms. More significantly, the heavenly voice unveiled his identity in theological or Gospel terms.

The precedent for John's baptism is irrelevant. The baptism of Jesus is described in an economy of words because Mark was a master of the skilful use of gaps which must be filled, keeping the reader alert and involved. The nature of John's baptism has been described and the reader naturally assumes that the baptism of Jesus followed the same pattern. It was a baptism of repentance for the forgiveness of sins and those who underwent it did so confessing their sins. Thus when Jesus called on his hearers to repent (1.15), he did so on the basis of his own public baptism.

Nevertheless, the significant action followed 'immediately' after his baptism. This word is used so frequently by Mark (forty-one times) that it loses its force and should be understood as meaning little more than 'next'. In this case it also indicates an essential connection with the preceding event, the baptism. While the significant action concerns the Spirit, it was not Jesus who baptised with the Spirit. He was apparently 'baptised' by the Spirit, though this term is not used. Perhaps we should think of the Spirit 'anointing' Jesus, though this term is not used either.

Reference to the heavens 'being torn apart' is characteristic of apocalyptic literature (cf. John 1.51; Revelation 4.1) and signals an act of divine revelation, making possible a vision of what is in heaven by those on earth. From the torn-open heavens the Spirit *was seen* descending like a dove, descending upon Jesus (see Isaiah 42.1; 61.1). This was seen by John, when he came out of the water. It is normally assumed that Jesus, who was baptised, came out of the water and saw the Spirit descending on *himself.* But this is not the most likely reading. Mark 1.10 does not specify who came up out of the water and saw. John must also have been in the water baptising Jesus. The previous sentence concludes with the mention of John as the agent of the baptism of Jesus, who was 'baptised in the Jordan by John'. John is thus likely to be the subject of 'he saw'. What he saw was 'the Spirit as a dove descending on him'. In this sentence 'him' is not a reflexive pronoun (not 'himself'). Thus we are to understand that John saw the Spirit descending on Jesus, as in John 1.31–34.

The scene is completed by reference to a voice from heaven, the *bat qol*, literally 'the daughter of the voice', signifying the echo of the voice of God, perhaps thought to take the place of the Spirit-inspired voice of prophecy. Here the Spirit descended upon Jesus and the heavenly voice declared, '*You* are my son, the beloved one, in *you* I am well pleased'. There is no suggestion that the words had any other audience than Jesus within the narrative. The readers or hearers of the Gospel are the other significant audience so that they have an advantage over the characters in the story.

The words echo Psalm 2.7 and Isaiah 42.1. At Qumran Psalm 2 was understood as an oracle predicting the coming of the Messiah. The term translated 'beloved' is characteristically used of an only child in the LXX (see Genesis 22.2). The final words (echoing Isaiah 42.1) express God's delight in his son and imply his obedience to the divine will.

> Behold my servant, whom I uphold, my chosen in whom my soul delights. I have put my Spirit upon him; he will bring forth justice to the nations.

At the baptism of Jesus, Mark provides the means to reinterpret Jesus' messiahship in terms of the Spirit-empowered servant. At the same time he has foreshadowed the outcome of the mission to the nations. Both the descent of the Spirit upon Jesus and the voice from heaven express Jesus' special relationship to God, which only becomes clear in the outworking of the narrative of the Gospel. Important in this is the interpretative model of the servant of Isaiah.

Apart from the recognition of Jesus by the unclean spirits (3.11; 5.7) Mark notes that Jesus is again called 'my son' by the heavenly voice in the 'transfiguration' (9.7), where the words are addressed to the three disciples. After the death of Jesus a Roman centurion declares, 'Truly this man was [a] son of God' (15.39). Perhaps the agent of this climactic announcement tells us something of the non-Jewish context of Mark's Gospel. The other two occasions involve the heavenly voice. Only in 15.39 is a human agent involved. It is notable too that the first revelation of Jesus as God's son was at the baptism, while the last was at his death. Mark 10.38–39 interprets Jesus' baptism in terms of his death. In the narratives of Jesus' baptism and death the verb 'to tear apart' is used. At the baptism John saw the heavens 'being torn apart', while at the death of Jesus the veil of the temple was torn apart from top to bottom. At the baptism the heavenly voice declared Jesus to be 'my son', while at his crucifixion a Roman centurion declared him to be '[a] son of God', 15.38–39. This framing of the mission of Jesus by the two uses of the verb 'to tear apart', and the two declarations of Jesus as son of God, is important. It implies that the rending of the veil of the temple, like the rending of the heavens, reveals Jesus. But the recipient of the revelation was a Roman centurion.

Mark 10.38–39 includes the participation of the disciples in Jesus' death. They also will be baptised with his baptism. John preaches and is delivered up to death, then Jesus preaches and is delivered up, and finally, the disciples will preach and be delivered up. Then the end will come.

The scene of the baptism with the heavens torn open reveals Jesus as the agent of God's action. He is the central figure of the drama, the subject of the good news confirmed as God's representative, his son, who performs his will, bringing it to fulfilment. That God acts through an intermediary is characteristic of apocalyptic literature. One reason for the distance of God from the world becomes apparent in the next scene.

## +THE TESTING OF GOD'S SON: THE SPIRIT DRIVES HIM OUT . . ., 1.12–13

The use of 'immediately' alerts the reader to the intimate connection between the baptism and the testing of Jesus in Mark's plot (see 1.10). It is precisely because Jesus has been revealed and empowered as God's son by the Spirit that he is now driven by the Spirit into the desert to face the testing by Satan. The desert was the place of the Exodus deliverance by God. It was also the place where Israel was tested and failed (Psalm 95.7–11), the place of demons (Deuteronomy 32.17; Isaiah 34.14), the stronghold of Satan. In Mark there is no statement of purpose but it is noted that, as a consequence, Jesus was in the desert forty days being tested by (the) Satan. In Job 1–2 Satan is a figure in the heavenly court who accused the servants of God. In later apocalyptic literature he is the principal demonic power opposed to God. It is in this sense that he is to be understood here. The wild beasts are linked with Satan (Test. Issachar 7.7; Test. Naphtali 8.4), just as the angels are associated with Jesus as God's son (Psalm 91.11–13). It is unclear whether the angels ministered to Jesus throughout the testing or only at the conclusion, as in Matthew 4.11. In Mark the statement that Jesus was with the wild beasts apparently applies to the whole period and this tends to weight the balance in favour of the ministry of the angels throughout the period also.

Reference to the forty days may relate allegorically to the testing of Israel (God's son) in the wilderness (see Numbers 14.34; Ezekiel 4.5–6 for the association of days and years). Whereas Israel failed the test in the wilderness it is implied that Jesus passed the test. This interpretation is clearer in Matthew and Luke than in Mark. Other uses of forty days relate to Moses on Mount Sinai (Exodus 34.28) and Elijah travelling to Horeb (1 Kings 19.8).

Mark gives no details of this struggle and no indication of the outcome. This weighs against the view that (for Mark) the encounter was a decisive victory for Jesus over Satan and that what follows in the body of the Gospel was a mopping-up operation only. Rather, as part of the Prelude, which provides the backdrop against which the story is to be understood, the narrative of the testing of God's son reveals the true nature of the conflict in which Jesus is involved. His opponents often appear to be simply human agents but, in and through them all, he encountered the Satanic power of evil.

Chapter 2

# Introduction to the Galilean mission, 1.14–20

## *FROM JOHN TO JESUS: AFTER JOHN . . . JESUS CAME, 1.14–15

The preacher to this point was John. The beginning of Jesus' ministry is marked by the arrest of John. Mark portrays the sequence of first John and then Jesus. Now Jesus came/returned into Galilee. Three important transitions occur at this point. 'From John to Jesus' marks the first change, which encompasses the other two. The second is from the desert region of the Jordan into Galilee. The third transition is from John's preaching of a baptism of repentance to Jesus' proclamation of 'the gospel of [the kingdom of] God . . .'. Mark (unlike Matthew 3.2; 4.17) starkly distinguishes the preaching of Jesus from the preaching of John. With the appearance of Jesus in Galilee, after his baptism and testing, his preaching carries a new urgency which distinguishes it from the preaching of John by asserting that the kingdom of God was now present in a new way. The new state of affairs was the ground for calling for repentance, but is also proclaimed as 'good news' in which the hearers are called to believe. While the call to repentance was common to the preaching of John and Jesus, Jesus' proclamation of the 'gospel' and his call to 'believe' in it were new. The 'gospel of God' was the good news which had God as its subject or, expressed more fully, concerned the presence of the kingdom of God. As preached by Jesus this was good news to be believed. This event was bad news for Satan and those who practised evil. It was good news for the oppressed who longed for liberation. Judgement and deliverance are two sides of the coming of the kingdom of God. The 'gospel of God' is also to be understood as good news from God declared by his messenger.

The *language* of 'the kingdom of God' is distinctive to Jesus in the Gospels. It is not used at all in the Jewish scriptures and is little used outside the Gospels in the New Testament (NT). Nevertheless, the affirmation of God's kingship is central to some parts of the Jewish scriptures and the usage of Jesus in the Gospels obviously grows out of this. In the Jewish scriptures the eternal kingship of God is affirmed, 'The Lord is king', Psalms 10.16; 24; 29.10; 47.7; 93.1; 95.3; 97.1; 99.1. Specific events of the past, like the Exodus, were proclaimed as manifestations of his kingship, Psalm 98, especially verses 6–9. In times of oppression the prophets looked to the future for a new and definitive manifestation of his kingship, Daniel 7; Isaiah 7; 9; 11 and see also Psalm 98.6–9. In Judaism there were divergent views about the way the future aspect would be fulfilled: (1) by reciting the Shema or the study of the Torah, an individualistic interpretation understood as taking on the yoke of God's rule; (2) by revolution, which was the Zealot understanding of the messianic cause; (3) by the direct intervention of God, which was sometimes bound up with another kind of messianism where the intervention was understood to be completely God's initiative, as in the case of Daniel 7.

In Mark Jesus' proclamation of the kingdom of God looked to the definitive manifestation of the reign of God. On the one hand it is clear that the kingdom had become present in a new way in the ministry of Jesus (1.14–15; 3.20–30), yet there is a clear expectation of future fulfilment, 9.1; 13; 14.61–62. Because the kingdom had become present in a new way it was possible to be 'not far from the kingdom' (12.34), 'to receive the kingdom' (10.15), and 'to enter the kingdom' (9.47; 10.15, 23–24). Thus Jesus not only proclaimed the presence of the kingdom, its presence is closely associated with Jesus, 1.15. The presence of the kingdom in Jesus is demonstrated by his overthrow of Satan's rule, 3.20–30. Hence the prominence of exorcisms (1.23–28, 34; 3.11–12, 15, 20–27; 5.1–20; 6.7, 14–29; 7.24–30; 9.14–29, 38–41), which demonstrate the plundering of Satan's kingdom and the assertion of a new reign. The parables of Mark 4 reveal the mystery of the hidden kingdom in which it is possible to perceive the presence of the kingdom in the ministry and activity of Jesus. God reigns through his Christ, but the fulfilment of God's final judgement lies in the future with the coming Son of Man. Thus the proclamation of the kingdom of God implied eschatology.

The scriptures quoted in 1.2–3 announce the coming of God in deliverance and judgement. Jesus distinctively proclaimed this in terms of the presence of the kingdom of God. The manner of its presence was a mystery bound up with the presence of Jesus himself. Judgement and deliverance are implied by the twofold call: (1) to repent and (2) to believe *in the gospel*. The call for repentance was in continuity with the ministry of John, but the call to believe in the gospel was new. The construction used by Mark is rare in the NT (see John 3.15; 20.31) but common in the LXX. Reference to the gospel forms an *inclusio* with 1.1 and opens the possibility that Mark implies that the gospel to be believed is not only the message of Jesus but the message of his book and of the early preachers commissioned by Jesus. In this summary there is no mention of healings or exorcisms, though they are essentially associated with the preaching and teaching of Jesus in the account that follows. Indeed, the healings and exorcisms are portrayed as active parables of Jesus' teaching and preaching and exorcism is seen as a manifestation of his new teaching with authority (1.22, 27). We should assume that this summary reference to the proclamation of the kingdom of God includes the accompanying healings and exorcisms.

Mark often describes the fact of Jesus preaching or teaching without reference to the actual content of the teaching. This definitive *summary*, under which all of Jesus' activity stands, has been placed at the beginning. Jesus appears as the emissary of the kingdom of God who not only announces its dawning, but is the one in whose ministry the kingdom is actually present. The summary is also a transition to the account of Jesus' Galilean ministry, which follows immediately. The opening scene of this provides an illustration of what it means to 'repent and believe in the gospel'.

## +THE FIRST DISCIPLES: 'FOLLOW ME AND I WILL MAKE YOU . . .', 1.16–20

Now, in a new scene, the location is made more specific by reference to the sea of Galilee. Two sets of brothers, Simon and Andrew and James and John, were called by Jesus. While they were not called on to repent and believe, they were called to leave all and follow Jesus. It seems that this is Mark's initial interpretation of what it means to repent and believe. With the first set of brothers Mark does not use the verb 'to call' (1.20 and see 3.13; 6.7; 8.1; 12.43), but depicts the call dramatically.

The brothers are carefully identified. Simon is mentioned first and Andrew is identified as the brother of Simon, not just 'his brother'. Certainly Simon (Peter) became better known than Andrew. James is described as the son of Zebedee and John is called 'his brother'. We know Zebedee only as the father of James and John, but it was common to identify someone as 'the son of . . .'. James had to be called the son of Zebedee because the name James became almost inseparably associated with the brother of Jesus, who would first come to mind with the use of the name. This is the major reason for the use of his father's name to identify him. John could then quite simply be identified as 'his brother'. In due course John became better known than this James (see Galatians 2.9 and Eusebius, *History*, 2.1.4–5), perhaps after the death of his brother James (Acts 12.2), and until that time the traditional order of Peter, James and John persisted (see Eusebius, *History*, 2.1.3) and Mark is consistent with this. It may be that in each case the elder brother is mentioned first, Simon and James.

The first set of brothers were casting their nets because, as we are told, 'they were fishers'. Jesus called them authoritatively 'Come after me and I will make you fishers of people'. Mark tells, 'And immediately they left their nets and *followed*' Jesus. The stress is on the authoritative word of Jesus and the 'immediate' response of Simon and Andrew. In the second call scene James and John were in their boat mending the nets. No words of Jesus are reported, only the fact that Jesus 'called' them and they left their father and the hired fishermen and followed (literally 'came after') Jesus, again emphasising the authoritative word of Jesus.

Nothing in the narrative suggests that the brothers had prior knowledge of Jesus, either before his baptism or after his return to Galilee. By calling two sets of brothers he established a basic group of 'followers' in a way that stresses the initiative and authoritative word of Jesus. The term 'disciples' is not used of them, though the *concept* of 'followers' contributes to the understanding of that term when it is used later in the Gospel. The term 'disciples' is used for the first time in 2.15 in the narrative of the call of Levi. See the discussion there for a list of references.

According to Mark the first 'followers' of Jesus responded to his word alone. Although the language of faith/belief is not used of them, the portrayal of them as 'followers' is an important insight into the Markan understanding of the meaning of belief. At this point there has been no mention of any miracles. The instant response of the four to the authoritative call of Jesus is, in Mark's terms, impressively in their favour. They were not amongst the crowds that were first attracted to Jesus by his healing activity or reports of it. Thus we have, at the beginning, a very positive introduction to the group we will come to know as 'the twelve' or 'the disciples' of Jesus.

This double scene confirms Mark's intentional use of the synonyms 'coming after' (1.7, 17, 20; 8.33, 34) and 'following' (1.18; 2.14, 15; 3.7; 5.24; 6.1; 8.34; [9.38] 10.21, 28, 32, 52; 11.9; [14.54] 15.41). Note in particular 1.17, 18, 20 and 8.33, 34. Yet 'following' alone did not qualify for Mark's use of the term 'disciple'. Many tax collectors and sinners (2.15), a great multitude from Galilee (3.7), a great crowd (5.24), Bartimaeus (10.52), the crowd going into Jerusalem (11.9), the women (15.41) are described as 'following' Jesus. Another essential element for Mark was the call of Jesus. Thus the four fishermen were constituted as disciples by the authoritative call *and* their own affirmative response. There are instances of others who wished to follow Jesus in this way. The Gerasene demoniac sought 'to be with' Jesus (5.18 and see 3.14). This is the essence of discipleship. But Mark indicates that Jesus would not permit him. Then there was the rich man, who was called by Jesus (10.21), but who failed to follow. All of this suggests that call plus affirmative response constitutes the follower as a 'disciple' of Jesus in Mark's terms. This is consistent with Mark's use of the term, which appears to be restricted to 'the twelve'.

The exceptional case is that of Levi (2.13–17, see the discussion below). Levi was certainly called and Mark notes that 'he followed'. Yet Levi is described as being *with* Jesus and his disciples, along with many tax collectors and sinners, and is not named amongst the twelve. Yet, in spite of the case of Levi, it seems best to conclude that call plus affirmative response constitutes the follower as a 'disciple' in Mark. Outside the small band of disciples, Mark depicts a host of followers. The term disciple signifies the close relationship to Jesus as the teacher.

The call scenes establish Jesus' mode of operation. His word is authoritative, calling for immediate response. From the beginning he did not act alone but in the company of 'followers'. Their presence signals the establishment of a new community and at the same time sets up a succession. Just as Jesus has caught them, they will also catch people. Jesus preaches and they will preach. This is explicit in the words of Jesus to Simon and Andrew, though expressed in a figure of speech. It is systematically set out in the commissioning of 'the twelve' (6.6b–13).

Chapter 3

# Miracles and conflict, 1.21—7.23

The Galilean mission can be viewed from two perspectives. The first concerns the *reception* of Jesus' mission. Initially, Jesus was received with a mixture of awe and enthusiasm. This phase of his ministry is conveyed by Mark through a series of miracle stories, 1.21–45. Even here a premonition of conflict is conveyed in the exorcisms where Jesus is challenged by the possessed (1.23–24, 34). Although Jesus' first exorcism was on the *sabbath*, his conflict with the Jewish authorities does not emerge until the healing of the paralytic in 2.1–10, when Jesus was charged with blasphemy by a group of scribes, 2.6–7. Conflict, not always with the scribes, dominates the section 2.1–3.35 and is expressed in a series of objection stories.

The scribes were experts in the law, not belonging to any one sect or party. Some would have been Pharisees by conviction, while others were Sadducees (see the discussion of 12.18–27). The latter were aristocratic and wealthy, belonging to the high priestly family. The scribes mentioned in 2.6 may have been local to Capernaum, and might have been Pharisees. In 3.22 scribes from Jerusalem are mentioned and it is likely that these were of Sadducaean persuasion.

The Pharisees were teachers of the law from the perspective of their own developing tradition, which was built on the law, prophets and writings. They were spread throughout Judaea and Galilee and indeed into the diaspora. Hence they were not concentrated in the wealthy aristocracy, nor were they a priestly group. Nevertheless, they, too, were opponents of Jesus.

The final group mentioned in opposition to Jesus is the Herodians. They were not a sect in the same sense as the other groups mentioned. Rather, they were 'retainers' of the Herodian dynasty with its pro-Roman position. All of these groups had their reasons for opposing Jesus.

Whether Mark was responsible for shaping the objection stories to bring out the conflict, or has used stories where the conflict already featured, is not easy to say. For example, Mark has placed the story of the call of four fishermen at 1.16–20 to demonstrate the authority of Jesus and to make clear that, from the beginning, Jesus did not act alone in his mission but with a group of disciples. In 2.13–17 Mark records a second call story. But the dominant theme of this story is the challenge of the scribes and Pharisees concerning the company Jesus kept. Obviously the intended slur of the criticism was that Jesus could be judged by the company he kept. The dramatic pronouncement of Jesus in 2.17, which is the climax of the story, is Jesus' response to that criticism. Later Jesus was challenged in similar ways on the basis of the behaviour of his disciples, concerning the failure to fast (2.18–22), plucking grain on the sabbath (2.23–28), the failure to wash hands before eating (7.1–23). After the initial concentration on Jesus' conflict with Jewish religious authorities this is a continuing feature in the Gospel, alongside the popularity of Jesus with the crowds in his teaching and healing.

Second, the Galilean mission can also be viewed from the perspective of Jesus' *itinerary*. Mark carefully charts Jesus' movement from place to place. More often than not locations are named, though sometimes as generally as the description 'beside the sea'. There are journeys to and fro across the sea. One of these, in the midst of the Galilean ministry (5.1–20), took Jesus outside of Galilee and into dominantly Gentile territory. There he performed an important exorcism. Nothing is said of the ethnic identity of the man Jesus healed. But Mark emphasises the location as the region of Gerasa and stresses that, after the exorcism, the man went throughout the Decapolis proclaiming what Jesus had done for him so that all marvelled. Thus this single incident, embedded in the midst of Jesus' Galilean mission, foreshadows Jesus' more extensive excursion into dominantly Gentile territory in 7.24–8.10.

## JESUS' GALILEAN MISSION A, 1.21–4.41

### Act One (collection of miracle stories): the revealed and hidden kingdom, 1.21–45

*+Teaching and exorcism in the synagogue at Capernaum on the sabbath, 1.21–28*

The scene is in two parts:

1 +Teaching, 1.21–22

The first part deals with Jesus' participation in the synagogue service (1.21–22) and forms the context for the second part. The call of the two sets of brothers took place at some unspecified place on the sea of Galilee (1.14, 16). Because 1.29 implies that Simon and Andrew lived in Capernaum, we should understand that Mark implies that the call took place beside the sea somewhere near Capernaum where the two sets of brothers lived. We are now told that '*They* came into Capernaum', 1.21. This unobtrusive use of the plural verb establishes that Jesus acts in the company of his newly acquired 'followers'. Having located Jesus and his 'followers' in Capernaum Mark indicates, 'And immediately on the Sabbath, having entered the synagogue he taught'. The flow of the narrative suggests that Jesus came to Capernaum for the sabbath in order to attend the synagogue. The first public act of Jesus, as the leader of a newly established band of followers, was to attend synagogue. It is as if Mark has announced to the reader, 'On the sabbath you may expect to find Jesus in the synagogue'.

Ruins of a synagogue in Capernaum come from a time later than Jesus, but an earlier synagogue might lie beneath it. While our knowledge of synagogue services comes from later texts, it is likely that in the time of Jesus and Mark the service included readings from the law and the prophets, with summary translations in Aramaic or Greek, an exposition or sermon, prayers and benedictions. Participation in the service was arranged by the ruler of the synagogue, who could authorise any gifted person to read or 'preach'. Given that Mark says that Jesus 'taught', we understand that he was recognised and asked to teach. Mark notes the amazed response to Jesus' teaching. This opening scene in the public ministry of Jesus gives an example of the typical practice of Jesus on the sabbath and sets the tone for his Galilean mission.

Luke 4.16–30 provides an account of the beginning of Jesus' ministry on a sabbath in a synagogue, but locates the incident at Nazareth. There Jesus was given the scroll of the prophet Isaiah to read from chapter 61. When he had done so he handed the scroll back to the attendant and 'sat down' *to teach.* This is implied by Luke, who says that 'the eyes of all in the synagogue were fixed on him'. Jesus did not disappoint them, affirming, 'This day is this scripture fulfilled in your ears'. The words are to be understood as a summary statement of the teaching of Jesus at that time. Luke follows this scene with the account of another sabbath synagogue scene in Capernaum (Luke 4.31–37, which corresponds to Mark 1.21–28), where Jesus encountered a person possessed by 'a spirit of an unclean demon'. Mark has Jesus in the synagogue at Nazareth somewhat later (in 6.1–6). Luke 4.16–30 is *a* reworking of that tradition. Luke has used the Nazareth tradition to show the customary practice of Jesus on the sabbath (Luke 4.16), attending the synagogue. In that context Luke provides a reading and summary sermon by Jesus which sets out a manifesto for his ministry. Characteristically, Mark is less concerned with the content of the teaching of Jesus at this point than with its powerful effects. Luke has also placed the rejection of Jesus, where Jesus was brought up (Luke 4.16) right at the beginning of Jesus' ministry. Mark, on the other hand, has held back the synagogue rejection scene to 6.1–6, with the result that this opening scene depicts a positive response by the synagogue congregation foreshadowing a successful Galilean mission.

At Capernaum Mark mentions no reading from either the law or the prophets, only that Jesus taught; no indication of what he taught, only that he taught as having authority and not as the scribes (1.22). There is no mention of any scribes present in the synagogue at this time. Yet their influence is already felt because of the way their practice intrudes on the minds of the those who then heard Jesus, bringing about a contrast of his teaching with theirs. From here on Mark develops a growing conflict between Jesus and the scribes: over the forgiveness of sins (2.5–7); and Jesus' authority over demons which 'the scribes *from Jerusalem*' attribute to Beelzebul, the prince of demons (3.22). No doubt Mark perceived the opposition to Jesus to be centred in Jerusalem.

Mark reports a contrast between the teaching of Jesus and the scribal tradition, which quoted various authorities on any issue without affirming what was right and true. Evidently, Jesus declared the truth unequivocally and with 'authority', not appealing to human authorities but announcing with certainty the way of the kingdom of God. If Mark was concerned to state the manner of Jesus' preaching, he was also concerned to state the response to that preaching. Those who heard 'were amazed'. In Mark amazement (1.22, 27, 32) or fear (16.8) are the regular responses to the words or actions of Jesus. The first point about Jesus' teaching in the synagogue at Capernaum was to show the authority expressed in his teaching and the amazement it produced in the hearers. The sabbath setting was, in the first place, the presupposition for Jesus' teaching in the synagogue. Only retrospectively does Jesus' action on the sabbath imply controversy (2.23–28 and especially 3.2 in 3.1–6).

2 +Exorcism: a hybrid quest/objection story, 1.23–28

The second part concerns another response to Jesus' participation in the sabbath synagogue service by a person with an unclean spirit, 1.23–28. Mark emphasises the connection by introducing this encounter with 'And immediately . . .'. If the response to Jesus' teaching by those who heard in the synagogue was amazement, there was a second response which can be perceived as an assault on Jesus, an *objection* to him, by the person with an unclean spirit. He appeared immediately in the synagogue. Jesus' authority was challenged by the power of evil manifest in a person with an unclean spirit. It is somewhat paradoxical that the kingdom encounters evil in *the synagogue* on *the sabbath.* Here there are hints suggesting opposition to Jesus by the synagogue.

The person with the unclean spirit should not have been in the synagogue. While the sabbath setting was necessary to provide the synagogue setting for Jesus' initial teaching, the encounter with the man with the unclean spirit did not have to be set there. There is something incompatible about that encounter in this context. Further, the exorcism on the sabbath had the potential to cause controversy concerning the breaking of the sabbath, as actions performed on the sabbath do in 2.23–28; 3.1–6. This did not eventuate in 1.23–28, perhaps because the scribes, Pharisees and Herodians were not present. The shadow of the scribes lengthens over this story with the comparison of Jesus' teaching with theirs. Nevertheless, the effectiveness of Jesus' exorcism by word was taken to reinforce the *authority* of Jesus' teaching, which is characterised as 'new' (1.27).

The encounter is tightly connected to Jesus' teaching and the response (1.21–22) by 'And immediately . . .' (1.23). The connection is further confirmed at the conclusion of the exorcism when the hearers again express their amazement (1.27). The encounter is introduced by the appearance of the person with the unclean spirit whose presence was announced by a loud cry. The opening words of the person possessed probably mean 'What have you got to do with *us*?' (compare Mark 5.7), though there might be some connection with a Hebrew expression of Judges 11.12 and 1 Kings 17.18 with the meaning 'Why are you interfering with us?' Even if the more straightforward Greek sense is followed, the sense of interference is implied. The question implies that Jesus has trespassed into the territory of the unclean spirit. This is the sinister element. It seems to be implied that the synagogue is the territory of the unclean spirit. The perceived threat of Jesus to the unclean spirit is confirmed by the second question, 'Have you come to destroy us?' The implied answer to this question is in the affirmative. On this reading the narrative is to be seen as an objection story, with the action of Jesus in casting out the unclean spirit providing the decisive pronouncement.

The man with the unclean spirit addressed Jesus first of all as 'Jesus Nazarene', recognising that Jesus was from Nazareth (see 1.9). While this identifies Jesus in social terms, there is a deeper truth about him that was revealed in his baptism. This, too, was known to the unclean spirit, 'I know who you are, the holy one of God'. For Mark this has the sense of the declaration of the heavenly voice. The 'holy one of God' is God's son. The title 'holy one of God' is known to us elsewhere only in John 6.69. There the ascription is used in a confession of faith by Peter which seems to be completely positive. Like the confession by Peter in the Synoptics (Mark 8.29–30, 33), however, the confession is followed by reference to the devil or Satan (John 6.70). Other than this the closest forms of ascription come in Acts, where Jesus is called 'the holy and righteous one' (Acts 3.14), and in quoting Psalm 16.10 in relation to the resurrection of Jesus it is affirmed that God did not allow his 'holy one' to see corruption (Acts 2.27; 13.35). There a different term is used for the 'holy one' and there is no full equivalence to 'holy one of God'. While the ascription is enigmatic, it is best to see it as the equivalent of 'son of God' but from the perspective of the unclean spirit, where the natural evaluation is in terms of the polarity of holiness or purity over against uncleanness. That equivalence is suggested by Mark 3.11, where it is said that whenever the unclean spirits saw him they fell down before him and cried out, 'You are the son of God' (compare 5.7).

There is thus a paradoxical element in Jesus' encounter with those possessed by unclean spirits/demons. It is, on the one hand, an expression of Jesus' conflict with evil, with Satan, 3.23. Yet there is more than a hint that the spirits, *or those possessed by them*, not only perceived the hidden identity of Jesus but submitted to his authority *in worship*. In this story (1.23), the man with the unclean spirit took the initiative and confronted Jesus in the synagogue. Even more pointedly, the Gerasene demoniac ran to Jesus and prostrated himself before him (5.6–7). Mark pointedly describes this in the language of worship appropriate to the behaviour of a lowly subject in the presence of the great king. There is thus a case for treating the specific exorcism stories as miracle quest stories in which the approach of the possessed to Jesus is understood as a paradoxical request for healing/exorcism. It is paradoxical because of the domination of the person by the demon(s). Thus the spirits also expressed fear in the face of the threat that Jesus posed for them.

Jesus' response shows that the worst fears of the unclean spirit were to be realised. That it is the unclean spirit speaking is confirmed in the question, 'Have you come to destroy *us*?' Nothing Jesus did threatened the man. It was the unclean spirit that was threatened and the threat was seen to be collective, to 'us'. The purpose of God in his son was to destroy evil. A later narrative confirms that Mark perceived the demonic destruction of the human personality resulting in a collective manifestation of evil (5.9). If the unclean spirit hoped to assert power over Jesus by revealing his knowledge, not only of Jesus' public identity but also of his secret identity or name, Jesus asserted his power by commanding the spirit to be silent and to come out of the person. The silencing of the unclean spirit was not only the first step in the exorcism. It seems also to be the indication of Jesus' refusal to allow the unclean spirits to make his identity known. See Mark 1.34; 3.11–12 and the discussion of the messianic secret below.

The result was a visible and violent tearing of the man as the unclean spirit cried with a loud voice and came out of him. The visible event convinced the spectators of the exorcism. This evidence confirmed the authority of Jesus' 'new teaching' so that they concluded that the unclean spirits were subject to him and obeyed him. A new and greater authority had appeared and so public was this event that the report went out throughout the whole region of Galilee.

In this account of the first miracle of Jesus in Mark the people in the synagogue identified Jesus' authority in performing an exorcism as a manifestation of his 'new teaching' (1.27 and see 1.22). It is not the exorcism in itself but the nature of the teaching that is in focus. This also seems to be the point made by the Markan Jesus in the Beelzebul controversy of 3.22–30. The exorcisms are authentications of his teaching. Thus there is a case for viewing the Markan Jesus as 'teacher', even though comparatively little of his actual teaching is recorded in Mark compared with narratives of his healing *activities*. Mark often notes that Jesus taught without reporting what he taught, see 1.21–22. This runs contrary to any tendency to interpret Jesus in terms of the so-called 'divine man' manifest by miracles. Nor should the disciples be seen to be advocates of this kind of christology (*pace* Theodore Weeden). After all, Mark narrates the call of the first disciples before any of Jesus' miracles. Indeed, the category of the 'divine man' appears to be a construct of modern scholars (see the work of D.L. Tiede and Carl H. Holladay). Nevertheless, 'signs and wonders' constitute a problem concerning which the Markan Jesus warns the readers (13.5–6, 21–23). This probably relates to prophets who promised eschatological signs of deliverance who are referred to by Josephus.

*+The healing of Simon's (Peter's) mother-in-law, 1.29–31*

The narrative confirms that the four disciples were with Jesus in the synagogue and tells us that 'coming out of the synagogue they went to the house of Simon and Andrew', implying that they lived in Capernaum (contrast John 1.44). There Jesus healed Simon's mother-in-law, who had a fever, by taking her hand and raising her. The healing was demonstrated by the way she ministered to them, apparently taking care of their material needs. The story confirms that Jesus acted in concert with his followers and is exceptional in showing him using his powers for the benefit of the family of one of those who will be named amongst the twelve.

**A summary statement: healings and exorcisms in Capernaum, 1.32–34*

A typical evening in the ministry of Jesus in Capernaum is now described. At the end of the day all the sick and demon possessed were brought to the door of the house of Simon and Andrew. Jesus healed many and exorcised many of those possessed by demons, refusing to let them speak 'because they knew him'. Some manuscripts read, with minor variations of wording, 'because they knew him to be the Christ'. This reflects a scribal failure to appreciate the revelation of Jesus' identity at his baptism (3.11–12). The silencing of the demons demonstrates the authority of Jesus in overthrowing the power of Satan. Thus even when Jesus was revealed formally he remained a mystery. The present kingdom remained a mystery to be explored in Jesus' teaching in parables, and to be demonstrated in his life, death and resurrection.

William Wrede argued that the secrecy motif was a theological construct to explain why the earliest tradition did not claim Jesus was Messiah. The solution to this problem for Mark was to argue that Jesus had kept his identity a secret. Wrede certainly identified an important issue. His solution has not proved to be completely persuasive. First, there is no non-messianic tradition concerning Jesus. Then, the components that make up the evidence for Wrede's unified theory seem to be a consequence of various causes, not the simple explanation offered by Wrede. There are various reasons for Jesus demanding secrecy from the demon possessed (1.24, 34; 3.11–12); after miracles (1.44; 5.43; 7.36); after Peter's confession (8.30); after the transfiguration (9.9). Not only did Jesus command secrecy, he performed secret actions, withdrawing from the crowds (7.24; 9.30), giving private instruction to his disciples about the mystery of the kingdom of God (4.10–12), that which defiles (7.17–23), prayer (9.28–29), messianic suffering (8.31; 9.31; 10.33–34), the *parousia* (13.3–37). Special teaching to the inner group of disciples does not provide support for Wrede's hypothesis.

There appear to be different reasons for silencing demons and requiring secrecy after certain miracles. Publicising the miracles of healing led to a situation where Jesus could not move freely, hindering his preaching itinerary. But residual problematic material remains. In Mark this material is used to show that, from the perspective of the death and resurrection of Jesus, the nature of Jesus' messiahship was misunderstood during his lifetime. For Mark the mystery was not that Jesus was the Messiah, but that the Messiah was to suffer and die. The mystery of the Messiah was bound up with the mystery of evil, which in turn leads to the mystery of the kingdom of God (Mark 4.11).

Whether Jesus claimed to be Messiah is perhaps impossible to say. That his teaching and actions raised the question of his messiahship in the minds of others during the time of his ministry is beyond doubt. Further, it seems certain that popular expectations were at odds with Jesus' understanding of his role. Conflict with role expectation is apparent in Mark's account of Jesus' dialogue with Peter after the confession at Caesarea Philippi. Certainly, Mark's understanding of Jesus' messiahship was at odds with the popular views of the day. Wrede was right to see that Mark gave a post-resurrection interpretation of Jesus, but his conclusion that the earliest tradition was non-messianic is at odds with all surviving evidence. Rather, Mark had to cope with the massive problem of proclaiming as Messiah, Jesus, who was known to have suffered and been crucified in circumstances of disgrace and indignity at the hands of the Romans.

Wrede called his book *Das Messiasgeheimnis in den Evangelien* because the messianic secret finds expression in all four Gospels. The first part of the title has been translated as *The Messianic Secret*. It is better translated as *The Messianic Mystery*. While the mystery encompasses the secrecy motif, it is not exhausted by it. For Mark, the nature of Jesus' messiahship constitutes the mystery because Jesus is Messiah precisely because he suffered and died. The secrecy motif is probably a construction of the early Christian tradition and one that Mark has developed and made use of in the construction of his Gospel, not because Jesus was not perceived to be Messiah but because Mark gave a radical reinterpretation to the messianic tradition.

*+The quest to find Jesus and the spread of the new teaching throughout Galilee, 1.35–39*

This transitional summary tells of another characteristic day in the ministry of Jesus. Early in the morning Jesus went to a desert place to pray. Simon and others found him and reported that everyone in Capernaum was *seeking* him, but Jesus indicated the necessity of preaching in all the other towns, which was the strategy of his mission. This, the narrator indicates, he did throughout Galilee, preaching in *their* synagogues and casting out demons. Again the activity of preaching and exorcism is seen to be typical and essential to the ministry of Jesus. Reference to 'their synagogues' could be taken as an indication that the narrative was written from the perspective of the church after the separation of synagogue and church. It is more likely that it simply indicates the synagogues in the various towns. The name 'Simon' continues to be used here prior to 3.16, where we are told that Jesus named Simon as Peter. Though named, Simon is not identified as the spokesman. Yet by being the only person named his leading role is maintained. While those with Simon are not named, the reader might suspect that Andrew, James and John were with him (see 1.16–20).

This summary account is not straightforward. Within it is set a complex quest story. It is a combination of a failed quest and a corrected quest. The quest is announced by Simon and those with him reporting, 'All are *seeking* you' (1.37 and see 3.22; 8.11, 12; 11.18; 12.12; 14.1, 11, 55; 16.6). As part of the 'All seeking', Simon and those with him are portrayed as seekers and, as it is reported that they *found* Jesus, it seems at first as if their quest was successful. The difficulty to be overcome if their quest was to be successful was that Jesus withdrew to a desert place. Of all the seekers, they alone found him. Yet success is qualified because their report suggests they were seeking Jesus on behalf of all the other seekers. Their report was their way of trying to bring Jesus back to those who sought him. If their quest is seen to be redirected by Jesus then their quest on behalf of all the rest failed. Jesus' impressive pronouncement declared that quest a failure, redirects the quest of Simon and those with him, and in so doing announces the Galilean mission, 'Let *us* go elsewhere into the neighbouring villages so that *I* may preach there; for this is the purpose for which I came out'. This might be a reference to the purpose of Jesus' coming out into the desert place, indicating that his action signified that he was not to be tied to one place because he had a mission to all the villages. It also is a statement concerning the purpose of Jesus' coming as such.

The narrator concludes the scene by noting that 'He went into the whole of Galilee preaching in their synagogues and casting out demons', applying this statement specifically to the Galilean mission. This confirms the correction of the quest of Simon and those with him, and the failure of the quest of all the others who sought and failed to find Jesus.

*+The quest of a leper for cleansing, 1.40–45*

The incident is set in Jesus' overall Galilean mission (1.39). No specific location is identified. A quest story is signalled by the approach of a leper. The supplicatory nature of the leper's request is strongly emphasised by noting that he knelt before Jesus (see 5.6). The omission of this from some texts was accidental. This attitude is reinforced by the verb used to express his request. He *besought* Jesus, saying, 'If you *will* you can make me clean'. This implied request identifies a difficulty to be overcome as the *willingness* of Jesus to act. He sought to overcome this difficulty by adopting the attitude of a suppliant. This is in contrast to the desperation of the father of the boy with the deaf and dumb spirit in 9.22 who, ignoring all formalities, appealed 'If you *can*, have compassion on us and help us'. There Jesus responded with what can be understood as affront at the suggestion, 'If you *can* . . .', 9.23. Nevertheless, in each case the request was successful.

Lepers, like those having an unclean spirit, were unclean. Jesus treated those possessed as victims and exorcised them without explicit request or in response to ambiguous requests because they had been overcome by evil powers. The leper was unclean but his personality was intact and his volition unimpaired. Thus he could request cleansing. While Jesus acted in reaction to the onslaught of the demonic, Mark says he had 'compassion' on the leper. A minority of texts say he was moved with 'anger' or simply omit any reference to compassion or anger. Because 'anger' *seems* to be the more difficult reading to explain, this might seem to be what was originally written. If correct it would seem to be anger at the situation of the leper who, by regulation of the Mosaic law (Leviticus 13–14), was isolated from normal human contact because of his disease. Touching him was a defiant act in the face of this convention. But compassion was also expressed by touching the leper, which was a show of fearlessness in the face of uncleanness. The response in word, 'I will, be clean', can equally be understood in relation to anger or compassion.

The textual evidence in favour of 'anger' is much weaker than supporting the reading of 'compassion' and, in the Markan context, 'anger' is not really the more difficult reading. Immediately after the cleansing the narrative indicates that Jesus 'sternly warned' the man. This verb is much more consistent with anger than compassion and might account for the minor scribal aberration, providing grounds for the reading of 'anger'. The strongly attested reading of compassion is to be accepted as the basis of Jesus' act of cleansing the leper. The result of his action and word is expressed in terms of instant cleansing, demonstrating again the authority of Jesus and his word, a new teaching with 'authority'.

Following the cleansing Mark narrates a solemn, even severe dismissal of the man he had cleansed. He 'sternly warned' him and 'sent him away'. This latter verb is the one used of exorcisms (1.34) and of the Spirit driving Jesus out into the desert (1.12). The forcefulness of the language suggests that Jesus needed to dissuade the man from following him (see 5.18–19). The stern warning appears to be related to the command, 'See that you say nothing to anyone [about this]' because the same verb is used in Matthew 9.30, where Jesus commanded the two blind men he had healed, 'See that you make this known to no one'. But they went out and made it known in the whole of that land, just as here the cleansed leper went out and began to preach much and to spread 'the word', a metaphor that has the potential to mean 'proclaiming the gospel', see 4.14, 15, 16, 17, 20, 33; 8.32. Reference here (1.45) to 'the word' is probably to be understood as a report of the cleansing. The result of his fame was that Jesus could no longer openly enter any city but was outside in desert places. Even so, they came to him from everywhere. Against this background the secrecy motif was, according to Mark, grounded in Jesus' wish to keep his mission on his own terms. His aim was to go into and preach in the cities and villages of Galilee (1.38). Publicising the healings made this impossible.

The second part of Jesus' instruction to the cleansed leper was in accord with the law of Moses. He was to go and show himself to the priest bearing the prescribed offering so that he could duly be recognised as cleansed on the evidence of the priest who acted on behalf of the people in this regard. He would then be in a position to re-enter normal life. The man did not do what Jesus commanded but did what he had told him not to do. What are we to make of this? First, it means that, although Jesus commanded secrecy, there was, according to Mark, no messianic secret because the man did not keep the secret. What is more, this is what happens again and again. Thus this motif provides no explanation for the absence of messianic recognition in the earliest tradition.

What of the man's failure to comply with the requirements of the law of Moses? Does Mark imply that when the followers of Jesus failed to comply with the law they did so in spite of the law-abiding mission of Jesus? At this point in Mark this is a difficult question to answer. The one clue that suggests a negative answer is that Jesus himself touched the leper, strictly speaking, rendering himself unclean. This he should not have done. Having done so he was required to undergo purification himself. There is no indication that he did so. As we read on, further evidence confirms that the mission of the Markan Jesus was not based on strict compliance with the law. Rather, it seems that the command to the man arose from practical concerns. Only when the man was officially confirmed as cleansed could he re-enter normal life.

Frequently, *conditions* are imposed after the quest has been made known. In this story Jesus first healed the man directly in response to his request before he laid down his requirements for the man. Neither of these was met by the man. Had his cleansing been dependent on these conditions his quest would have failed. Nevertheless, the outcome for the man is important for the story, as is his failure to comply with Jesus' command.

### Act Two: growing conflict (collection of objection stories): an assault on the kingdom, 2.1–3.35

The first act of Mark revealed Jesus' conflict with the kingdom of Satan. The second act opens up another dimension of the conflict, between Jesus and the Jewish authorities. In a series of five objection stories (2.1–3.6), Jewish authorities object to sayings or actions of Jesus or his disciples, and Jesus answers with telling and powerful words and actions. This sequence of objections is without any explicit indication of a developing plot against Jesus until its conclusion (3.6). Repeated objections create a sense of seriousness. In Jerusalem this conflict is shown to develop in intensity, giving rise to the plot which ultimately led to the death of Jesus (14.1–2, 10–11). The issues over which the conflict is portrayed were also relevant to the conflict between the followers of Jesus and Jewish authority.

#### *+Healing a paralytic: authority to forgive sins, 2.1–12*

This quest/objection story is the first of a number of objection stories. Certain scribes objected to words spoken by Jesus. He responded with a dramatic and memorable saying, the validity of which, he claimed, was demonstrated by his healing activity by means of his spoken word. At the end of the story there is no sign of the objecting scribes. Their role in the story was fulfilled by raising the objection.

At this point in Mark's story we have the first indication of objection to Jesus by Jewish 'authorities'. No attempt is made at this stage to show an implacable opposition. For the moment the reader might conclude that Jesus had successfully overcome this objection. The healing, which is the context of the objection story, was performed in response to an implied request so that the overall story is to be understood as a miracle quest story.

Mark notes that after some days Jesus returned to Capernaum, suggesting that his purpose of preaching in the synagogues in the other towns in Galilee had been completed (1.39). Alternatively, Mark may imply that the task had to be given up because of the press of the crowds (1.45), which continued on his return to Capernaum. When it was heard that he was in a house the crowds gathered so that there was no room even at the door. This happened either some days after leaving Capernaum or, more likely, some days after he returned. On the latter reading Jesus slipped back unobtrusively into Capernaum and it was some days before his presence was located in a house.

There is no reason to think that Jesus had a house in Capernaum. If we can identify the house – the reference is quite indefinite – it would seem to be the home of Simon and Andrew (1.29), where Jesus had been previously. It might simply be a house where Jesus was offered hospitality. The motivation of the crowd in gathering is not indicated. Jesus took the opportunity 'to speak the word to them'. We must understand this as a reference to proclaiming the gospel of God, the kingdom of God. The motivation of the crowd might be illuminated by the four carrying a paralytic. Obviously they had brought him with the hope that Jesus would heal him, though no other healings are mentioned in this context.

The story illustrates the popularity of Jesus. The presence of the crowd is only intelligible in the light of the previous healings and exorcisms in Capernaum (1.21–28, 29–31, 32–34), and more widely in Galilee (1.39, 40–45), which led to people coming to Jesus from everywhere.

The action of the four in bringing the paralytic to Jesus was an expression of their *quest* for healing and the crowd constitutes a challenge to their resolve. This problem was overcome by making a hole in the roof and lowering the paralytic on a stretcher. Jesus recognised this as an act of faith which, for the first time in Mark, is made a presupposition of healing.

The complexity of the story now comes to light. In the midst of the healing, the scribes became embroiled in a controversy with Jesus. Indeed, the manner of healing chosen by Jesus was aimed at the scribes. Jesus said to the paralytic, 'Child, your sins are forgiven'.

Given the pervasive view in the ancient world that sickness and suffering were a punishment for sin, a view identified in Deuteronomy, debated in Job, and assumed by the disciples in John 9.1–3, the words of forgiveness might be seen as essential to the process of healing. For Mark, however, the healing is the evidence that demonstrates the reality of the words of forgiveness.

Jesus' words of forgiveness produced no effect on the paralytic. The effect was on the scribes who, we are now told, were sitting there. The effect was in the reasoning *in their hearts* that Jesus had spoken blasphemy, assuming for himself what only God could do. Mark indicates that Jesus knew immediately in his spirit what they were reasoning. Because knowing the hearts or minds was perceived to be a divine activity, Jesus' response was itself a challenge to the assessment of blasphemy. His words of forgiveness also turn out to have been chosen in order to provoke objection which can then be definitively answered. The question, 'Which is easier . . .?' (2.9) shows, in this case, the healing has been used to demonstrate that Jesus has the authority to forgive sins and therefore stands on the side of God. The logic is that anyone can say, 'Your sins are forgiven', and there is no way of judging whether or not this is true. But to say to a paralytic, 'Take up your bed and walk', is to produce a situation where the effectiveness of the word can be tested. Jesus therefore asserts that the testable effect should be made the evidence for the untestable. In this context he told the man to get up and take his bed and go to his house. This the man did immediately in front of everyone.

The story follows the well-known pattern of a miracle story. The illness is stated. The manner of healing is described and the evidence of the healing is attested by the crowd that witnessed the man carrying his bed home. But there is more to the story than this. The *quest* motif is introduced by the narrative description of the bringing of the man to Jesus, overcoming the separation from Jesus resulting from the crowd. Then Jesus' words of forgiveness provoked the *objection* raised by the scribes who were sitting there. Reference to their presence has a sinister ring in the light of the role they are to play in the story.

The story has become the instrument bearing the all-important saying of Jesus, 'The Son of Man has power on earth to forgive sins'. Mark has used Son of Man as a christological title of dignity. In this story it is set in the context of the claim that only God can forgive sins. Jesus adds that 'The Son of Man has power on earth to forgive sins'. Thus this healing provocatively places Jesus on earth in the place of God in a context where he has shown that he has the divine power to read the thoughts and reasonings of the heart.

The result of this healing in front of the crowd was astonishment and praise to God because, they said, 'We have never seen anything like this before'. The christological focus of this story is clear. The note of serious conflict with Jewish authority also emerges here for the first time. But what happened to the scribes at this point? Were they caught up in the amazement and praise to God which is expressed at the end of the story? Mark says this of *all*, but the scribes have vanished. Mention of the dissenting scribes with the charge of blasphemy is but the first note of conflict between Jesus and Jewish authority which re-echoes throughout the rest of the Gospel.

*A note on the use of Son of Man in Mark*

The use of this title is virtually restricted to the Gospels, Acts 7.56 being an exception. In Mark, as in the other Gospels, the title is used by Jesus speaking of the Son of Man in the third person, although there is no doubt that the evangelists understood it as a self-reference by Jesus. The sayings have been classified into three groups, though some of the references overlap the categories: (1) concerning the present authority of the Son of Man (2.10, 28); (2) predicting the suffering, death [and resurrection] of the Son of Man (8.31; 9.9, 12, 31; 10.33, 45; 14.21, 41); (3) concerning the future vindication and coming of the Son of Man (8.38; 13.26; 14.62). In the Gospels, Son of Man is clearly used in relation to the reference to one like a son of man in Daniel 7.13–14. By the time of Jesus and Mark, Son of Man was understood as a reference to the Messiah as an individual heavenly figure (in 1 Enoch 37–71; 4 Ezra; 2 Baruch). For Mark, as for all of the Gospel writers, Son of Man was the title chosen by Jesus as best able to convey the sense of his messiahship and has become a key christological title. The mystery surrounding the use of this title by Jesus in Mark is associated with the mystery of the kingdom of God.

In Daniel 7, one like a Son of Man comes to the throne of the ancient of days in heaven and an everlasting kingdom is given to him. That kingdom was God's response to the successive 'bestial' kingdoms represented by the beasts which arose from the sea. The imagery used was drawn from the creation myths of ancient

Mesopotamia in which God triumphs over the forces of chaos. In the apocalyptic literature which has influenced Mark the forces of chaos have taken on a diabolical character. Thus, for Mark, Son of Man gives expression to the way the kingdom of God encounters and overcomes the powers of evil in the world. The mystery associated with this was the manner in which God encountered the powers of evil in Jesus. For Mark this was to be seen in the authoritative preaching of Jesus, his healing of the sick and predominantly in his power over demons in casting them out of those they oppressed. What then are we to make of the suffering and death of the agent of the kingdom of God? Because the suffering Son of Man is the model for discipleship it is clear that the struggle goes on. Nevertheless, the coming Son of Man provides hope for the ultimate triumph of the kingdom of God and the overthrow of evil.

*+Teaching the crowd beside the sea of Galilee, 2.13*

This summary brings Jesus back beside the sea of Galilee, presumably still around Capernaum. Mark has established the popularity of Jesus and now tells us that all the crowd came to him. For whatever reason the crowd had come (for healings?), Jesus taught them. Thus, although Mark contains little of the content of Jesus' teaching, he portrays Jesus as the teacher. It has already been noted that this new teaching is with authority (see 1.22, 27).

*+Jesus and the outcasts: the calling of Levi, 2.14–17*

The new scene continues beside the sea, 2.13. A town is implied by reference to Levi, the tax collector and son of Alphaeus, sitting at his seat of business where scribes/Pharisees are present. Because no change of location is mentioned the reader assumes Jesus was in Capernaum beside the sea.

The story, the second objection/testing inquiry story, provides interesting details concerning the mission of Jesus. It concludes with the arresting saying of Jesus answering the objection. As in the story of the healing of the paralytic, the role of the scribes/Pharisees was to raise the objection.

The story commences in a way similar to the accounts of the calling of Simon, Andrew, James and John, noting the profession of Levi as a tax collector just as it had been noted that the four brothers were fishers. The story fills out the varied make-up of Jesus' group of 'followers'. In this case the occupation of Levi also provides the grounds for the testing inquiry that is to follow. Like the other call stories, this one also highlights the authoritative word of Jesus, who calls and those called instantly *follow*.

While the first four 'followers' called by Jesus are numbered amongst the twelve, the name Levi is not to be found there (Mark 3.13–19). For the first-time reader this comes as a bit of a surprise. That this constituted a problem is evidenced quite early by Origen, who noted that some manuscripts inserted the name of Levi in place of Thaddaeus (3.18). The problem had already been noticed when Matthew was written. There the solution was to change the name of Levi to Matthew in the call story (Matthew 9.9–13), Matthew's name being listed amongst the twelve (Mark 3.18; see Matthew 10.3, where he is called 'the tax collector'). In Mark the omission of Levi from the list of the twelve has led to textual variants, so that the name of Levi is changed to James the son of Alphaeus in some texts of 2.14, thus numbering him amongst the twelve where his name appears, 3.16–19. This is clearly a scribal attempt to harmonise what was perceived to be a discrepancy.

It is possible that Mark wished to treat Levi as a representative of the many tax collectors and sinners who followed Jesus (2.15) rather than as a member of the small band of disciples. This solution is put in question by the identification of Levi as 'the son of Alphaeus' (2.14) and the coincidence that one of the twelve is named James 'the son of Alphaeus'. With the two sets of brothers called in 1.16–20, their relationship as brothers is clearly stated. There is no mention of any relationship between Levi and James. On the other hand, there is no explicit indication that Levi was one of the twelve. It is just that, of the five people explicitly called by Jesus, four of them are named amongst the twelve. It is hard to credit that Mark was unaware of the discrepancy created by the conjunction of the names of Levi and James as 'the son of Alphaeus'. If he was, he has failed to provide any clues that enable us to solve this problem.

The story of the call of Levi is linked to the account of a meal at which Jesus was present with his *disciples* and many tax collectors and sinners. It is natural to read this as if Jesus, a notable teacher and guest of honour, attended a meal at the house of Levi. This is the way Luke (5.29) has understood the story and it makes good sense of the presence of large numbers of tax collectors. They were people from Levi's social circle who, due to the influence of Levi, had followed Jesus. Mark distinguishes the many tax collectors and sinners *who followed Jesus* ( 2.15c refers to them) from those he describes as Jesus' 'disciples'. This is clear from the comment that Jesus and his disciples ate with them (2.15b, 16). Mark implies that Levi, although specifically called by Jesus, is numbered not with the disciples, but amongst the others who followed on their own initiative.

Reference to 'the disciples' occurs for the first time in 2.15–16. They were with Jesus and the Pharisees put a testing inquiry 'to his disciples'. From the beginning the disciples were a nucleus amongst the wider group of those who followed Jesus. The next reference to disciples (2.18) sets a contrast between the fasting practices of the disciples of Jesus and the disciples of John and the Pharisees. In Mark 'disciples' is always used by the narrator, except in 2.18 where it was used by the questioners. Because Jesus does not use the term we are to understand it as Markan shorthand to describe an inner circle amongst the followers of Jesus. Yet Mark's use has built on conventional practice. He has set the question in the context of a note by the narrator indicating that the 'disciples' of John and of the Pharisee were fasting. This early comparison with other disciples suggests that the term indicates a well-known social role. At the same time, the fact that the disciples of Jesus differed in practice from the others warns the reader to pay attention to the way those described explicitly as *Jesus'* disciples are portrayed before drawing too many conclusions. See 2.15, 16, 18, 23; 3.7, 9; 4.34; 5.31; 6.1, 35, 41, 45; 7.2, 5, 17; 8.1, 4, 6, 10, 27, 33, 34; 9.14, 18, 28, 31; 10.10, 13, 23, 24, 46; 11.1, 14; 12.43; 13.1; 14.12, 13, 14, 16, 32; 16.7. To these, references to 'the twelve' need to be added, 3.14[16]; 4.10; 6.7; 9.35; 10.32; 11.11; 14.10, 17.

In none of the references to 'disciples' is it clear that a group larger than 'the twelve' is intended. In many instances, such as Jesus being in a boat with the disciples (3.9; 6.45; 8.10) or in a house (7.17; 9.28; 10.10; 14.12, 14), a group much larger than the twelve is unlikely. Thus for Mark 'disciples' means 'the twelve' or, prior to the appointment of the twelve, the growing nucleus that would become 'the twelve'. Confirmation of this is to be found in a number of places. For example, after the mission of the twelve (6.6b–13) Mark reports the return of the 'apostles'(6.30) and, at the initiative of Jesus, they departed with him by boat to a desert place. Nevertheless, it is with the 'disciples' that Jesus discussed feeding the crowd (6.35) and to them that he gave the broken bread and fish to distribute (6.41). That there were twelve of them might be confirmed by the twelve baskets full of fragments collected after all had satisfied their hunger (6.43). There is no doubt that a much wider group *followed* Jesus, sometimes referred to as the crowd or crowds. In one instance a wider group is described as 'those around him [Jesus] with the twelve' (4.10). But Mark does not call them 'disciples'.

The location for the meal mentioned in 2.15 is not made specifically clear; 'his house' could refer to the house of Levi or Jesus. Some commentators argue that Jesus was the host and that the meal was held in his house. This is unlikely. Nowhere is there any suggestion that Jesus had a house at Capernaum. If the meal is understood to be in the house of Levi, the situation can be taken as demonstrating the transformation that took place in his life. From a Pharisaic position, a meal hosted by Levi for such a group would not be regarded suitable for their participation. Just how the participation of Jesus and his disciples in a meal with tax collectors and sinners became known to those Mark calls 'the scribes of the Pharisees' (those scribes who were Pharisees) is unclear and unimportant. Their knowledge of the situation is essential to the conclusion of the story.

The company kept by Jesus (and his disciples) is mentioned three times. We are told that many tax collectors and sinners were in the house with Jesus and his disciples. Then it is noted that the scribes of the Pharisees saw Jesus eating in this company, and finally Mark records the words of the complaint about the company. That Mark himself names them tax collectors and sinners rules out the possibility that reference to the sinners is simply a prudish Pharisaic reference to the tax collectors. Rather, it must mean that Jesus welcomed into his company some who were notable sinners. Tax collectors, by virtue of their profession, would have been social outcasts but not necessarily regarded as notable sinners.

The punctuation of what the scribes said is unclear. If they asked a question, 'Why does he eat with tax collectors and sinners?', we have a testing inquiry story. If they made a statement, 'He eats with tax collectors and sinners', we have an objection story in which guilt is assumed to be self-evident. The question formally allows for a legitimate explanation, though the reason for asking it was probably to encourage the disciples to incriminate Jesus. The use of the imperfect tense ('the scribes were saying') may imply a repeated rather than casual accusation, though this is less than certain in the light of Mark's frequent use of the imperfect (see 4.13, 21, 24, 26, 30, 35). Certainly the accusation 'He eats' implies habitual practice.

Jesus' response to the criticism, by implication a criticism of his own failure to keep the law, was to draw attention to the nature of his mission. He had come to bring healing to the sick, not to the healthy who had no need. He had not come to call the righteous but the sinners. The saying is notable and brings to light the nature of his mission. Interestingly, it reverses the order of preaching and healing/exorcising which is normally found in the summaries of his mission. Nevertheless, both elements are present in this proverbial saying. The saying justifies Jesus keeping company with the outcasts and needy. In this way the story of the call of Levi introduces a situation of conflict with the experts and exponents of Jewish religion, providing Jesus with the opportunity to state the purpose of his own mission in a memorable proverbial saying. As with the healing of the paralytic, the forgiveness of sinners appears to be central to his mission. In calling sinners we may assume that 'to repentance' is implied. See 1.14–15. 'The Son of Man has power on earth to forgive sins.'

Jesus' acceptance of those who were 'outcasts' was perceived as bringing his mission into conflict with the law. In this way the 'outcasts' can be seen as pointing in the direction of the mission to the nations. Mark maintains the historical perspective which recognised that Jesus restricted his mission to 'Israel', though he allows two explicitly exceptional stories and a saying of Jesus from which he draws a conclusion upon which the Gentile mission *could* be based. See the discussion of 5.1–20; 7.1–23, 24–30.

*+The question of fasting, 2.18–20*

To a third objection or testing inquiry Jesus responded with another proverbial saying at the conclusion of the story. The testing inquiry is a subtle variation on an objection story because a question is asked with a view to establishing, by way of an admission, grounds for objection. There is no indication of the identity of those who raised the inquiry. The narrator sets it in the context of the observation that the disciples of John and of the Pharisees were fasting. Whether a particular fast was in mind, such as at the Day of Atonement (Leviticus 16.29), is unclear. It may only reflect the practice of fasting twice a week (Luke 18.12) on the second and fifth days (Didache viii.1). While John (the Baptist) announced the coming of Jesus as the coming judge, according to Mark, John stands with the old dispensation. Thus the disciples of John, like the Pharisees, fast.

In the question put to Jesus the questioners refer to the 'disciples' of John and the 'disciples' of the Pharisees conforming to the practice of fasting. Strictly speaking, the Pharisees did not have disciples. Perhaps what is in mind is disciples of the great Pharisaic teachers such as Hillel. The overall point is clear. The disciples of John and of the Pharisees fast. The disciples of Jesus did not. Here, as in the next story, Jesus' disciples are used as evidence of the teaching and practice of Jesus so that the complaint was brought to him. His defence came in the form of an arresting proverbial pronouncement. 'Surely the bridegroom's attendants are not able to fast while the bridegroom is with them, are they?' The form of the saying implies a negative answer, 'Of course not!' This contrast between the practice of Jesus and John fits well with the acknowledged ascetic practice of John according to Q and the non-ascetic practice of Jesus (Luke 7.33–35; Matthew 11.18–19). The presence of the bridegroom is an image for the presence of the eschatological kingdom of God. Banqueting, not fasting, is the appropriate response to the presence of the kingdom.

Mark, of course, reflects the situation of the early church in which fasting had become an essential part of the Christian religious practice (see Matthew 6.16–18; Didache viii.1). Mark allows that, after the departure of Jesus, fasting will become an essential part of Christian piety. But the reasons for fasting will be quite different from those motivating the disciples of John and the Pharisees. The disciples of Jesus will fast because the bridegroom (Jesus) has been snatched away violently from them. The conflict between the old and the new remains clear, even though fasting became a practice of the early Christian community.

The disciples of Jesus are mentioned here by the questioning critics of Jesus. They are identified as comparable to the disciples of John and the Pharisees. Mark assumes that knowledge of other disciples throws light on the way to understand Jesus' disciples, although it was a point of difference between Jesus' disciples and the others that provided the basis for the story.

**Old and new, 2.21–22*

What appears to be a complex of separate proverbial sayings contrasting old and new has been attached to the *chreia* on fasting. Analysed in detail the sayings do not make the same point, but such an approach is probably mistaken. Rather, the sayings emphasise that the old and new cannot be mixed. It is probably implicit that the new is superior to the old.

*+Sabbath controversy I: Lord of the sabbath, 2.23–28*

A fourth *chreia* deals with an issue in which the new comes in conflict with the old, represented again by the Pharisees. It is an objection story in which the most important response to the objection is made by Jesus in a dramatic saying at the end of the story. For a second time an objection is raised to Jesus on the basis of the practice of his disciples (2.18, 23–24). The issue emerged when Jesus and his disciples passed through a corn field on the sabbath and the disciples plucked ears of corn as they went. The Pharisees objected that such a practice was unlawful on the sabbath. The language in which Mark introduces the objection ('The Pharisees were saying', which is in the imperfect tense) suggests repeated objection and the action of the disciples ('they are doing', which is described in the present tense) suggests habitual practice rather than a single act, though Mark's use of tenses makes this less than certain (cf. 2.16).

Jesus might have responded that Deuteronomy 23.25 allowed such a practice, the casual picking of a few ears of corn, which was distinguished from harvesting, and that only scribal interpretation (M. Shabbath 7.2) excluded it. This sort of approach is to be found in the early Christian interpretation of Jesus (see Mark 7.3), but not in Mark at this point.

First, Jesus responded in terms compatible with Pharisaic debate, appealing to scriptural precedent to the record of what David did when he and those with him were in need and hungry (1 Samuel 21.1–6). Jesus asked them, 'Have you never read' how David entered the house of God when Abiathar was high priest and ate the bread offered to God, which he also gave to those with him although it was not lawful for any but the priests to eat this sacred bread? The question is asked in a form that presupposes the answer, 'Yes, of course we have read this!' While this story has nothing directly to do with what is permissible on the sabbath, it is a case which demonstrates that *need* takes precedence over such regulations. This approach admits that sabbath law covers such practices as plucking a few ears of corn, thus siding with the strict scribal interpretation of sabbath law. That law is, however, overridden by need. But is the sabbath on the same level as the bread offered in the temple? Jesus, according to Mark, assumes this to be so. If in a time of need it was legitimate to eat that bread, in a time of need it is legitimate to pluck ears of corn on the sabbath and to eat them. Crucial to his case also is the equivalence of the need and hunger of David and those with him, which is stated explicitly, with the need and hunger of the disciples, which is implied. While there is no evidence that the disciples were desperately hungry, this is to introduce a detail which complicates the Markan case in a way that obscures the point of the story.

A second response seems to be quite independent of the first. In it a memorable saying of Jesus identifies the *chreia* as a pronouncement story. 'The sabbath was made for man not man for the sabbath; so that the Son of Man is Lord of the sabbath.' Closer inspection shows that this saying provides the basis for extrapolating the principle involved in the incident with David to issues concerning the sabbath and other legal matters. The sabbath was made for man. Consequently, sabbath law applies only in cases where it leads to human well-being. Where application of the law is opposed to human well-being the law does not apply. Naturally it might be argued that the law as a whole was for human well-being. Normally it would be argued that God had commanded only what was good for humanity. The principle put forward by Jesus becomes the test of whether a particular law is applicable or not. If this loosened the universal applicability of the law, who was to decide when a law was for human well-being or not? The final part of the saying answers this question, 'The Son of Man is Lord of the sabbath', and arbitrates all matters concerning the demands of the law. Jesus' authoritative interpretation, based on a principle which human minds could understand, is set over against Pharisaic interpretation of the law. The law was for human good and this was to be the test of the applicability of all particular laws.

This is the second of two Son of Man statements in Mark 2. The first (2.10) asserted that the Son of Man had power on earth to forgive sins, a claim which set the Son of Man on the divine side of reality and was validated in the story by Jesus' ability to heal a paralytic. Now Jesus claims that the Son of Man is Lord of the sabbath (2.28). The justification of this claim is less clear. It may be understood as follows. If Jesus, in his scriptural appeal to the example of David, has shown that human need overrides the demands of the law, that in fact the law was given for human well-being, he has shown himself to be the authoritative interpreter of the law. The Son of Man is Lord of the sabbath.

*+Sabbath controversy II: the person with the withered hand, 3.1–6*

A fifth *chreia* is a variation on the objection story. Jesus anticipated the objection of Pharisees and Herodians. His justification, in the form of a question, neutralised the force of any objection to his proposed action. Nevertheless, although the question cut the grounds of objection from under their feet, when Jesus had acted they began to plan how they would destroy him (3.6). This is an important development in the Markan plot. Conflict with Jewish authority, which began in 2.1–12, has now reached a climax in the decision to destroy Jesus. Yet it is important to note that, in the Markan narrative, the objectors were not able to find a flaw in Jesus' justification of his action. This draws attention to the fact that, in an objection story, the response is directed to the reader rather than the objectors. Objection stories leave the views of the objectors unchanged.

Reference to Jesus' entry *again* into the synagogue (3.1) looks back to the synagogue in Capernaum (1.21). In a matter-of-fact way we are told that a man was present with a withered hand. The first healing on the sabbath led to amazement at the new teaching with authority, which forced unclean spirits to obey, so that Jesus' fame spread throughout Galilee (1.27–28). Now we are told of those whose only concern was to see whether Jesus would heal this man on the sabbath so that they might accuse him (3.2). What has happened in the synagogue in Capernaum between the two acts of healing? Mark does not specifically address this question. Reference to the role of the Pharisees and Herodians in 3.6 suggests that their presence and activity is a new dimension expressing reaction to the growing fame and influence of Jesus, and awareness that he performed healings on the sabbath. Mark has traced the growing objections to Jesus, first by the scribes (2.6), then the scribes and Pharisees (2.16), then the practice of the disciples of Jesus is contrasted with the disciples of John and the Pharisees (2.18), then again by the Pharisees (2.24). In each of these cases the objection expressed is apparently met successfully by Jesus.

In 3.1–6 the presence of the man with the withered hand appears to be a 'set-up', a provocation of Jesus to act on the sabbath. Jesus dramatically anticipated the objection to his action. First, the man with the withered hand was made to stand in the middle of the synagogue congregation where all could see. Then Jesus put his question, 'Is it lawful on the sabbath to do good or evil, to save life or to kill?' The question is the dramatic pronouncement of the story. Those who wished to accuse him were silent. Mark obviously intends his readers to conclude from this that the question had cut the ground from under the feet of Jesus' opponents, that the necessary answer must be 'To do good, to save life'. Jesus commanded the man to stretch out his hand and in stretching it out Mark says it was restored. Although they could make no answer the Pharisees and Herodians withdrew from the synagogue and took counsel how to destroy Jesus. They did not fault Jesus' defence; nevertheless, they determined to destroy him. Mark's purpose was to show that, in spite of Jesus' ability to justify his action, by this stage in the story the Jewish authorities had become implacably opposed to him. This opposition had already reached the decision to destroy Jesus, although it would be some time before this decision could be carried out.

Yet the Markan account has oversimplified the situation. The question put by Jesus did not include as an option what appears to be the correct approach consistent with the law. The man with a withered hand was not in a life-threatening situation. Had this been the case the Pharisaic approach to the law would have allowed his healing, even on the sabbath. His hand could wait and be healed on the following day, thus keeping the sabbath and bringing him healing. Mark extends the principle that recognised the legitimacy of life-saving action on the sabbath. That principle is taken to justify all doing of good. It will not allow that the keeping of the sabbath law is *in itself* good and therefore a criterion of what may be done. It may be that the sabbath principle is, in general, good for human life. According to Jesus, it can also be contrary to what is good for human life and in these circumstances is not binding. While the Pharisees and Herodians made no public objection to Jesus' justification, their decision to destroy him was based on a real difference between his position and theirs, his growing fame and their entrenched opposition to him on the basis of the law.

## Discipleship: counter-attack in the midst of assault, 3.7–19

*+Multitudes from all over Israel followed Jesus with his disciples beside the sea, 3.7–12*

This summary confirms that Jesus now acts in concert with his disciples and that he had become an immensely popular figure. While there are some textual problems, the general sense is clear. Jesus, with his disciples, withdrew to the sea of Galilee, followed by a huge crowd, from Galilee, Judaea, Jerusalem, Idumaea and Trans Jordan and the region surrounding Tyre and Sidon, who had heard of the things that he did. Why Jesus withdrew is not stated. It could be because of the decision to destroy him taken by the Pharisees and Herodians. Jesus healed many with diseases and they crowded in on him in order to touch him. Because of the great crowd Jesus instructed the disciples to have a boat ready for him so that the crowd would not press on him. Whenever the unclean spirits saw him they fell down before him and cried out, saying 'you are the son of God'. And he gave them strict instructions not to make him known (3.11–12).

Nothing new emerges in this summary, which confirms and completes what has already been narrated. Reference to the disciples as a group here and in 2.18 seems to assume that the four fishermen went to Capernaum with Jesus, 1.21. Now (in 3.7) the disciples go with Jesus and assist him with practical matters (3.9). The summary extends the regions within which Jesus' fame has spread, now not only in Galilee. Consequently, there is emphasis on the size of the huge crowd that Jesus had drawn. News of the healings had drawn them, and when Jesus healed many this increased the crush of those who were sick as they sought to touch Jesus in the hope that this would heal them. The encounter with the unclean spirits continued but without mention of exorcisms, though they may be implied. The unclean spirits recognised Jesus as son of God, but Jesus forbade them to make him known. Jesus is announced to be son of God, possibly in the opening verse of the Gospel, certainly by the heavenly voice at his baptism and transfiguration, and at the crucifixion by a Roman centurion (15.39). Only the unclean spirits are silenced in their revelation of the identity of Jesus. The heavenly voice is opposed to the unclean spirits, though each makes the same announcement concerning Jesus. The readers of the Gospel hear both voices but in the story Jesus' sovereign authority silences the unclean spirits. This act demonstrates that he has brought the reign of evil to an end.

### +*The appointment of the twelve, 3.13–19*

The process of gathering a group of disciples, described in call stories, culminates in the present narrative, which suggests that the twelve were chosen from a larger group of followers. Given the importance of the twelve in the early Christian tradition, it is not surprising that this short passage contains a number of textual variants, the most significant being the attempt to attribute the naming of the twelve as *apostles* to Jesus. This scribal addition was probably made on the basis of Luke 6.13. At this point in Mark the group has no special title other than 'the twelve' (but see 6.30), although the twofold purpose of the appointment, stated in 3.14, might suggest and justify both names as 'disciples', who were appointed 'to be with' Jesus, and 'apostles', to be sent out to preach and have authority over demons.

Mark sets the scene by noting that Jesus went up the mountain. The name of the mountain is not mentioned, nor is it important. The mountain scenario recalls the place of divine revelation and action (see Exodus 18–19) where Israel was constituted the people of God. Significantly, Mark 3.7–12 has recorded the response of the nation to Jesus and, although it follows reference to the plot to kill Jesus by the Pharisees and Herodians, that response is in largely positive terms. From his position on the mountain Jesus sovereignly called those he wished and they came to him. Mark not only says Jesus *called* but that he *appointed* them and numbered them as *twelve*, perhaps implying a renewed/reformed Israel. Apart from Levi, the other four called in earlier stories are numbered amongst the twelve. Thus it is unclear whether or not the story of Levi is somehow to be understood as a story of one of the twelve, as Matthew assumed, as did the scribes who produced textual variants. See the discussion of 2.14–17.

According to Mark, the twelve were appointed for two purposes: *to be with* Jesus and *to be sent out* to preach and to have authority to cast out demons. In Matthew the account of the appointment of the twelve (10.1–4) and their mission (10.5–15) forms a single episode. Mark has separate accounts of their appointment (3.13–19) and their commission to mission (6.7–13). This separation is consistent with Mark's statement of the *twofold* purpose of the appointment of the twelve. Matthew mentions only the single purpose of the mission for which the twelve were chosen. Mark's recognition of the twofold purpose finds expression in the structure of the Gospel. From 3.13 the twelve were 'with Jesus' as disciples or learners until Jesus sent them out on their mission (6.7–13). They returned as *apostles* (6.30), but on return from their mission they recommenced their relationship as *disciples* (6.35).

The purpose of being with Jesus is not explained, but it is probable that the earlier references to disciples being with Jesus (2.18, 23) imply that the purpose was to learn from the teacher so that the disciples' words and action were a reflection on the teacher. From the second purpose of being 'sent out' the designation of the twelve as 'apostles' has arisen here in the text of Mark 6.30. They were to be sent out to preach and to have authority to cast out demons. They were to replicate or, perhaps better expressed, to extend geographically the mission of Jesus. Jesus preached; now they will preach also.

The twelve are named: Simon, to whom Jesus gave the name Peter; James the son of Zebedee and John the brother of James, to whom he gave the name 'Boanerges', which is 'Sons of Thunder'; and Andrew, Philip, Bartholomew, Matthew, Thomas, James the son of Alphaeus, and Thaddaeus, Simon the Cananaean and Judas Iscariot, who also betrayed him.

This is the first reference to Peter in the narrative. The occurrence of the two names together (Simon and Peter) should be compared with the Gethsemane scene, where the narrator indicates that Jesus addressed *Peter*, but when he does so he calls him 'Simon' (14.37). The name Simon is used otherwise only until the appointment and naming of the twelve (1.16–20, 29, 36; 3.16), while 'Peter' is used of him from that point onwards (3.16; 5.37; 8.29, 33; 9.2; 11.21; 13.3; 14.29, 31, 33, 66–67, 72; 16.7). This makes Jesus' address 'Simon' in 14.37 notable and significant, and may reflect the fact that, by falling asleep, Peter has failed a crucial test, he has fallen back. Mark does not explain the name Peter as Matthew (16.18) does, relating the name to the Aramaic *Kephas*, meaning rock or stone. He is mentioned first, as he was in the first 'call story' (1.16). Andrew is not here mentioned next with him, nor is he identified as the brother of Simon. He was dislodged from his position following Peter in the list by James and John.

James and John are also given a name ('Boanerges') by Jesus and Mark explains this to mean 'Sons of Thunder'. The etymology of this Aramaism is unclear. For other Aramaisms see 5.41; 7.11, 34; 14.36; 15.22, 34. The meaning of Boanerges might relate to their character (see 9.38 and Luke 9.54), their fiery preaching (see Revelation), or it might be a term for twins. These first three, who were given names by Jesus, are the most prominent disciples in Mark (5.37; 9.2; 14.33) and were thought to have played a notable role in the earliest church (see Eusebius, *History*, 2.1.3). In Mark they made up an inner group, causing the separation of the two brothers Simon and Andrew in the list of the twelve. Andrew had to settle for fourth place in this list, which is also the order in the list of those named accompanying Jesus on the Mount of Olives (13.3) and as the audience of the apocalyptic discourse (13.5–37). Relegation to fourth place was preliminary to the reduction of the inner group to three.

Levi is not mentioned in spite of the special call story (2.13–14). This might indicate that Jesus called more than the twelve, that those called in 3.13 were more inclusive than the twelve appointed in 3.14. But there is a puzzle here in that the call of Levi the son of Alphaeus is narrated in detail, yet he is not listed amongst the twelve, while James the son of Alphaeus is listed amongst the twelve but there is no account of his call. Should we think that they were brothers, or is there confusion here? See the discussion of 2.14–17 above.

The other name over which there is confusion is Thaddaeus. Luke (6.14–16) and Acts (1.13) have Judas the son of James in the place of Thaddaeus, and some variants of Matthew (10.2–4) have Lebbaeaus. Simon the Cananaean is identified as Simon the Zealot by Luke (6.15), recognising the derivation from an Aramaic word. It is unclear whether the term here indicates a member of the Zealot party, revolutionary opponents of the Romans whose political aspirations became evident in the Jewish war (66–73), or, more generally, some sort of enthusiast. Last, Judas Iscariot (there are some variants for the second part of his name), whose name has been explained as a reference to his place of origin, 'man of Kerioth' (the village of Kerioth of which there was more than one in Judaea), or as a corruption of *sicarius*, that is, the dagger man. This meaning would be appropriate because Judas is further identified as 'the one who betrayed him [Jesus]'.

The narrative commences on a positive and triumphant note. Jesus called and chose whom he wished. It finishes dismally. One of those chosen and appointed, one of the twelve, betrayed him.

This prepares the way for the next scene. The disciples, chosen with high hopes and expectations, failed to live up to the expectations the reader has been led to develop. There is a warning to the reader not to expect too much of these disciples. One of them betrayed Jesus.

## Opposition: the assault continues, 3.20–35

Four different groups are shown to be in varying degrees of opposition to Jesus. Opposition arises from different levels of misunderstanding. The crowd, disciples, scribes from Jerusalem and Jesus' own family are involved in these scenes, and the most serious, indeed damning, misunderstanding occurs in the middle scene (3.22–30).

### +*The attempt to restrain Jesus, 3.20–21*

A new scene, signalled by the movement to a new place, provides a double *objection* to Jesus. It deals with the accusation that Jesus 'is beside himself' and the misguided attempt of those with Jesus (οἱ παρ' αὐτοῦ) to '*restrain*' him . In 6.17; 12.12 this verb is used of attempts to '*arrest*' Jesus. It indicates a negatively violent action against Jesus. Some texts attribute this action to 'the scribes and the rest', linking this action closely with the evaluation of the scribes from Jerusalem that follows (3.22–30). The motivation for this textual change is clear. The negative action is more appropriately ascribed to the scribes than those closely associated with Jesus. The same motivation might have led to another piece of textual confusion.

At the beginning of this narrative some texts read, '*He* came into a house', while others read '*They* came'. The weight of the textual evidence slightly favours the plural reading. Nevertheless, the use of the singular verb has been widely adopted. If Jesus came alone there is no room for any others with him to act and it is natural to look for another group to be responsible for the attempt to restrain Jesus. The adoption of this reading may have led to the introduction of the scribes as the agents of this attempt. This is clearly secondary. An attempt has to be made to interpret the phrase οἱ παρ' αὐτοῦ in a way that does not imply that they came with Jesus. There are two ways of doing this which assume that the phrase is a reference to the family of Jesus.

The first assumes that the house Jesus came into was his family home and that his family was already at home. He came in alone, but with the arrival of the crowd he went out to them and the press was so great that it was not possible to get a meal break. The family inside the house heard of this and concluded, 'he is beside himself' and went out to 'restrain' him. The evaluation of Jesus as being 'beside himself' is the popular idiom for madness, which can also be described as possession by demons or unclean spirits.

A second approach takes the house which Jesus entered to be his own establishment in Capernaum. News of the situation travelled to his family in Nazareth. They set out from Nazareth with a view to restrain Jesus (3.21), arriving only at 3.31.

In each of these approaches the singular verb is adopted at the beginning of 3.20, signalling that Jesus was acting alone. In each case the family of Jesus is understood to be acting in a negative way in relation to Jesus.

Another reading seems more consistent with the flow of the Markan narrative. Jesus had chosen twelve (disciples) *to be with him* (3.13–19, especially 3.14). It is likely that they are to be understood as travelling with him in 3.20, even if the singular verb is correct. More than likely the plural verb is original so that we understand that 'they [Jesus and his disciples] went into a house'. There is no reason to think that Jesus maintained a house in Capernaum or anywhere else. This house might be any at which he was offered hospitality. The mission charge of Jesus to the twelve (6.6b–13, especially 6.10) lays down the principle of conducting the mission on the basis of hospitality in houses which welcomed their presence. If it is intended to be a particular house the most likely conclusion is that it was the house of Simon and Andrew (1.29) in Capernaum.

The phrase οἱ παϱ' αὐτοῦ does not explicitly identify the subject, similar expressions of the disciples in 1.36 (οἱ μετ' αὐτοῦ); 3.14 and cf. 4.10 (οἱ παϱ' αὐτοῦ). There is a precedent for the use of this phrase in relation to friends, family and associates (LXX and other contemporary Greek manuscripts). No evidence suggests this is a technical term for 'the family'. Given that the family has not been mentioned in Mark to this point, it would be extraordinary if the reader were expected to recognise this as an oblique reference to them. Rather, Jesus had appointed twelve associates expressly *to be with him*. It follows naturally that the reader would assume that a group described as οἱ παϱ' αὐτοῦ, immediately after their appointment, was a reference to them. Reluctance to accept this conclusion arises from what this group *appears* to have done. First, they may have evaluated Jesus' behaviour in terms of madness, saying of him, 'He is beside himself'. As a consequence of this evaluation they went out to restrain Jesus. But this is a more negative assessment of Jesus' associates than it is necessary to draw from the text.

In 3.21 we are told that it was when the associates heard that they went out to restrain Jesus. What they heard was people saying, 'He is beside himself'. This was not the evaluation made by the disciples but by the crowd. Nevertheless, the disciples set out to restrain Jesus. Thus, although Jesus had chosen them, their actions show that they did not, at this point, comprehend the significance of Jesus or the role for which they had been chosen. Forewarning of this is already given at the end of the list of the twelve, which mentions Judas Iscariot who betrayed Jesus, although he was one of the twelve.

On this reading Mark narrates two objections to Jesus, the first raised by the crowd in its assessment that Jesus was 'beside himself', and the second in the action of the disciples in the attempt to restrain Jesus. Mark records no response of Jesus to either of these objections, perhaps because it becomes obvious that the attempt to restrain him had failed and a more serious form of the accusation against him was about to be expressed.

### +*Exorcism: the Beelzebul accusation, 3.22–30*

A new scene is signalled by a new group, scribes who 'came down' from Jerusalem. Mark may distinguish the Jerusalem scribes from other scribes present or simply mean that the scribes came from Jerusalem (compare 7.1), making clear the Jerusalem base of this serious opposition and *objection* to Jesus. These scribes had come from Jerusalem specifically to investigate Jesus the exorcist. While their assessment of Jesus is closely related to the view that Jesus was mad (beside himself), it is expressed in 'theological' rather than popular idiom. They *were saying* 'He has Beelzebul'. This was a repeated accusation rather than a casual assertion (see Matthew 10.25, but see Mark 4.13, 21, 24, 26, 30, 35).

Beelzebul may be derived from the Hebrew *baalzebul*, meaning 'lord of the house', and makes good sense in relation to Jesus' parabolic saying about the house of the strong man in 3.27. The variant Beelzebub (probably from *baalzebub*), found in some of the versions, means 'lord of the flies' and refers to the God of Ekron (2 Kings 1.2). Whereas the popular perception appears to have been based on the unrestrained involvement of Jesus with the crowd, the scribal view was based on Jesus' activity of casting out demons. While the language of Mark could be understood to involve two charges, the probable interpretation takes the second statement as an explanation of the first. The charge that Jesus had Beelzebul meant that he cast out demons by [the power of] the prince of demons. This was, of course, a much more serious charge than the popular accusation of madness, which was not specifically based on Jesus' encounter with the demonic and his activity of casting out demons. This then is an objection story in which the scribes from Jerusalem object to the practice of Jesus the exorcist.

It is not mentioned how Jesus heard of the accusation made by the scribes. Nevertheless, he called the scribes and answered them *in parables*. This is the first use of *parable* in Mark, used by the narrator to describe Jesus' teaching and, on the precedent of the sayings that follow, it is possible to identify earlier parabolic sayings in Mark 2.19–22; 3.4. In the LXX the term translates the Hebrew *mashal*, which is used to denote a variety of literary forms, stories, fables, proverbial sayings, riddles. A wide range of forms is also covered by this term in the Gospels, from brief sayings to stories of some length.

In Mark 3.23–30 we are dealing with enigmatic riddle-like sayings. 'How can Satan cast out Satan?' First, this question makes clear that Jesus understood the Beelzebul, prince of demons, accusation as a reference to Satan. Then, the riddle-like question proves to be no riddle. Rather, the question is aimed at showing the absurdity of the accusation. Logically, the outworking of the question in 3.24–26 suggests that Satan's kingdom was not under siege and was not falling. This is to miss the point of the saying, which is rather that Satan is not so stupid as to attack his own kingdom. In 3.27 the assumption is that Satan's kingdom is indeed under siege from without, that the house of the strong man was being plundered by a stronger one who had first bound the strong man. Logically, this saying suggests that Satan had already been defeated (perhaps Mark 1.12–13) and his house was now being plundered (from 1.23 on). The strong man might be bound but the battle continued.

The conclusion of this debate was summed up by Jesus in a solemn 'Amen' saying. In Judaism 'Amen' was used at the conclusion of liturgical sayings, affirming their truth. It is a distinctive characteristic of the sayings of Jesus that his solemn sayings were *introduced* by this word, which was an assertion of his authority. This saying declares unforgivable the blasphemy of the Holy Spirit. Reference to the Holy Spirit draws attention to the tradition that asserted that the exorcisms of Jesus were performed by the Holy Spirit and were evidence of the power of the kingdom of God in action (Matthew 12.28; Luke 11.20). All other sins and blasphemies committed by *people* will be forgiven; 'the sons of men' is a Semitism for 'people' (Psalms 21.10; 115.16). Blasphemy is here used in a rather general sense of speaking against God. The unforgivable sin was to attribute the work of God through his Spirit to the prince of demons (3.22), to Satan (3.26), to an unclean spirit (3.30). If God is confused with the devil, then . . . ?

The unclean spirits recognised Jesus (1.24; 3.11; 5.7), but Jesus' human opponents lacked this insight. The lines of conflict have now been drawn. Jesus, baptised and empowered by the Spirit, is the agent of the kingdom of God in the assault on the powers of evil and the deliverance of the oppressed.

### +*The true family of Jesus*, 3.31–35

This failed quest story concludes with the dramatic pronouncement of Jesus in 3.34–35. The inquiry was initiated by the family approaching Jesus, calling him, *seeking* him. Their approach raised the question of the place of the family of Jesus in the 'Jesus movement' or, in more universal terms, in the kingdom of God, which Jesus answered with a memorable saying.

A new scene is marked by the arrival of the mother and brothers of Jesus. The narrative provides the first reference to any members of the family. Mark apparently takes their arrival to indicate that the family was making some claim of family obligation on Jesus. Mark not only reports that the family arrived and were calling Jesus, but also narrates the report of this to Jesus by the crowd sitting around Jesus. Whereas the report of the arrival of the family indicated that they were '*calling*' Jesus, the crowd reported to Jesus that they were '*seeking*' him. There is nothing in either the account of their arrival or the report of it that suggests a negative purpose. Indeed, the arrival of the family is described in terms that suggest a respectful approach. The family arrived at the house and waited, '*standing outside*', sending a message to him, calling him.

Jesus was inside, surrounded by the crowd. The family stood *outside.* The interpretation that takes 3.31 to be the resumption of the movement of the family, begun in 3.21, assumes a continuous scene in the house mentioned in 3.20. If this is the case, the scribes from Jerusalem are to be thought of as in the crowd gathered around Jesus. It is hardly likely that Jesus would address the words of 3.34–35 to them. Rather, it seems that these scenes are loosely connected. Although there is no explicit mention of Jesus' exit from the house, it is likely that Jesus' confrontation with the scribes from Jerusalem took place outside. It is also likely that those who went out to restrain Jesus also went out from the house Jesus had entered with them in 3.20.

Thus the arrival of the family of Jesus is a new scene and does not complete the description of the attempt to restrain Jesus, of which there is no sign in 3.31–35. Mark's reference to the family mentions only the mother and brothers of Jesus. Reference to sisters has been introduced in the crowd's report to Jesus in some manuscripts. Almost certainly this is because, in Jesus' explanation of his true family, he mentions not only mother and brothers but also sisters. That Jesus had sisters is not in question and reference is made to them in Mark 6.3. Neither there nor in the present passage is there any mention of Joseph as the father of Jesus. There is speculation that this could be because he was dead. By the second century references to brothers and sisters were taken as an indication that Joseph had children by a previous marriage when he became betrothed to Mary. Later Jerome argued that those called brothers and sisters were actually cousins, being children of the sister of Mary who was also called Mary. These are desperate attempts to preserve the virginity of Mary even after the birth of Jesus. While Matthew and Luke affirm the virginal conception of Jesus by Mary, no document in the New Testament shows any awareness of the continued virginity of Mary, let alone teaches it. Reference to brothers and sisters of Jesus in the same context as reference to Mary as his mother clearly implies real brothers and sisters. No one suggests that Mary was mother of Jesus in anything but the natural sense.

Reference to the natural family of Jesus is presupposed by the words of Jesus. He asked rhetorically, 'Who is my mother and my brothers?' At the natural level the answer obviously was, 'Those waiting *outside!*' Jesus had another level of meaning in mind, which he indicated by his action, looking around him at those seated around him. His words then made the meaning of the action unambiguous, 'Behold my mother and my brothers'. So far the idiom has been constrained by the make-up of the family group that had come seeking him. But the interpretation was also constrained by the nature of the movement Jesus had initiated and Mark's understanding of this. Thus the interpretation continues, 'Whoever does the will of God, this person is my brother and sister and mother'. Certainly in any universal movement, such as Mark perceived the Jesus movement to be, the relation of the founder of the movement to his natural family constituted a serious problem that needed resolution, and this is evident in accounts of the movements of Jesus' day. Here, in Mark, Jesus deals with the question of the claims of his natural family. They have no special claim on him. Whoever does the will of God is true family. Interestingly too, according to Mark, Jesus has expressed this in terms that allow no advantage to men over women. Indeed, mother and sisters provide double the reference for women compared to men as brothers. True family depends only on doing the will of God. There is no special place here for the natural family who, especially in Mark, *seem* to be left out. They remained standing *outside* while Jesus names those gathered around him as his true family. It may even be that Mark expects the readers to pick up the reference to the family as outsiders in the sense *to be* referred to in 4.11. Those inside, gathered around Jesus, are given to know the mystery of the kingdom of God, while the family, standing outside, must be content with parable. But this sense of 'outside' is yet to come in the narrative and it is probably fanciful to read it into the text at this point.

The purpose of this *chreia* in Mark was not to establish the family as 'outsiders'. Rather it was to show that the natural family had no special claim on Jesus, no privileged place in his movement. Indeed, on the basis of the criterion set out by Jesus in 3.35, neither did the twelve have any privilege. Mark's purpose was to make clear the basis of the Jesus movement as a universal movement in which family and friends had no advantage. In such a movement Paul, who had not met the earthly Jesus, was at no disadvantage in relation to the most powerful members of Jesus' family, such as James, or of the twelve, such as Peter.

In the reading of 3.20–35 adopted here, three different groups respond to Jesus. First, those chosen to be with Jesus, appropriately described as οἱ παρ' αὐτοῦ, attempted to restrain him when they heard the report from the crowd that, 'He is beside himself'. Then the scribes from Jerusalem attributed Jesus' activity of exorcism to the power of Beelzebul, the prince of demons. Finally, the mother and brothers of Jesus arrived on the scene, calling him, enabling Jesus to affirm that those who do the will of God are his true family.

## Assurance of the kingdom: a collection of parables, 4.1–34

This collection of parables comes at the conclusion of a section dominated by challenges to Jesus' authority expressed in objection stories. In these a striking pronouncement of Jesus, sometimes combined with his action, provided his response to the challenge to his authority. On one occasion (3.22–30), in response to the charge that he was possessed (3.22), Jesus responded in a pronouncement in the form of a series of parables, 3.23–30. These parables took the form of enigmatic riddle-like sayings. In Mark 4 we learn something more of the range of sayings that can be described as parables. Specific reference to Jesus' teaching in parables comes here at the end of the first major section dealing with the challenge to Jesus' authority, 3.23; 4.2, 10, 11, 13, 33–34. The next use of the term 'parable' is in 7.17, where the Markan narrator says the disciples asked Jesus about the parable, Mark's description of the enigmatic saying Jesus had used to justify the failure of the disciples to observe the Pharisaic practice of hand-washing. The pattern of Mark 4 is in view in 7.17. Jesus spoke to the crowds in parables, but when they were alone, the disciples asked (4.10; 7.17) and he explained the meaning of the parables (4.10–20, 33–34; 7.17–23). Parable (and explanation to the disciples) is then Jesus' response to the challenge to his authority. This context helps to elucidate two apparently conflicting motifs in Mark 4. The parables are instruments of judgement to those opposed to Jesus. But the parables are also told in a context emphasising the need and importance of hearing and responding to Jesus, assuring the *hearers* of the certainty of the dawning of the kingdom.

### +*The parable of the soils, 4.1–9*

A new scene is signalled by the move from a house, perhaps the house of Simon and Andrew in Capernaum, to a situation beside the sea (of Galilee); from an audience of a crowd around Jesus in the house (3.32) to a great crowd beside the sea (4.1). The scene opens with the indication that Jesus *again* began to teach beside the sea, which looks back to previous occasions, 2.13 and 3.7–12. Again Jesus' teaching attracted a great crowd, though here there is no reference to the regions from which the crowd was drawn (contrast 3.7–8). On the previous occasion Jesus had instructed the disciples to have a boat ready, because of the press of the crowd (3.9). Here Jesus actually embarked and sat in the boat to teach the great crowd that remained on the sea shore. Previously, *that* Jesus taught has been frequently mentioned. Now something of the content of his teaching is given in a parable and in the interpretation of it in the form of explanation and other parables.

His teaching is introduced by the statement that Jesus taught them many things in parables. This is the second use of the word 'parables' in Mark (see 3.23 and comments). Further important indications of the meaning of parables in the Gospel are given here. What Jesus said in his teaching was, first, 'Listen!' The first word, in the imperative or commanding mood, is arresting. It stands starkly alone in a single word sentence. If we are tempted to think that this is simply an instruction to the crowd to be quiet so that the real business of teaching might begin, let us note that the parable ends with another imperative, 'Let the one who has ears to hear listen!' (4.9). Thus at the beginning and the end Jesus calls on his audience to listen.

Jesus repeats the concluding call to listen, almost verbatim, in the interpretative explanation to those around him with the twelve (4.23). This is followed by his call, 'Take care how you hear!' (4.24). The interpretation concludes with the summing up of the narrator, who indicates that Jesus spoke to them (apparently the crowd) in many such parables, as much 'as they were able *to hear*' (4.33). The narrator also distinguishes teaching in parables, limited only by the ability to hear, from Jesus' explanation to his own disciples privately (4.34). The narrator's comment here apparently explains the situation outlined in 4.10–12. Having spoken a parable to the crowd (4.1–9), Jesus was asked for an explanation by those around him with the twelve, when they were alone (away from the crowd). His explanation was that 'To you [the insiders] is given the mystery of the kingdom of God, but to those outside [the crowd] everything is in parables'. The fact that they have to ask the meaning of the parable shows that they do not understand. The Markan narrator has *partly* explained this by interpreting Jesus' words to mean that he explained the parables to his disciples when they were alone

(4.33–34). The problem bound up with the parables concerns seeing and hearing leading to perception and understanding (4.12). Jesus called on outsiders and insiders alike to 'Listen!' The call to listen is the theme of the parable and not simply the preliminary act before teaching begins.

Between the two calls to listen in 4.3 and 4.9 the well-known parable is told. Matthew and Luke reinterpreted this parable for their own distinctive purposes. In Matthew the parable of the sower is elaborated by a second parable, in which weeds were sown by an enemy (the devil) alongside the good seed sown by the Son of Man (Matthew 18.37–39). Matthew's version has been influential to the extent that the parable has become known as the parable of the sower (Matthew 13.18). For Matthew the christological message is dominant, making critical the identification of the sower *of the good seed* with Jesus as the Son of Man. In Luke the key to the parable is recognition that 'the seed is the word of God', Luke 8.11. Thus for Luke it is *the parable of the seed.* The reason for this may be that Luke is looking to the ongoing effect of the word of God in and through the early Christian preachers and does not wish to restrict the application of the parable to the time of Jesus. But neither of these approaches emphasises the main point made by Mark. Mark would not have denied the significance of Jesus as sower, nor would he have denied the power of the word of God preached by Jesus and his followers. Certainly he recognised that the one who sows the seed stands for the one who sows the word (of God), Mark 3.14. Nevertheless, his emphasis in understanding this parable lies elsewhere.

The parable begins and ends with calls to 'Listen!' From the beginning to the end the focus of attention is on the role and responsibility of *the hearer*. What is more, the parable is about hearing or *reception*. Neither the authority of the sower, nor the power of the word, can guarantee the harvest. In the idiom of the parable, '*everything* depends on the soil'. Consequently, the parable elaborates the various kinds of soil upon which the seed falls. There is no question of different sowers or of good and bad seed (as in Matthew). The one variable is the soil: the wayside; the stony ground; the thorny ground; and finally, the good ground. Only the good ground produced any harvest and this it did to varying degrees, thirtyfold, sixtyfold, and one hundredfold.

*+The purpose of the parables, 4.10–12*

A new scene is signalled by reference to Jesus being *alone*. It soon becomes apparent that this means only that he was away from the crowd, who are perceived as 'outsiders'. Then those around him (οἱ περὶ αὐτον) with the twelve asked him about the parables. Who were those around Jesus? Are they to be identified with 'those sitting in a circle around him' in 3.34? But this group is described as a crowd in 3.32, which makes them correspond more to the crowd of 4.1 though Jesus does imply that they are his potential true family, *if* they do the will of God. It is probably a mistake to try to equate too closely groups appearing in different scenes. Rather, Mark's point here is to show that those viewed as 'insiders' were more inclusive than the twelve. After 4.10–12 Mark does not carefully signal changes of audience.

Who then asked the question about the parables? It could be that *those around him*, who were with the twelve, asked the question, though Mark might mean that the question arose from the whole group. No single spokesperson is mentioned. They asked Jesus about the *parables*, but Jesus had told only one parable on this occasion. Jesus' response also made reference to parables. He said, 'To you [plural] is given the mystery of the kingdom of God; but to those *outside* everything is in *parables*'. Perhaps there is this vacillation between singular (parable) and plural because, in the interpretation, this parable is made the key to all the parables (4.13).

For Mark, the kingdom of God is a mystery to be revealed which, even when it has been revealed, remains a mystery. William Wrede referred to *Das Messiasgeheimnis*, which is commonly translated as the messianic secret but is better understood as the messianic mystery. The secrecy motif is but a small part of the mystery and the messianic mystery in Mark is an integral aspect of the mystery of the kingdom of God. The mystery of evil in the presence of the kingdom of God is partly illuminated by the struggle of Jesus with the demonic powers, and it is this that gives the exorcisms their prominence in Mark. The exorcisms not only throw light on the presence of the kingdom, they also have implications for understanding the role of Jesus and Mark's interpretation of the crucifixion.

Jesus affirmed that those gathered around him had been given the *mystery* of the kingdom of God. This is sometimes understood as if Jesus had said that they had been given to *know* the *mysteries* of the kingdom of God, which is to read Mark through the eyes of Matthew (13.11) and Luke (8.10). Matthew and Luke indicate that the disciples have been given detailed knowledge about the mysteries of the kingdom. The mysteries can be understood as secrets that, once disclosed, can be known. But Mark says, 'To you is given the mystery of the kingdom of God'. Nothing is said about knowing, and a single mystery is in view. The kingdom of God is itself the mystery. The mystery of the kingdom has been given to them, but they do not understand it. Indeed, for Mark, the kingdom is intrinsically mysterious and, while the disciples increasingly come to some knowledge of it, the kingdom remains a mystery to them. The disciples progressed from being outsiders and were given the mystery of the kingdom of God, but the kingdom remained intrinsically mysterious.

The difference between 'outsiders', for whom everything is in parables, and the disciples as 'insiders', to whom is given the mystery of the kingdom of God, is that the parables were explained to them by Jesus (4.33–34). The purpose of the parables is stated in Mark's use of a quotation of Isaiah 6.9–10, which was widely used by the early Christians to explain why Jesus was rejected by his own people. Mark has Jesus assert that all his teaching to outsiders was in parables so that the purpose and consequence of this is

> that seeing they may see and not perceive, and hearing they may hear and not understand, lest they turn and it be forgiven them.

The problem with this quotation is that it seems to suggest that Jesus taught in parables in order to blind and confuse the crowd, which is not consistent with the portrayal of Jesus in Mark, nor does it agree with the consequences of his teaching or the content of the parables that have been preserved in Mark. In particular the parable of the soils solemnly calls on the audience to 'Listen!' It is a parable that highlights the significance of the response of the audience. What distinguishes the crowd of 4.1 from those gathered around Jesus (4.10) is response, even though it is a questioning, not a knowing, response. The parable of the soils is oriented to producing a response. 'Let the one who has ears to hear listen!' For those who listened and responded there was the gift of the mystery of the kingdom of God. For those who made no response, no move from the position of 'outsiders' to 'insiders', there were only the parables. The parables were designed so that no response meant no perception, no understanding, no forgiveness. The saying from Isaiah 6 is significant because, although probably relating to the call of Isaiah, it is a reflection from the perspective of the end of his ministry and expresses the *judgement* of God on the unfaithful, unresponsive nation. God's judgement is expressed in the hardening of the heart, the blinding of the eyes and the deadening of perception. God judged the nation as beyond hope. In the same way, the parables are instruments of blinding judgement for those who do not respond to them. Everything depends on response. In Isaiah too, although the nation was unresponsive and therefore judged, there was a remnant that proved to be faithful. In Mark it is to the responsive remnant that the mystery of the kingdom of God was given.

Mark was deeply conscious that the majority of Jesus' own people had rejected him. This indeed was a mystery. Mark did not see this in terms of the failure of Jesus or of the kingdom of God. It was rather a manifestation of the mystery of the kingdom of God. While the insiders were given the mystery, it is of the nature of a mystery that, even when it is given, it remains intrinsically mysterious because it is bound up with the mystery of God himself. Nevertheless, it is possible to grasp elements of that which is mysterious. For this reason Jesus provided some explanation to the perplexed questioning from those around him.

### +*The parable of the soils explained, 4.13–20*

According to Jesus the meaning of this parable is the key to the meaning of all the parables (4.13). Obviously the sower sows the word. The various soils represent the different levels of reception. Satan has a role to play only with those represented by the wayside. Because there is no depth of soil the birds, here a figurative representation for Satan, can snatch away the seed, the word. But this does not make Satan responsible for the failure of the seed, the word, to bring forth its desired consequences. Had the seed been received, as it is in the good soil, it would not have lain on the surface ready to be snatched away by the birds, by Satan. For the rest, apart from the good ground, various circumstances inevitably prevent the seed from growing because it has not been received deeply into the soil. Such reception happens only in the good soil, which produces a varied but manifold crop. The various circumstances which prevent the seed from growing are all described in terms appropriate to the problems encountered by the early church rather than the ministry of Jesus. Thus the interpretation in particular appears to be oriented to the needs of the early church.

The main teaching in this parable is clear. Everything depends on the kind of reception given to the seed, the word. The reception given to the word depends on listening, hence the stress of Jesus, 'Listen!' In the group of sayings following the formal explanation of the parable Jesus again says to his disciples, 'If anyone has ears to hear, let that person listen' (4.23), and 'Take care [Watch out] how you hear' (4.24). The 'visual' image is used to heighten the auditory image ('Listen') found appropriately in the telling of the parable itself where, at least in the interpretation, 'the sower sows the word' or, in Luke's more straightforward analogy, 'the seed is the word'. Elsewhere, in the context of the apocalyptic discourse, Jesus appropriately calls on his disciples to 'watch', 13.5, 9, 33. Here, in 4.24, by using visual and auditory images together, the quotation of Isaiah 6 is recalled (4.12) and Jesus emphasises not only the necessity of hearing but also of *hearing in the right manner.* There is a hearing in which what is heard 'goes in one ear and out the other'. This is not serious listening. There is a hearing which enjoys and assents to what is heard but never leads to anything because there is no commitment. There is a hearing which listens as long as there is 'nothing better to do'. None of these kinds of hearing qualify for what Jesus has called for in the parable.

The parable portrays varying levels of good ground with proportional percentages of harvest, though even thirtyfold was a good harvest. Concluding with the harvest draws attention to the eschatological orientation of Mark. The extraordinary harvest assures the reader that in spite of the challenges to Jesus' mission and the hiddenness of the kingdom in the present, the kingdom would dawn in a spectacular way *in the end.*

### +*Parables and similes on the theme, 4.21–32*

Separate groups of sayings are signalled by a new quotation formula, 'And he said [to them]', 4.21, 24, 26, 30. The first two groups of sayings (4.21–23 and 24–25) are made up of what appear to be separate traditions. Matthew has scattered these sayings through his Gospel. But since Matthew seems to have fragmented traditions in the interest of his own arrangement, this proves little. The strongest evidence that four separate traditions have been brought together is the way the sayings have been loosely linked together. Each of the two groups is made up of two sayings linked by 'for'. These two groups of sayings would seem to be understood as addressed to the group mentioned in 4.10–12, because no change of audience has been signalled and there, as here, it is said 'And Jesus said to them'. This is put in question, however, by the conclusion on the use of parables in 4.34, where the narrator (Mark) contrasts Jesus' teaching in parables to the crowd with his private teaching to his own disciples (see 4.36).

The first group of sayings is linked linguistically by the relationship between light (the lamp) and revelation. The saying that what reveals is light, 'All that manifests is light' (Ephesians 5.14), probably expresses a widely held tradition. The sense of the Markan sayings is that the mystery of the kingdom, though withheld from the crowd (the outsiders), is *given* to the disciples (the insiders). It is given to them because of their response. But there is no ground for complacency and this is signalled by warning at the end (4.23), which echoes the words at the end of the parable of the soils (4.9). 'If anyone has ears to hear let that person [hear] listen.' Though they have responded to Jesus the disciples must remain sensitively open because the mystery of the kingdom of God, though given to them, remains a mystery beyond them to which they must attend as they are drawn on by the light.

The second group of sayings opens with the warning 'See how you hear!', taking up the first two metaphors of response in the saying of Isaiah 6.9–10, 'that seeing they may see but . . . hearing they may hear but . . .'. The combination of the metaphors in 4.24 brings them together, by the connection of 'how', in the single metaphor of watchful hearing. Both metaphors express alertness, the visual from the perspective of apocalyptic vision and the auditory from the perspective of the prophetic proclamation of the word. If being given the mystery of the kingdom has suggested the image of receiving, it is now affirmed that those who *give* will *receive*. This might well develop out of the parable where the seed in the good ground *bears fruit*. In the parable it bears fruit, thirtyfold, sixtyfold and one hundredfold. Now it is taught that the measure measured out (given) determines the measure received.

The next two parables are introduced by 'And he said', introducing new sayings but with no suggestion of a change in audience. Only the second of these uses the word parable but, like the groups of sayings in 4.21–25, they are implied parables (4.33–34).

Both 4.26–29 and 4.30–32 are formally comparisons or analogies intended to throw light on the kingdom of God, addressing the mystery of the kingdom of God on the assumption that the nature of the mystery is such that the kingdom cannot be spoken of directly, only by analogy.

In the first, 'The kingdom of God is *like* a man who casts seed upon the earth' (4.26). While the man was asleep the seed grew, although he had no knowledge of it; the earth *automatically* bore fruit, first the blade, then the ear, then the full grain in the ear. When the crop is ripe the harvest follows immediately.

In the second, 'How shall we liken the kingdom of God or in what *parable* shall we describe it?', it is likened to a mustard seed which, when sown, is small but grows into a large plant in the branches of which all of the birds can shelter.

Two important points develop out of the original parable, focusing attention on the mystery of the kingdom of God, a theme not explicitly dealt with in the original parable but essential to its meaning (4.11). The authority of Jesus was seriously challenged in Mark 2–3. Just where was the kingdom of God whose presence Jesus had announced? The answer of the first parable is that the kingdom, though hidden and growing imperceptibly, would produce its results. Emphasis on the harvest implies an eschatological fulfilment. The kingdom, though present in a hidden way, would be fully manifest at the judgement. The major emphasis is on the certainty of the harvest because the seed would produce first the blade, then the ear, then the full grain in the ear. This assurance makes sense in the context of the challenge to Jesus' authority (2.1–3.6) and the subsequent mystery of the death of Jesus, and would have been a comfort to the early Christian movement as it struggled to make its way in the Graeco-Roman world.

The second parable is also a response to the challenge to the authority of Jesus and makes the point that humble beginnings do not rule out an impressive and effective conclusion. Ineffectual as the kingdom seemed to be as the authority of Jesus was challenged, the effectiveness of the kingdom was promised and guaranteed by this parable, from the tiniest of seeds to the mighty shrub which could give shelter to all of the birds of the air. In the parable, reference to all the birds of the air is almost certainly a reference to the universality of the kingdom, encompassing people from all nations (see Ezekiel 17.23; 31.6; Daniel 4.12, 14, 21). We might be right to suspect Markan interpretation at this point.

+*On the use of the parables, 4.33–34*

Mark tells us that Jesus spoke *to them* in many parables like these. Both references to Jesus speaking to them in parables in 4.33–34 use the imperfect tense and might imply that Jesus habitually spoke to the crowd in parables. But see 4.9, 11, 21, 24, 26, 30 for the use of the imperfect tense in quotation formulae. Context alone makes clear that this is Mark's meaning, regardless of the use of the imperfect tense. There is no mention of a change of audience from the group last mentioned in 4.10–12. Yet 4.33–34 asserts that the parables were spoken to the outsiders and explanations given to the disciples. The Gospel is sometimes made up of loosely connected units which were read/heard by believers, for whom the distinction between the audiences of the parables and the explanation dissolved when addressed to the reader.

Jesus' teaching is further elaborated by saying in or through these parables Jesus spoke *the word* to them. Reference to 'the word' echoes the idiom of the early church, reminding us that Mark wrote from this perspective, telling the story of Jesus as good news, gospel (Mark 1.1), which does not suggest that Jesus held back or intentionally hid his meaning in this teaching. The only limitation suggested was that of the audience, 'as much as they were able to hear' or 'in so far as they were able to hear'. In this concluding summary concerning the parables, it is made clear that response is crucial, that only response limits the teaching of Jesus. Like the parable of the soils and its interpretation, the teaching about Jesus' use of parables stresses the importance of hearing. That is not surprising because, according to the Markan Jesus, that parable is the key to all the parables (4.13). Right hearing is attentive, committed, determined, obedient hearing which bears fruit. To such hearing the mystery of the kingdom of God is given.

Mark maintains the distinction of parables only to outsiders while explanations were given to the disciples. In the light of 4.10–12 this looks like a severe limitation. Yet again we have an apparent paradox. On the one hand, Mark stresses that Jesus held back his explanation from the crowd, giving it privately to his disciples. On the other, the teaching to the crowds appears to be limited only by the limitations of the crowd. Three points need to be made in response to this observation. First, Mark recognises the possibility of the movement from being an outsider (crowd) to insider (disciple). Thus, in one sense, explanation is available to all who will hear.

Second, the distinction between outsider and insider is dissolved for the reader who hears the word in both the parable and the explanation.

Third, in telling the story of Jesus' ministry to his own people, awareness of the mystery of the rejection of Jesus hovers in the background as something which calls for explanation. The *mystery* of the kingdom of God finds expression in the parables. Jesus' teaching in parables is used to help explain the rejection of Jesus in a way that preserves the credibility and authority of Jesus and the kingdom he proclaimed.

## Three miracle stories – four miracles, 4.35–5.43

### +*Calming the storm – the disciples and faulty faith, 4.35–41*

Without any indication of a change of audience 4.35 begins 'And he said to them'. The time setting is on the same day when evening had come. It becomes clear, however, that the disciples were spoken to by Jesus because, at his suggestion, they left together in a boat to cross the sea, *leaving the crowd* (4.36). In the light of 4.33–34, it is implied that they are Jesus' own disciples, which, given that they left in a boat, cannot be a group wider than the twelve in spite of the reference to others in 4.10.

Other boats accompanied them, perhaps suggesting that some of the crowd attempted to follow them. The other boats and the crowd play no further part in the story. The failure to be specific about the audience in 4.21–32 after indicating private teaching to the disciples in 4.10–20 makes the reader uncertain about the audience in 4.35–41, having only the narrator's words in 4.33–34 concerning the practice of Jesus to teach in parables except to his own disciples. Now (4.35–41), after private instruction from Jesus, the faith of the disciples is shown to be faulty, just as the credibility of the (twelve) disciples was put in question in 3.20–21, immediately after Jesus had appointed them (3.13–19).

In this correction story the disciples, who had been privately instructed by Jesus, might be expected to have some understanding of Jesus and of their own role in relation to him. Jesus, by his action and word, corrected their understanding and commitment, or lack of it. The story, though commencing with Jesus and his disciples in one boat, accompanied by other boats, concerns just the one boat with Jesus and his disciples. At the opening of the description of the journey we are told a great storm of wind arose. Waves broke over the boat, filling it with water while Jesus slept on a cushion in the stern. Six matters call for attention. The significance of (1) the storm; (2) the description of Jesus sleeping; (3) the response of the disciples to Jesus sleeping; (4) Jesus' response to the storm; (5) Jesus' response to the disciples; and (6) the disciples' final response.

In Middle-Eastern mythology the sea with its storms was seen as the place of potential chaos caused by powers often spoken of in demonic terms. This line of interpretation is confirmed by Jesus' response, silencing the storm.

Jesus slept while the storm raged. The reader knows that numbered amongst Jesus' disciples were fishermen well used to the sea. Does Jesus' sleep indicate his trust in the disciples' seamanship? Such a psychological interpretation has no place in Mark. Mark may use this incident to demonstrate Jesus' trust in God as a reproof to the disciples, a line of interpretation confirmed by Jesus' words to his disciples. But Mark also intends Jesus' sleep to be a test for the disciples. It is through this act that the weakness of the faith of the disciples is exposed, enabling Jesus to challenge and correct it.

The response of the disciples exposes their faulty assessment of Jesus. They called him 'Teacher', which is the Greek equivalent of 'Rabbi'. For Mark this is appropriate but hardly adequate as a statement of faith. The question as to whether he cared 'if *we* perish' might suggest that they thought he could act to overcome the storm. This need not be the case. Whether he could help or not, his behaviour appeared to indicate that he did not care. The disciples' words after the storm had been calmed also show that they did not expect him to save them. The use of the first person plural ('if we perish') might or might not include Jesus himself with them as those who were about to perish. The concern of the disciples was for their own safety.

Jesus' response to the storm is expressed in terms similar to his first encounter with the man with an unclean spirit in 1.25. Just as he had 'rebuked' it, he now 'rebuked' the wind. Just as he commanded the spirit to 'be silent', so he 'silenced' the wind. While the silencing of the unclean spirit seems to have been because it knew him, this is not the case with the wind. Nevertheless, because it was also an expression of the demonic forces, Jesus silenced it, revealing the complexity of the secrecy motif. In response to Jesus' words of command the wind ceased and a 'great' calm descended.

Between the *great* storm of wind (4.37) and the *great* calm (4.39), the dynamic word of Jesus interposed.

Jesus' words to the disciples followed without any indication of a response by the disciples. His words to them are a rebuke and correction: 'Why are you fearful? Do you not yet have faith?', indicating the inappropriate behaviour of the disciples. What is in view is craven fear, cowardly fear, and Jesus diagnosed its cause as the absence of faith. But what is the meaning of faith here? Perhaps this emerges in the contrast between the way the disciples addressed Jesus in the midst of the storm and the fearful, bewildered questioning at the conclusion of the story.

The disciples' final response takes the form of the final pronouncement in this story. It was that sense of mystery, not the storm which had ceased, that produced in them the sense of great fear. The expression 'They feared with great fear' is a Semitism. This fear, like the amazement at the authority of Jesus in his teaching, is an appropriate human response to the divine. It is not the term itself that indicates this. For example, the ruler of the synagogue feared the death of his daughter and in this context Jesus told him not to fear but to believe, 5.36. Similarly, fear of a ghost meets Jesus' word, 'Don't be afraid!', 6.50. Those following Jesus up to Jerusalem were afraid, not in response to the mystery revealed in Jesus but of the danger of death, 10.32. The response of the women to the announcement of the resurrection was fear, and it is on that note that Mark ends (16.8). There fear paralysed the women and prevented the fulfilment of their commission.

On the other hand, the fear of the disciples in response to the authority of Jesus in the stilling of the storm was appropriate. No word of rebuke comes from Jesus at this point. Instead the disciples themselves express the climactic pronouncement in the story, 'Who then is this, that even the wind and the sea obey him?' His authority, expressed now in relation to the wind and sea, raised an awareness of mystery in relation to him. The question may point to an awareness that what Jesus does here is appropriate to God who controls the sea, Psalm 89.8–9. Nevertheless, the fear they expressed at this point in response to a manifestation of the divine was the awe of ignorance, 'Who is this?' While the disciples have made some advance, there is not too much to be said for their ignorance.

## AN EXCURSION INTO THE REGION OF GERASA: PREMONITIONS OF THE MISSION TO THE NATIONS, 5.1–20

*+The Gerasene demoniac: (an interlude in Jesus' Galilean ministry foreshadowing 7.24–8.10), the significance of the Decapolis and an elaboration of exorcism, 5.1–20*

This quest/objection story is marked by the movement of Jesus and his disciples, by boat, to a new location beyond (to the eastern side of) the sea. There is textual confusion concerning the name of the region as 'of the Gerasenes', or 'Gergesenes', or 'Gadarenes'. The variants seem to have arisen because the distance of Gerasa from the sea (about thirty miles) creates problems for the story which occurs 'immediately' after Jesus has disembarked. Precise location is not important. The reader need know only that Jesus left Galilee and moved into 'Gentile' territory. This is confirmed at the end by reference to the man preaching throughout the Decapolis, the league of ten Greek cities on the eastern side of the sea and the Jordan river, by reference to the large herd of pigs, which, for Jews, were unclean animals, and by the name the demoniac used for God. No reason is given for this move. In terms of the structure of Mark's Gospel it foreshadows Jesus' more extensive mission into dominantly Gentile territory in 7.24–8.10.

It is the occasion for the second detailed account of Jesus' encounter with a person with an unclean spirit (see 1.21–28). The first took place in the synagogue at Capernaum, while the second is set at no specific location, only a general region. The significance of Gerasa is that it places Jesus on Gentile soil. Jesus disembarked and the possessed person came out from the tombs to meet him. Given that such a person was not fit for human society, dwelling among the tombs, an unclean place, was characteristic. Contrast the synagogue setting of 1.23–28. Here, as in 2.15–17, Jesus dealt with one who was an outcast from society, not only from Jewish but also from Gentile society.

The exorcism is narrated following the pattern of the traditional miracle story. (1) The circumstances of the possessed man are described in some detail. (2) Jesus' authority and words of exorcism are recorded. (3) Impressive evidence is recorded to demonstrate the effectiveness of the exorcism. Because the man came out to meet Jesus it can be viewed as a miracle quest story, the act of coming to meet Jesus being viewed as an implied request by the man for healing (exorcism). Yet, because he was possessed, coming to meet Jesus can be viewed as an act of objection or as a challenge to Jesus by the unclean spirit(s). From this perspective it can be viewed as an objection story. The objection can be seen in the challenge, 'What is there between me and you?' and 'I beseech you by God not to torment me'.

The story is told in characteristic Markan fashion in which a summary is first given, followed by a more detailed account. Having described the encounter in the briefest terms (5.2), 5.3–5 sets out more fully the circumstance, demonstrating what a bad case of possession this was. The circumstances accentuate the remarkable nature of the exorcism performed by Jesus. So powerful was the possession that chains could not bind the man. All night long he cried out and cut himself with stones. His behaviour was anti-social and self-destructive. The latter is further emphasised when, in response to Jesus' question concerning his name, the possessed person replied, 'My name is Legion, for we are many'. The man's own identity was destroyed or obscured, leaving only the fragmented voice of the demons.

Having described the condition of the possessed man, Mark turns back to describe the circumstances of his meeting with Jesus (5.6–13), which had been noted briefly in 5.2. First, the initiative of the man in coming to meet Jesus is now confirmed in detail. He saw Jesus when he was a long way off, ran to him and 'prostrated himself' before him in worship. The term is appropriate to the response of a lowly subject to a great king. All of this is consistent with a quest story in which an entreaty is about to be made. What follows is somewhat inconsistent with this. The demoniac cried out in a loud voice with words similar to those addressed to Jesus in the synagogue in Capernaum, 1.24. Surprisingly here, in the incident in which the man is shown to be possessed by a legion of spirits, he asks, 'What is there between *me* and you . . .?', whereas in 1.24 the plural 'between *us* and you' and 'Have you come to destroy us?' asserts the fragmented consciousness of the possessed.

Here (5.7) Jesus is addressed as 'Jesus son of God most high', which combines together two equivalent statements in 1.24 which named 'Jesus of Nazareth' and claims to know who he was, naming him 'the holy one of God'. 'God most high' is the common address for the God of Israel by non-Israelites in the Old Testament (OT) (see Genesis 14.18–20; Numbers 24.16; Isaiah 14.14; Daniel 3.26, 42 and compare Acts 16.17). The use of this name for God is appropriate to the Gentile setting of the story and confirms the Gentile identity of the demoniac. Precisely what 'son of God most high' means has to be understood at two levels: the appropriate level for the demoniac and the Markan level which the reader will discern as the narrative unfolds. If the approach of the demoniac and his act of worship (*proskunesis*), combined with the words of recognition, suggest a positive relation to Jesus, his concluding words suggest he perceived himself to be under siege by Jesus. 'I beseech you by God not to torment me!' The positive words and action imply an approach to Jesus to request healing, whereas the final words suggest that Jesus was perceived as a threat. Mark explains the threat in terms of Jesus' command, 'Unclean spirit come out of him!' Perhaps Mark has developed this dramatic paradox to portray the predicament of the man needing exorcism, on the one hand, and the destructive will of the unclean spirit(s) on the other.

In spite of the order of events in the narrative, it is implied that Jesus first called on the unclean spirit(s) to come out of the man, who then responded (or is this the voice of the unclean spirit(s)?), requesting Jesus not to torment him. Certainly there is no reason to think that Jesus intended to torment the man. There is every reason to think that, in Mark, the unclean spirits feared destruction. Alternatively, we may think that the process of exorcism was itself painful (see 1.26), though there is no sign of pain for the man in this exorcism. The conclusion of the story leaves no doubt that the man was grateful to Jesus for his deliverance from the unclean spirit(s) because he asked to stay with Jesus.

Not only did Jesus command the unclean spirit(s) to come out of the man, he demanded to be told its/their name. What is more, it was the spirit(s) that replied 'My name is Legion, for we are many'. What follows is a negotiation by the spirit(s) to ensure survival. The entry of the spirits into a herd of pigs and their destruction, rushing down a cliff into the sea, provides one level of evidence of the success of the exorcism. The herdsmen fled to the town, and the townspeople came to see what had happened and found the man who had been possessed by Legion sitting clothed and in his right mind. From our point of view this is a more important level of evidence of the exorcism.

Mark is also concerned to show a variety of responses to the exorcism. When they saw the evidence of the man, the townspeople 'were afraid'. After they heard what had happened to the pigs they besought Jesus to leave. This Jesus did by boat.

The response of the healed man was to beseech Jesus to allow him *to be with* Jesus. This language suggests that the man sought to enter the relationship for which Jesus chose his disciples (3.14). Jesus would not permit him but sent him back to his own house to report what *the Lord* had done for him. The man did not restrict himself to his own house, but preached throughout the cities of the Decapolis, the league of ten Greek cities in the region. If the response of the townspeople to the exorcism was fear, the response to the man's preaching was *amazement*.

Jesus would not permit the man to go with him. Being healed did not qualify a person to become a member of Jesus' mission. Jesus chose and appointed the twelve. But this incident is unique in Mark in that only here does someone *seek* 'to be with Jesus' (to follow), and in this instance Jesus would not permit him. Mark has signalled by geographical location and by the name the demoniac used for God that a Gentile is involved. Jesus did not have a Gentile as part of his mission team and Mark does not press Jesus into a universal mission with disciples who were not Jewish. It is no coincidence that, according to Mark, Jesus did not himself preach in this region. But the man who had been healed did and, it seems, with some success. Yet, this was not at the instruction of Jesus, who had sent the man back to his own home. Mark has foreshadowed the Gentile mission without making Jesus directly responsible for it. What he has done, however, is to show that the mission to the Gentiles was a direct (and legitimate) consequence of Jesus' own mission.

## GALILEAN MISSION B, 5.21–7.23

### *+A miracle within a miracle, 5.21–43*

Two miracle quest stories have been combined to form a single narrative in which the second story interrupts the first. This is described as a sandwich structure or an intercalation which some redaction critics take to be a sign of Markan redaction (C. Clifton Black, *The Disciples according to Mark*, p. 34 and note 96). The two stories are connected by the general theme of the restoration of life to two women, each of whom is referred to as 'daughter', and specific reference to twelve years, being the period of the woman's affliction and the age of the young girl, which might reflect a traditional connection of the two stories.

+The daughter of the ruler of the synagogue, 5.21–24a, 35–43

The new episode is initiated by Jesus' return to the western side of the sea to dominantly Jewish Galilee. Probably a scribe has introduced reference to the boat to make clear the means by which Jesus (and the disciples) travelled. The new scene took place somewhere beside the sea where a great crowd gathered around Jesus. No specific location is mentioned, but some scholars suggest Capernaum because a ruler of the synagogue is mentioned and Mark earlier placed Jesus in the synagogue at Capernaum. The name Jairus is omitted by some texts and might have been imported from Luke 8.41.

The ruler of the synagogue came and fell at Jesus' feet. This is what we are told the unclean spirits did (3.11). In the preceding narrative the Gerasene demoniac ran from afar to fall down and worship Jesus, 5.6. In each of these narratives the act was accompanied by a loud cry in which Jesus' secret identity was confessed. No verbal confession was made by the ruler but the act of falling down before Jesus makes a statement, especially when the status of the ruler is kept in mind. The posture of the ruler makes clear that he made persistent *requests* rather than commands. His action implies an acknowledgement of the significance of Jesus.

This story, like the one embedded in it, is a miracle quest story, which embodies the features of a miracle story but includes some additional distinctive features. As with a miracle story: (1) The condition of the person to be healed is specified. The ruler's daughter was at the point of death. He was desperate because the condition was critical. (2) The method of healing is described. (3) Evidence of the healing is confirmed by the girl arising and taking food. The distinctive elements are: (1) The coming of the ruler and the request for the healing of his daughter. His request that Jesus should come and lay his hands on her probably assumes the common practice of healers at the time, but does not correspond to the practice of Jesus *described so far* (but see 6.5) or to what actually happened in this case. The request is an essential element in the miracle quest story. (2) In these stories normally an obstacle emerges between the request and the successful fulfilment of the quest, an obstacle that the quester must overcome if the quest is to be fulfilled. In this case the interruption by the woman, whose story is embedded in the first story, allows time for the little girl to die and news of this to be brought to the ruler. On arrival the reality of the little girl's death is stressed. Consequently the ruler's reliance on Jesus is tested to a new level. He had to trust Jesus beyond the limits of death if his daughter was to be restored to life. In this way the symbolism of salvation and resurrection becomes apparent.

The purpose of the ruler's request is spelt out in language designed to evoke the understanding of salvation, 'that she will be saved and will live'. Thus when news of the death of the little girl is confirmed, although Jesus asserts that she sleeps, his words and actions can be understood as raising the dead or awakening her from sleep. His words to the girl, recorded in transliterated Aramaic, are consistent with contemporary healing practice of using mysterious foreign words. But in this case they are only an indication of Jesus' use of Aramaic language. There is nothing mysterious in the words which Mark also translates. Taking the little girl by the hand he told her to 'arise'. The command is consistent with sleep or death and reflects the Christian euphemistic speech about death as sleep precisely because of belief in the resurrection.

The healing was performed by Jesus privately, away from the crowd of mourners, in the presence only of the girl's parents and of Peter, James and John. The crowd, which mocked Jesus for his suggestion that the girl slept, might have been excluded for this reason. But why were the majority of Jesus' disciples excluded? We might note that, according to Mark, the same three disciples accompanied Jesus at the time of the transfiguration (9.2) and in the garden of Gethsemane (14.33). These three were named amongst the first four called by Jesus (1.16–20), only Andrew, Simon's brother, is missing, though the four of them are mentioned as the audience of the apocalyptic discourse of Mark 13 (13.3). But the secrecy motif goes further than exclusion from the performance of the miracle. Those who were present were commanded not to make it known. Given that the girl's death was widely known, how could the event be kept a secret?

+The woman with a haemorrhage, 5.24b–34

The second miracle (5.24b–34) within the first not only provides narrative space in which the little girl can die, it reinforces the connection between faith and healing as a symbol for faith and salvation, 5.34. Again the story has the marks of a traditional miracle story. (1) The woman's condition is described and the seriousness of it emphasised by reference to the duration of the condition (twelve years); the failure of the physicians to produce any improvement, in spite of the woman's expending all of her resources. Despite this her condition had become worse. The condition appears to have been some form of vaginal bleeding, which would have made the woman unclean (Leviticus 15.25–30). Thus she should not have been in the crowd and should not have touched Jesus. (2) The means of healing is described. In the press of the crowd the woman decided that if she could touch Jesus' clothing 'I will be saved'. Here also healing has become the image of salvation, as is confirmed at the end of the *chreia* in the striking saying of Jesus, 'Daughter, your faith has saved you; go in peace'. (3) Confirmation of the healing is given by the woman, who knew of the change in her body immediately, and by Jesus, who indicated that healing 'power' had gone out from him because someone had touched part of his clothing. Because this might seem to be less than conclusive, there is a discussion between the disciples and Jesus about how he could know that someone had touched him in a crowd that pressed in on him from every side.

The quest story is signalled by the initiative of the woman. Her first obstacle was the pressing crowd, which she had to overcome to get near Jesus. She turned this to her own advantage. Assuming that Jesus would not be aware of her touching his clothing, she did this and was healed instantly. The story has the appearance of magic about it. Jesus himself is the source of the healing power (5.30), not his clothing, and the woman's faith was the key. To make this clear it was necessary for Jesus to confront the agent of the secret action. Under Jesus' searching gaze the woman was 'afraid', 'fell down' before Jesus (see 3.11; 5.6, 22, 33) and told him all she had done. While this aspect of the story is not presented as a condition of healing, it is understood (by Mark) as a condition to be fulfilled by the woman if the story is to end successfully. Only after this is Jesus' final impressive pronouncement made, confirming not only the healing but the salvation of the woman, 'Daughter, your faith has saved you; go in peace and be *whole* [see John 5.6, 9, 11, 14, 15; 7.23] from your affliction'.

## Three responses, 6.1–30

*+Rejection at Nazareth, 6.1–6a*

Wherever the home of the ruler of the synagogue was, this objection story is set in Jesus' 'home town'. The term translated 'home town' was suggested by the proverb Jesus used in response to his reception there. Mark does not identify where this might be. Luke names Nazareth, which probably makes explicit what Mark presupposes (see 1.9, 24). The change of location is marked by the occurrence of another sabbath upon which Jesus again taught in the synagogue.

While Jesus' teaching was again met by a response of amazement (compare 1.22), this was expressed in a series of questions concerning: (1) The origin of Jesus' wisdom and miracles ('mighty works'). Again (see 1.27), teaching and miracles are connected. (2) Jesus' known family, which made his activity unlikely. Evidently, because he was 'a local boy', whose family connections were known, the people of his home town *were scandalised/stumbled* at the authority implied by his teaching and miracles.

Jesus is described as 'the carpenter', the son of Mary. His brothers are named as James, Joses, Jude and Simon. His sisters are mentioned but not named. Mark does *not* say the family were scandalised by Jesus' behaviour. Rather, Jesus was identified by his relationship to them.

In response to the scandalisation, which implies an *objection*, Jesus spoke a proverb which is covered by Mark's use of the term *parable*. This proverb appears in slightly different wording in the other Gospels (including that of Thomas 31), and a different context in John 4.44. In Mark Jesus said, 'A prophet is not without honour except in his home town among his fellow country men and in his own house'. The proverb was Jesus' response to what must be viewed as his rejection in his home town. The rejection is expressed in paradoxical terms, but the proverb suggests clear-cut rejection and specifically names groups not otherwise mentioned. It is doubtful that the proverb is meant to provide accurate details concerning those who rejected Jesus, though Mark had no concern to clarify the role of the family of Jesus. Readers regularly conclude that the brothers were amongst those who rejected Jesus at this point. The same conclusion is not drawn concerning Mary, who is also named by the townspeople and would be covered by the terms of the proverb *if* it is to be taken as a list of those who rejected Jesus. This line of interpretation seems to be mistaken. Rather, the proverb is used to challenge the unbelief of the townspeople.

The proverb provides an explanation for the rejection of Jesus in his home town which, if accepted by the townspeople, could lead to a revision of their assessment. Jesus' use of it, with reference to himself, implies that he perceived himself to be a prophet. The origin of the proverb is not known but the logic is clear. Every prophet must have a home town where he and his family are known, providing grounds for objection to prophetic authority. The use of the proverb failed to persuade the people to revise their judgement of Jesus. To confirm this Mark says that Jesus was unable to do many miracles there, except that he laid hands on and healed a few sick (compare 7.32). Laying hands on the sick was a common practice with healers. While Jesus is sometimes portrayed as acting in this way, it was not his *regular* practice.

Mark was not afraid to indicate limitations in Jesus' ability, though he is quick to note the reason for them. The townspeople were scandalised by him. He marvelled at their *unbelief*. This confirms that their unbelief was the cause of his inability to perform many miracles.

*+Mission of the twelve, 6.6b–13*

Mark described the calling of a number of disciples (see 1.16–20; 2.13–17; 3.13–19). Immediately following the rejection at Nazareth he narrates the mission of the twelve. The placement of these two narratives (6.1–6a, 6b–13) implies that Jesus' mission is to be seen as distinct from his home town and family. Distancing from family was a necessary development for a universal movement and has been discussed in relation to Jesus' family in 3.31–35.

The dual purpose of the appointment of the twelve was: to be with Jesus, and to be sent out by him to preach and to cast out demons (3.13–19). From then until this point in the narrative the twelve had been with Jesus, sometimes surrounded by crowds and sometimes with a wider circle of 'followers' (4.10, 34). Now Jesus commissioned them for the second task. Thus the present narrative forms an *inclusio* with the account of the appointment of the twelve and their response. In contrast to the response of the people of Jesus' home town, their response must be considered a positive one.

+Summary of Jesus' mission activity, 6.6b

There is no indication where Jesus was when he sent out the twelve. He had been going about the villages teaching (6.6b). Mark introduces the sending out of the twelve with their tasks in the context of a summary statement concerning Jesus' own mission of going around the villages teaching. What Jesus does, the twelve are to do also. With the exception of the brief excursion to the eastern side of the sea (5.1–20), Jesus' mission had been concentrated in Galilee and there is no reason to think that the villages of 6.6b are not Galilean villages. Summaries like this put in question the view that Jesus did not visit places not specifically mentioned, such as Tiberius and Sepphoris. Cf. 1.38–39.

+The mission of the twelve, 6.7–13

The sending out of the twelve in pairs implies a wider mission, perhaps foreshadowing the Gentile mission. The prescribed 'style' of the mission of the twelve makes explicit the style of Jesus' own mission, though the sending out of the twelve, in six pairs, marks a new phase. The significance of this might be the requirement of two witnesses (Deuteronomy 17.6; 19.15), though they do not seem to be sent to give legal evidence. The command to 'shake off the dust from your feet as a *witness* to them' might be construed as an enigmatic legal action. Perhaps mutual support was more the point, see 14.13. The evidence of Acts (8.14; 13.1–2; 15.22, 39) suggests the early church found this model to be useful. Initially, the mission of the twelve is elaborated in terms of being given *authority* over unclean spirits by Jesus. This is only half the task nominated in 3.14–15. The task of preaching must have been presupposed because, when they went out, we are told, they preached.

The Markan terms of the mission are clearly set out. They differ in some details from the accounts of Matthew and Luke. The requirements reflect an eschatological urgency in which the twelve were to extend the scope of Jesus' mission. In some ways they were to be like the beggar philosophers, like the Cynics. Light equipment was the order of the day, a staff, sandals and tunic, but no bread, purse or even a small coin in the belt. Sandals signify provision for arduous journeys. The principle of the mission assumed hospitality. The 'missionaries' were to stay in one house in a village until the mission to that village was complete. But if they were rejected, they were to shake the dust from their feet and move on to the next village. This might reflect the practice of a Jew returning to Israel, shaking the dust of Gentile lands from his feet (see M. Oholoth 2.3; M. Tohoroth 4.5; B. Shab. 15b). It presupposes the notion of Israel as 'the holy land'. Mark says that this act was to be done 'as a witness to them'. Perhaps it was intended as a symbolic act which proclaimed that those who refused the messengers were no longer part of Israel and their villages were to be treated as Gentile territory. As such they must face the final judgement.

Having set out the terms of the mission Mark tells us, 'They went out and preached that they should repent'. This confirms that, although not mentioned, preaching was one of the essential terms of reference. They also cast out many demons. Given that the terms of reference speak of authority over unclean spirits, this confirms the equivalence of unclean spirits and demons for Mark. Unmentioned either in the account of the appointment or the terms of reference given above is the practice of anointing the sick with oil to heal them. Accounts of Jesus' healings generally mention no ritual acts although, in the account of the rejection at his home town, we are told he laid hands on a few sick people (6.5). The action of the twelve in anointing the sick with oil is unprecedented in Mark's account of the healing ministry of Jesus. It was a Jewish practice reflected in James 5.14, which might suggest that Mark's silence about aspects of Jesus' mission should not be taken to mean nothing happened. Here again the mission practice of the twelve probably reflects Jesus' own practice.

The terms and purpose of the mission of the twelve were: to preach, to cast out demons, and to heal the sick. The content of their preaching, 'Repent', has more in common with the preaching of John (the Baptist) than Jesus, though it should be remembered that Mark summarised Jesus' preaching as 'Repent and *believe* the gospel'. What is missing from the summary is any reference to believing the gospel. Because the twelve concentrated only on the message of repentance it may be that we are to think of their ministry as preparatory, presupposing that Jesus himself was to follow them as he had followed John.

*+Execution of John, 6.14–29*

The sending out of the twelve forms an *inclusio* with their appointment (3.13–29) and the account of the death of John (the Baptiser) forms an *inclusio* with the summary account of his arrest, 1.14. The arrest of John marked the transition from John to Jesus and the beginning of Jesus' ministry *in Galilee.* Now, after the account of the extension of Jesus' mission by the sending out of the twelve, Mark introduces the account of the death of John so that it comes immediately before the account of the return of the twelve, now designated 'apostles', from their mission (6.30).

The account of John's death is introduced here because news of Jesus had reached 'king Herod', not because John had just died. Herod associated Jesus with John. The narrative implies that Herod was in Galilee, in his palace at Tiberius, and provides us with Herod's response to Jesus. In the process it reports a variety of responses. This Herod (Herod Antipas), the son of Herod the Great, was tetrarch (not king) of Galilee and Peraea from 4 BCE to 39 CE. According to Mark, Herod supposed that Jesus was John, whom he had beheaded, risen from the dead. He concluded this because of what he heard being said of Jesus. There is some textual confusion. A minority of texts attribute the saying (6.14) that 'John the Baptiser is risen from the dead' to Herod. The correct reading attributes this saying to others whose sayings Herod heard. Some said that Jesus was John 'the Baptiser' risen from the dead and because of this the powers were at work in him. Herod heard the other reports as well, but agreed with this assessment, 6.16. The textual variant in 6.14 probably arose from the statement of Herod's view in 6.16.

Some Jews believed in resurrection, generally understood as a corporate event of the end time, not something that happened to individuals in the present. The notion of an individual resurrection was not incomprehensible at the time, but the identification of Jesus with John implies that Jesus was relatively unknown until John was arrested. Jesus was seen to be continuing the work of John, to be John again. It was impossible to get rid of him. But unless a greater sense of identity was perceived there was no need to express this in terms of resurrection. There were plenty of examples of succession like Moses and Joshua, Elijah and Elisha. Even to the common mind the miracles of Jesus, 'the powers at work in him', distinguished him from John.

In the report Herod heard, 'the powers' of Jesus were said to be a consequence of resurrection. By asserting that the powers were at work in him because of the resurrection it is implied that John did no miracles (John 10.41), while maintaining his identification with Jesus. Because news of Jesus' activity had spread throughout Galilee (1.28) we must consider that Mark has held back the news so that it reached Herod only at this point in the narrative. The narrative assumes that John had been dead for some time, allowing the activity of Jesus to take place in the narrative space between the death of John and the time when Herod heard of Jesus. The report of Herod hearing of Jesus provided the opportunity to tell of the circumstances of John's death. This retrospective account fills the narrative space between the sending out of the twelve (6.6b–13) and their return (6.30–31).

The narrative provides opportunity to: (1) give an account of John's death, alerting the reader to the continuing importance of John in Mark's time; (2) set out the various responses to the teaching and healing mission of Jesus. What is common to all of these responses is the perception of Jesus as a prophet. We can say also, according to Mark, Jesus claimed prophetic status in his use of the proverb of 6.4. The common conclusion drawn from his activity inferred that he was to be seen in prophetic terms. The expression 'a prophet like one of the prophets' affirms Jesus' continuity with the line of prophets known in the Jewish scriptures. If there were those who thought that prophecy, in these terms, had ceased, Mark gives evidence of those who did not accept that view. The view that Jesus was Elijah differs from this. It does not identify him with an ongoing tradition of prophecy but with a prophet from the past, one who, according to tradition, did not die but was caught up to heaven in a fiery chariot (2 Kings 2) and who was to come again before the dawning of the day of the Lord (Malachi 3.1; 4.5–6). Others, no doubt concentrating on the rumours of the miraculous activity of Jesus and knowing of his connection with John, asserted that he was John risen from the dead. The mystery surrounding Jesus is preserved in the clamour of these opinions. For Mark, John was the returning Elijah and Jesus was something more. This incident is used to raise the question of the significance of Jesus in a new way, a question here expressed in terms of his hidden identity. These views about Jesus were later reported to Jesus by his disciples in response to his direct question as to what people were saying of him (8.27–28). Jesus then asked them what they had to say, to which Peter alone responded, 'You are the Christ!' and Jesus solemnly charged them to tell no one of this (8.29–30).

Mark's account of the death of John is an anecdote unlike anything else in this Gospel. It is a lengthy story about a character other than Jesus, confirming the significance of John for Mark. It might be justified by the assumed identity of Jesus with John. But Mark did not accept that view and could easily have given the account of John's death in summary form. Josephus (*Antiquities*, 18.5.2) indicates that John was held at the fortress of Machaerus to the east of the Dead Sea. Josephus' account of Herod's marriage and the reason for John's execution differ from Mark. According to Josephus, Herod Antipas was married to Herodias but (contrary to Mark 6.17) his half-brother Philip was married to Salome, the daughter of Herodias. Family relations here are complex because king Herod (the Great) was married to a number of wives by whom he had children. Four of these children, being half-brothers, were also related by marriage. Aristobulus, a half-brother of Herod Antipas, was the father of Herodias, who was a half-niece of Herod Antipas and became his wife, having first been married to another Herod. Her daughter, Salome, married Philip. Herod Antipas also had a previous marriage to the daughter of Aretas, the king of Arabia.

According to Josephus, John was executed because Herod Antipas feared a popular uprising/rebellion, of which Josephus gives a number of examples. Josephus is normally scathing in his description of these movements, referring to the leaders as impostors, but he had a reasonably high view of John. He records a link between the death of John and Herod Antipas' marriage to Herodias. When Herod divorced the daughter of Aretas to marry Herodias, any treaty between the king of Arabia and Herod (confirmed by that marriage) was broken and Aretas made war on him, inflicting a shameful defeat on his army. The people saw this as the judgement of God on Herod for the murder of John.

While Roman women could divorce their husbands, according to the Jewish law, only a husband could divorce his wife (Leviticus 18.16; 20.21). Apparently, Herodias had not been divorced by her first husband and was therefore not free to marry by Jewish law. This was the ground of John's objection according to Mark. In Mark's account the narrative of John's struggle with Herodias is depicted in terms similar to those that describe Elijah's struggle with Jezebel, who was his real opponent and dominated king Ahab.

Whereas Elijah triumphed in that struggle, Herodias succeeded in manipulating Herod, bringing about the execution of John. Details of the plot at the birthday feast of Herod are worthy of a Hollywood blockbuster epic. The cameo illustrates the dramatic skills of Mark. Herod is portrayed as a weak man who, in spite of his evaluation of John as a righteous and good man (6.20), allowed himself to be manipulated to execute John. While the arch-villain was Herodias, the role played by the daughter was at least that of a very willing accomplice. Here there is some textual confusion. The daughter is probably described as the daughter of Herodias, and might have been Salome, her daughter by a previous marriage. An alternative reading makes her his daughter Herodias, probably making her the daughter of Herod and Herodias, that is, the daughter of the union condemned by John. If so, her hatred of John probably equalled that of her mother. Against this background Herod appears as a weak figure and there is a dramatic parallel with Mark's treatment of Pilate's role in the execution of Jesus. Each was manipulated to execute a person he believed to be innocent. Weakness in these cases is portrayed as wickedness, perhaps not as great as the wickedness of those who manipulated them.

Mark concludes this story by telling that when John's disciples heard of his death they came and took his body and laid it in a tomb. The continuing role of the disciples of John is indirectly evidenced here as elsewhere in a few places in the New Testament. There are two independent pieces of evidence concerning the reputation and status of John. Herod regarded him to be a righteous and holy man and his disciples, even in the face of the danger that the death of their 'master' signalled, came and took his body to ensure that it was given appropriate burial. Similar concerns were shown to provide appropriate burial for the body of Jesus by Joseph of Arimathea and some women, not by his disciples, certainly not by the twelve.

### +*The return of the twelve, 6.30*

A summary account is given of the return of the twelve (6.30), now referred to as *apostles*. This is the only use of 'apostles' in Mark, the textual variant in 3.14 being an assimilation to the text of Luke 6.13. Reference to them as apostles reflects the fact that Jesus 'sent' them out on a mission with carefully defined terms (see 6.6b–13). In the LXX the term is used to translate the Hebrew *shaliach*, which is used in Rabbinic texts of a person commissioned to perform a specific task for which the person sent carried all the authority of the sender. Hence the saying, 'A person's *shaliach* is as himself'.

## Three Galilean miracle stories, 6.31–56

*+Feeding of the five thousand (*inclusio, *feeding of the four thousand, 8.1–10), 6.31–44*

This is a hybrid objection/correction story. On the one hand the disciples *objected* to Jesus, who had compassion on the crowd and taught them (6.34), telling him to send them away (6.35). The reason for their objection was the need of the crowd for food. Jesus answered the objection, telling the disciples 'You give them [what they need] to eat' (6.37). The story then provides a correction to the views of the disciples.

1 Where Jesus was when the 'apostles' returned is as unclear as the location from which he sent them out (6.7, 30). It is often supposed that, because Jesus sent the 'apostles' back to Bethsaida after the feeding (6.45), Mark implies that this was also their point of departure.

On return from their mission the 'apostles' reported to Jesus all that they had done and taught. No details are given but Jesus invited them to come away alone with him to a desert place to refresh themselves for a little while. The reason for this suggestion was the press of people coming and going, giving no opportunity even for normal meals. Here, unlike the situation in 3.20, Jesus invited the 'apostles' to avoid the press of the crowd. This move sets the scenario, a desert place, for the next event, but *not* without the crowd.

2 The desert place to which Jesus and the 'apostles' went by boat (6.32) was on the western side of the sea of Galilee because, after this episode, Jesus and his disciples again embarked to cross to 'the other side' to Bethsaida (6.45) which, though on the northern side, is close to the eastern side. The traditional site is Tabgha, about twelve kilometres north of Tiberius. Wherever the desert place was, many people from all the 'towns' saw them and knew where they were going and ran there before him. There is no indication that the crowd included many sick or demon-possessed people, and there is no mention of any healing activity on the part of Jesus. Thus Mark has set the scene for Jesus in a desert place with the twelve and with a great crowd also.

3 Jesus saw the crowd as sheep without a shepherd (see Ezekiel 34.5). 'Shepherd' is a symbol of leadership (see Numbers 27.17; 1 Kings 22.17; Jeremiah 23.1–6; Ezekiel 34) and was used in the critique of the leaders of Israel (Ezekiel 34.2–10). The ideal against which they were judged was God, the true shepherd of Israel (Ezekiel 34.10–22, 31; Psalm 80.1). This led to the ideal of the shepherd like David, appointed by God (Ezekiel 34.23), which became understood in messianic terms. Thus, when Mark commented that the crowd was leaderless and Jesus had compassion on them, the reader is led to expect that his action would provide the lacking leadership, that he would act messianically. He did this by beginning to *teach* them (compare 4.1, 33–34) much, or at length. Whereas Mark tells us in 4.33–34 that Jesus taught the crowd only in parables, here nothing is said of his mode of teaching. Certainly the compassion of Jesus for the crowd does not suggest that in his teaching he was concerned to conceal his meaning from them.

What or how Jesus taught is unimportant for Mark, only that he taught for a long time so that, when he finished, it was late. Mark's account then proceeds via a series of dialogues between Jesus and the 'disciples'. The reported words of the disciples imply that the homes of the people were too far away for them to return that day. Because of the late hour the disciples told Jesus, 'Send them away' to buy 'something to eat'. Following the appointment of the twelve they attempted to restrain Jesus at a time when he was so involved with the crowd that it was impossible to eat (3.20–21). The summary introduction refers to the return of the '*apostles*' (6.30). Having rejoined Jesus in *his* mission, Mark indicates that the *disciples* came to Jesus and *instructed* him, 'Send them away!' (6.35). Jesus instructed them to continue their mission by providing food for the crowd. '*You* give them [what they need] to eat.' If they could give instructions like *apostles*, let them act like apostles. But they could think only of what it would cost to buy food for so many people. Although they were successful 'missionaries' (apostles), they had learned nothing.

Having failed the challenge laid down to them by Jesus, they were now given a lesson on the way to act in such a way that their involvement and learning continued. Although Jesus was in charge they had to produce the five loaves and two fish. Jesus commanded the crowd to sit down in groups, *took* the five loaves and two fish. Looking up to heaven he *blessed* and *broke* the (loaves of) bread and *gave* them to the disciples, and he divided the two fish also.

In this account the disciples are the 'go-betweens', mediating Jesus' action on the broken bread and the fragments of fish to the crowd. The language of taking, blessing, breaking and distributing is often thought to be indicative of the Christian celebration of the Eucharist. The use of 'blessed' rather than 'gave thanks' is not significant as both verbs were used to describe the Jewish practice of giving thanks. Here, and in the narrative of the Last Supper, we have the description of a customary Jewish meal. That later readers understood this narrative in terms of the Eucharist need not be doubted, but the narrative has another function in the overall plan of the Gospel.

Mark assumes that Jesus had performed a remarkable miracle. The point of the desert place is that no natural resources lie close at hand. They had only five loaves and two fish which Jesus took, blessed, broke and distributed.

4 In 6.43–44 Mark makes three points. (1) They all ate and were satisfied. (2) Twelve 'baskets' full of fragments of bread and fish were collected from what was left over, thus confirming the satisfaction and preparing the reader for the magnitude of the miracle. (3) Mark here numbers the *men* who ate at five thousand. While it is not impossible that we should understand this to mean 'people', this is unlikely. The result is the description of a remarkable miracle.

5 The context of the desert place recalls the provision of manna in the wilderness in the time of Moses. This is explicitly the case in John's interpretation of the feeding miracle. Mark gives no comparable indication that Jesus is to be understood as the one like Moses giving manna in the desert. While Mark believed Jesus to be the Messiah, it is not possible to say that he was appealing to the tradition that, just as Moses gave manna in the desert, so also would the Messiah. Rather, the desert place sets the context for the miracle with no easy supply of food available. A detailed account is given of the means by which the miracle was performed, establishing how little food was available and the actions performed by Jesus. Finally, the proof of the miracle is clear in the attested satisfaction of hunger, the amount of food left over, and the number of men who ate.

The miracle is a success story for Jesus. But those who start the story as *apostles* do not fare so well as *disciples*. The story serves to magnify the power of Jesus but also casts a shadow of doubt over the role and activity of the disciples. At the height of their achievement they again encountered the depth of failure.

+*Walking on the sea* (inclusio, *calming of the storm, 4.35–41 and 8.14–21*), *6.45–52*

Very likely this correction story came to Mark attached to the feeding miracle. It presupposes that Jesus was on the western side of the sea and that the disciples were returning to Bethsaida by boat. Jesus' previous time of teaching the crowd (4.1–9, 33–34) was also followed by a sea crossing from west to east (4.35–41) in the form of a correction story. On that occasion Jesus was in the boat with the disciples. Nevertheless, they did not give a good account of themselves. Here again the disciples appear in a poor light in a journey from west to east.

On this occasion the disciples, sent off alone in the boat, headed north-east across the sea for Bethsaida, while Jesus dismissed the crowd. This happened 'immediately' after the feeding miracle, leaving no doubt that Mark intended the two events to be understood together. Mark reinforces the connection by recalling (at the conclusion, 6.52) the feeding story as the key to understanding this one.

Having dismissed the crowd, Jesus went into the mountain to pray. Just as the desert place was unidentified, so is the mountain. In the story the separation of Jesus from the disciples is crucial and the refreshment for the returning 'apostles' (6.31), which was the original purpose of the journey, is unfulfilled and forgotten. The purpose of this narrative was to place the disciples in a boat in the middle of the sea by evening while Jesus remained on land.

Jesus saw the boat fighting against a contrary (north-east) wind. About the fourth watch of the night, in Roman terms about three o'clock in the morning, Jesus came walking on the sea. In spite of the wind, Jesus overtook the disciples in the boat. For some unexplained reason, he wished to pass by them. They saw him walking on the sea and thought him to be a 'phantom' or ghost. They were terrified and cried out. Their response to the presence of Jesus was similar in the last sea-crossing story (4.40). Jesus met their fear with his word, 'Be of good cheer, it is I, do not be afraid'.

There is no suggestion that the disciples were in any danger, or afraid of the storm, or that Jesus rescued them. Nevertheless, when Jesus entered the boat the wind dropped, a motif consistent with a rescue story. The disciples were astounded. It is not clear whether it was because Jesus came in this manner or because the wind ceased when he entered the boat, or as a consequence of this combination of events. Their astonishment was, according to Mark, because they did not understand about the loaves. But what is it about the loaves that the disciples failed to understand? Is it that the one who fed so many with so little ought to be expected to walk on water? Or is the point rather that the provision of bread in the desert and the miraculous crossing of the sea belong together (Psalm 78.13–25)? Mark makes no specific connection with the Exodus. The disciples failed to understand because their heart was hardened. This explanation seems to hark back to the treatment of Isaiah 6.9–10 in Mark 4.10–12. Immediately following the part of Isaiah 6 quoted there by Mark it is said,

> Make the heart of this people fat, and their ears heavy, and shut their eyes; lest they see with their eyes, and hear with their ears, and understand with their hearts, and turn and be healed.

The fat heart is the thickened, hardened heart. The disciples are here shown to be no better off than those *outsiders* spoken of in Mark 4.10–12.

*+Healing of the sick at Gennesaret, 6.53–56*

This summary tells of the arrival of Jesus and his disciples in the region of Gennesaret, not Bethsaida, for which the disciples had set out, according to 6.45. Mark does not call the sea Gennesaret and is probably referring to the northwestern shore, south of Capernaum. Mark again notes that the events summarised occurred 'immediately' Jesus had disembarked. Immediately this was known the people ran throughout the region and brought the sick on stretchers to any place Jesus was known to be, laying them in the market place, begging Jesus to allow them to touch 'the fringe of his garment', and those who did so were healed.

This summary is in contrast to the story of the great crowd that followed Jesus to the western side of the sea to be taught by him (6.33–34). It is true that they were fed by Jesus, but there is no hint that they were motivated by the desire for healing miracles. Now, on return to the northwestern side of the sea, the motivation of the crowds was only for miracles of healing. Perhaps this alternation between teaching and healing miracles was a literary strategy to bring out these dual aspects of the ministry of Jesus. By featuring one then the other, Mark ensured that neither was overlooked.

*+Bridging conflict: purity laws and the traditions of the elders, 7.1–23*

This complex objection story and the following story of the Syro-Phoenician woman deal with questions of purity and are relevant to an understanding of the basis and scope of Jesus' mission according to Mark. See also the issue of Jesus dealing with the outcasts of society (2.13–17) and the exorcisms of 1.23–28; 5.1–20.

*+Conflict with Pharisees and scribes: the tradition of the elders, 7.1–13*

The practice of some of Jesus' disciples led to a testing inquiry and the statement of its basis by the Pharisees and scribes from Jerusalem. (Compare 2.18–22; 2.23–28.) The objection of 7.5 led Jesus to the striking saying expressed in the parable of 7.15. This saying provides the answer to the objection and lays down principles for the mission to the nations.

There is no change of location for this new scene. Jesus was somewhere in the region Mark designated Gennesaret (6.53). A new scene is signalled by the entry of new characters identified as Pharisees and certain scribes *from Jerusalem*, signalling a new phase in the opposition to Jesus.

In 3.22 the scribes *from Jerusalem* charged Jesus with casting out demons by the prince of demons. Here (7.1, 5) the coalition objecting to Jesus is described as 'the Pharisees and *certain* scribes coming from Jerusalem' (7.1). Does 'from Jerusalem' cover both groups? Does '*certain* scribes coming from Jerusalem' mean that all the scribes present came from Jerusalem, or that only certain of the scribes present, the ones from Jerusalem, were involved? Most likely Mark has brought together the scribes with the Pharisees, identifying the origin of the opposition to Jesus with them and Jerusalem. Later, in the dispute with Jesus, having established their origin, they are simply described as the Pharisees and the scribes (7.5). The objection to Jesus in 3.22 was raised by the scribes alone. The combination of the scribes with the Pharisees now marks a new phase in the intensity of the opposition. In this dispute the Pharisees are named first, giving them the leading role, because of the issue involved in the dispute (see 7.3).

The sequence of the narrative is puzzling. That the Pharisees and certain of the scribes who came from Jerusalem 'came together' to Jesus, 7.1. Coming to Jesus might have looked an open and responsive act. The description of them 'coming together to him' has the appearance of an official delegation. Only then does the narrator tell us that 'some' of Jesus' disciples were seen eating with 'common' (unwashed) hands (7.2). Characteristically, Mark first tells of the coming together before providing the reason for the gathering. In this delegation the Pharisees, mentioned first on both occasions (7.1, 5) played the leading role. The reason for this is that Mark (the narrator) explains that the Pharisees played a leading role in establishing the common Jewish practice of not eating with unwashed hands, establishing this as 'the tradition of the elders' (7.3–4).

In Rabbinic Judaism, which developed after the Jewish war after Mark was written, issues of purity were of central importance. While the treatment of these issues was based both on biblical laws concerning purity and Pharisaic traditions, which Mark calls 'the tradition of the elders', the Rabbinic treatments also reflect considerable development. Because we lack detailed knowledge of Pharisaic interpretation and practice it seems best simply to accept what Mark says, although there must be doubt that 'all the Jews' did not eat without washing their hands. Mark implies that, on the lead of the Pharisees, Jews generally recognised that they *should not* eat with unwashed hands. This is the only use of 'Jews' outside the passion narrative, where Jesus is repeatedly referred to by Pilate as 'king of the Jews', a title that reflects a Roman perspective. Here the narrator adopts an 'outsider's' perspective, writing of 'the Jews' as 'others', not of the group of which he was part.

The precise manner of hand-washing described by Mark is unclear. This probably gave rise to a textual variant meaning 'thoroughly' when the original seems to have something to do with the 'fist'. Whether this means that the fist is washed or that the hand was washed with a fist full of water is unclear. The precise details are not important for Mark, who also describes the necessity of cleansing vessels as an aspect of purification, though vessels are not involved in this incident.

Mark's editorial outlines the coming together of Pharisees and scribes, notes that the practice of some of the disciples was noticed, and explains why this was a problem. Only then is the objection of the Pharisees and scribes reported in the form of a testing inquiry. 'Why do your disciples not live [*walk*] according to the tradition of the elders but they eat food [bread] with common hands?' The wording of this question has been prepared for by Mark's introductory summary. This is the third occasion when Jesus has been called to give account for the behaviour of his disciples (see also

2.18–22, 23–28). Because Jesus was their teacher, it was natural to judge him by the words and actions of his disciples.

Jesus' answer to this question was in two parts expressed to three groups, the first addressed to the Pharisees and scribes (7.6–13), and the second addressed to the crowd (7.14–15(16)), which led to an explanation to the disciples when Jesus was alone with them (7.17–23). Verse 16, 'If any one has ears to hear, let him hear', is omitted by some of the best manuscripts.

Jesus responded to his accusers by attacking them, 7.6–13. He addressed them as 'hypocrites' in a way that implies that this was the evaluation of them implied by Isaiah 29.13 (LXX). Although that term was used originally of actors, in the Gospels it is used by Jesus in the sense that is evident in his quotation from Isaiah. 'This people honour me with their lips, but their heart is far from me; vainly they worship me, teaching as doctrines the commandments of men.' The sense of hypocrisy is clearest in the first part of the quotation, which contrasts words with heart, that is, appearance with reality. But the point taken up arises in the last part of the quotation. Jesus' point is that his critics have displaced the commandment of God in order to keep the traditions of men. This is aimed at the assertion of the validity of the tradition of the elders. But it is difficult to see how the tradition of hand-washing was opposed to any commandment of God. It was an addition to the biblical commandments but not obviously opposed to them. Consequently, it is difficult to see the relevance of the practice of 'Corban', declaring something to be a gift to God (to temple and priesthood) when it should have been an expression of honouring father and mother, a requirement of the fifth commandment. It may be that those who stood to benefit from the gift encouraged those who might make it by promising freedom from some obligation to parents. In other words, the gift would not cost *the giver* anything. The Markan Jesus used this as a typical example. No specific answer has yet been given concerning the behaviour of the disciples. The direct response to the Pharisees and scribes was scathing and abusive. In so far as any answer was given, it was a rejection of the authority of the tradition of the elders.

+*Teaching the crowd about purity, 7.14–15(16)*

Generally, in Mark, the crowd spontaneously gathers around Jesus. That Jesus 'called' the crowd, just as he had called those from whom he chose the twelve (3.13), implies a positive relationship to the crowd that responded to his call. With this new audience Jesus addressed the issue directly. His teaching is introduced in a way similar to the parable of the soils, 'Listen!' (4.3), and might conclude in almost identical words (4.9), in fact the same words as 4.23, 'If any one has ears to hear, let that person listen!' The more closely Mark has based this incident on the earlier one, the more likely it is that 7.16 is not a scribal addition. Thus we note that Jesus' words to the crowd are introduced and concluded in a way similar to his earlier parable. With the parable of the soils in mind, the opening words of Jesus are the more remarkable. He not only called on the crowd to 'Hear!' but 'Hear . . . and understand!' According to 4.11–12 Jesus taught in parables so that 'hearing they may hear and not understand'. But Jesus now gave expression to the parable of 7.15, which dealt directly with the issue but also went beyond it, as Mark saw and explicitly noted. 'There is nothing from outside a person that entering into him is able to make him unclean [to make him common], but the things proceeding out of a person are the things that make a person unclean.' No explanation of the parable was given to the crowd and no comment is recorded from the crowd, which was left to draw its own conclusions.

+*Teaching the disciples about purity, 7.17–23*

Then, as in Mark 4.10, when the disciples were alone with Jesus in a house they asked him about the 'parable' (7.17–23). The house is not identified and there is no reason to think it was Jesus' house or any other house that we can identify. It is another case indicating Jesus' acceptance of hospitality as a principle of the way his mission was conducted.

As in Mark 4.13, Jesus questioned the disciples about their lack of understanding (7.18) and went on to explain the parable to them (4.13–20; 7.18–23). In asking their question the disciples are portrayed as 'lacking understanding' and they are asked, 'Do you not understand?' If the parable was not clear, it is now explained by Jesus and further clarified *for the reader* by an editorial comment by Mark (7.19). The point Jesus makes is simple. Food does not affect the heart, entering the belly and passing from there into the sewer. Evil thoughts and actions proceed from the heart and defile, make a person unclean, 'common'. At this point Jesus' quotation of Isaiah 29.13 to the Pharisees and scribes becomes relevant to their question about purity. It is what makes the heart of a person unclean that defiles. It is the unclean heart that makes a person unclean, not such practices as eating with unwashed hands. It is Mark, not Jesus, who drew the conclusion that with this parable Jesus had declared all food to be clean, 7.19. In this Mark clearly followed the logic of the parable but proceeded to a conclusion Jesus did not draw. Matthew, in recording this incident, only applies the parable to the tradition of hand-washing. What Mark has done is to bring out the continuity of the principles of Jesus' mission with the mission to the nations as pursued by Paul and others. The reader perceives this, but there is no indication that the disciples have made any progress.

Chapter 4

# Jesus' mission to the regions beyond Galilee

## Three more miracle stories, 7.24—8.10

What holds these three stories together is that they all happen outside dominantly Jewish areas. The first involves a Gentile, while the second and third do not indicate the ethnic identity of those encountered by Jesus. This was also the case in 5.1–20 in the story of the Gerasene demoniac. There, and in the first and second episodes here, there is no suggestion of Jesus preaching to or teaching Gentiles. In the third episode the crowd had been with Jesus for three days and, apart from the healing of the deaf and dumb person in the previous episode, there is no reference to healings. Given the extended period of time it is implied that Jesus was teaching them, though Mark did not make this or the ethnic identity of the crowd explicit.

### *THE DAUGHTER OF THE SYRO-PHOENICIAN WOMAN: AN EXORCISM, 7.24–30

For the first time since 1.14 we have a major section that does not begin with 'And . . .'. Nevertheless, there are eight uses of 'and . . .' in seven verses. This narrative is a concise miracle quest story which, like a miracle story, describes the problem condition, the manner of healing, and finally sets out the evidence of the successful healing. The traits of the quest story are evident in the approach of the suppliant with a request. An objection is raised which the suppliant must overcome if the quest is to succeed and the outcome of the quest is stated.

The new scene is introduced by the note that Jesus moved from the unnamed place at which his debate over hand-washing had taken place. Mark used the parable of 7.15 to prepare the way for the extension of Jesus' mission into Gentile territory. The new location is identified as the regions of Tyre, perhaps Tyre and Sidon, which is supported by some texts, though Sidon might have been imported from 7.31. No reason is given for this move. There is no suggestion that Jesus had embarked on a Gentile mission. The move may be seen as an extension of his Galilean mission to the Jews outside Galilee. He entered a house to escape notice but his presence could not be kept secret. The use of a house again demonstrates that the principle of hospitality was crucial for Jesus' mission.

The new region, like the region of Gerasa (5.20), was not free from Jewish presence. Nevertheless, these were regions in which Jews would inevitably come in contact with Gentiles. Because Jesus' presence became known, a woman, described as a Greek, Syro-Phoenician by race, came and threw herself at Jesus' feet. Her behaviour is like that of Jairus (5.22) and the demon possessed described in Mark 3.11; and compare 5.6. The attitude expressed in this posture is that of a suppliant before a great and powerful person. The woman was not herself possessed, though her daughter, on whose behalf she had come, was. Her behaviour implies that, like those possessed, she recognised Jesus' secret identity. Unlike the Gerasene demoniac who fell down and 'worshipped' Jesus but whose ethnic identity is not mentioned, the woman is identified. There is no doubt that she was a Gentile. That could be the meaning of 'Greek' here, but it is probably a statement about her cultural identity. She was a product of the Greek cities established by Alexander to disseminate Greek language and culture. She is also described as Syro-Phoenician 'by race'. Thus there is no doubt that she was not Jewish and that is crucial for the following story.

The woman had a daughter with *an unclean spirit*, 7.25. She came to Jesus as a suppliant and, throwing herself at his feet, implored him to cast the *demon* out of her daughter, 7.26. Here we have the statement of the problem combined with the expression of quest. Jesus raised the objection with a parabolic saying. 'Permit first the children to be satisfied, for it is not good/fitting to take the children's bread and to throw it to the dogs.' Such a stern rebuff is typical in a quest story. If the woman's quest was to succeed she must find some way around this objection. This she did in her response, 'Sir/Lord [or Yes Lord], even the dogs under the table eat from the children's crumbs'. This is not just a clever saying. From the perspective of Jesus' mission it takes account of the priority of the Jewish people. In common with some prophetic teaching her words affirmed that the blessings bestowed on Israel overflowed to the nations and a foundation for this hope can be found in Genesis 12.1–3. Jesus accepted the woman's response, which successfully negotiated his objection. 'Because of this word, go! The demon has come out of your daughter.' The exorcism is confirmed by the narrative conclusion, which tells us that the woman went home and found the child lying on the bed with the demon come out of her. In this way Mark has foreshadowed the mission to the nations without making Jesus himself a universal missionary.

## +A DEAF AND DUMB MAN HEALED, 7.31–37

A new episode is signalled by Jesus' movement from Tyre through Sidon, which is about thirty kilometres to the north, and through the regions of the Decapolis to the sea of Galilee. While this is a circuitous route and Mark provides no reasons for Jesus' choice of it, there is no good reason to think it does not fit Mark's plan for Jesus' mission. After all, Jesus was engaged in a mission, not attempting to travel as quickly as possible from A to B. This is not an argument about historical accuracy but about the credibility of Mark's narrative. Mark implies that Jesus was still in dominantly Gentile territory by first outlining his route to the eastern side of the sea of Galilee, then locating Jesus in the midst of the region of the Decapolis, where this incident took place. The overall journey inclines the reader to conclude that Jesus continued to deal with Gentiles.

This episode is another example of a miracle quest story. The scene is set with Jesus surrounded by a crowd. A deaf person with a speech impediment was 'brought' to Jesus. For a person with a hearing and speech problem 'led' might have been more appropriate, but Mark appears to have a preference for 'brought' (see 2.3; 8.22). The term translated as 'dumb' indicates a speech defect and was used because of the LXX version of Isaiah 35.5–6. The healing takes on an aura of the messianic age. When he was healed we are told that his tongue was loosed and he spoke correctly or plainly (7.35).

The bringing of the person was an expression of the quest for healing, made explicit in the request that Jesus should lay his hand on him (see 6.5). Unlike the previous episode, no clear objection was raised to this request. Nevertheless, Jesus did not straightforwardly comply with the request. He took the man apart from the crowd in an attempt to maintain some secrecy concerning what he was about to do. He did not just lay a hand on the man. Rather, he put his fingers into the man's ears and spat and touched his tongue. Such actions were common amongst healers of the day. Jesus' most important action was yet to follow. Looking to heaven, to acknowledge the source of his power, he groaned and said, '*Ephphatha*'. Groans and foreign or mysterious words were often used as magical spells and Mark gives the impression that Jesus had resorted to such a practice. As in 5.41, this is immediately clarified because Mark translates the command, 'Be opened'. Thus the means of healing are concisely described. The healing is confirmed by the assertion that the man's ears were opened and the impediment loosed from his tongue so that he spoke clearly. This healing story is one of only two in Mark that appears in no other Gospel. As in the other story (see 8.22–26) Jesus uses physical means, common amongst healers of the day, to produce this healing. The other Gospel writers may have been sensitive to this likeness, or simply reacted against such 'crude' physical means. But in this story, unlike the one that is to come (8.22–26), Jesus did use his healing word of command, 'Be opened'.

Given that Jesus had taken the man apart from the crowd, the conclusion is puzzling. Jesus commanded *them* to say nothing. Perhaps those who brought the man also came with him and they, as well as the man, were commanded to say nothing. According to Mark, Jesus did not want to be swamped by crowds of people seeking healing. But the more Jesus commanded them the more they 'preached' or 'announced'. What they announced was the astonishing (pronouncement) news, 'He has done all things well, he even makes the deaf to hear and the dumb to speak', which echoes Isaiah 35.5–6, implying that Jesus belongs in a messianic context.

## *FEEDING OF THE FOUR THOUSAND (*INCLUSIO*, FEEDING OF THE FIVE THOUSAND, 6.31–44), 8.1–10

For only the fourth time in a major section of the Gospel so far, this episode does not begin with 'And . . .'. For the earlier instances see 1.1, 14; 7.24. Nevertheless, 'and . . .' is used fifteen times in ten verses here. The new episode is not marked by a change of time, being introduced by 'In those days . . .'. Nor is there a clear change of characters because Jesus was still with a crowd, though it is now described as 'a great crowd'. There is no more indication of where the crowd had come from here than in the previous episode (7.33). Its ethnic anonymity is in contrast with the Galilean crowd that followed Jesus (6.33) to the desert place and was fed by Jesus. The anonymity is consistent with the subtle suggestion that the crowd has been drawn from Gentile territory. Just as Jesus had fed a Jewish crowd of five thousand men, he now fed a Gentile crowd of four thousand. Mark implies a twofold mission and this is one reason for the two parallel feeding stories.

Like the previous feeding story, this is also a correction story. Some days have passed because Jesus notes that the crowd had been with him for three days (8.2). They cannot be sent away without food because they will faint on the way. Again the disciples failed the test. Although they did not instruct Jesus to send the crowd away (as in 6.36), they asked where they could get sufficient bread in the desert to satisfy the crowd, 8.4. Again Jesus corrects them, indicating that he intends to satisfy the need from existing resources. Yet the only food available was seven loaves and a few small fish. Again Jesus commanded the crowd to sit down, though no details are given of the arrangements. Jesus' action, *taking* the loaves, *giving thanks*, *breaking* and *giving* the broken loaves to the disciples to distribute to the crowd, follows the same pattern as the previous feeding. But here the distribution of the fish is described with a separate *blessing* using the verb that was used in the earlier feeding.

The proof of the miracle was that all ate and were satisfied. About four thousand *people* were fed and *seven* baskets of fragments were collected. The importance of the seven is not obvious within the Markan narrative. In Acts 6.1–7 *seven* 'Hellenists' were chosen to 'minister/serve' and to have special responsibility for the Hellenists. What we hear of the seven subsequently is that they spread the mission to regions beyond Jerusalem and beyond other Jews. Such an association makes good sense of the Gentile setting of this story in Mark.

The episode ends when Jesus and the disciples re-embarked to travel by boat to the region of Dalmanoutha, which must have been as unknown in early times as it is now, given the textual variants. The journey closes this episode and the excursion beyond Galilee.

The two feeding stories are sometimes thought to be based on two accounts of the same story. This may be true but Mark has carefully arranged the episodes to suit his own plot development. Each is an important part of two phases of the mission of Jesus. The emphasis on the role of the twelve and the twelve baskets in relation to a Galilean crowd suggests a feeding in relation to Jesus' mission to Israel. The geographical setting of the second feeding and the symbolic role of the seven baskets implies a mission to the nations, though Mark's reticence to make this clear suggests that he has written this story very much in the light of the later reality of the Gentile mission, but constrained by the awareness that Jesus restricted his mission to Israel.

Chapter 5

# Hard hearts and blindness, 8.11—10.52

This central section of the Gospel is characterised by the journey motif and the theme of discipleship. Two stories of the healing of blind men, one near the beginning (8.22–26) and one at the end (10.46–52), frame this section. In the first story the blindness of the disciples is treated parabolically. In the end the twelve remain blind and Bartimaeus *follows* Jesus in the way.

## +THE DEMAND FOR A SIGN, 8.11–13

Following the feeding of the four thousand Jesus made two journeys by boat. The first journey closes the feeding story and brings Jesus to a new destination. The journey is not important in itself and we are told no details of it. At the end of it, where this episode begins, we assume Jesus is on the western side of the sea, most likely near one of the larger towns because he encounters the Pharisees there. Their presence introduces an objection story.

Jesus' arrival brought out the Pharisees. Their confrontation with Jesus is expressed in an *objection* to his mission. They disputed with him, demanding a *sign* from heaven, testing him, objecting to the authority which he assumed and manifest in his mission. The validation of a sign from heaven implies that the Pharisees recognised that the claims of Jesus' mission implied a heavenly authority. These claims demanded validation. John alone of the Gospel writers called the miracles of Jesus *signs*. Mark generally describes Jesus' actions specifically, he heals and casts out demons, though he can group these together as 'mighty works' (6.2), which is about as close as Mark gets to what we mean by the term 'miracles'. Built into the perception in the ancient world is the recognition that powerful people can perform mighty deeds. The more powerful the person, the mightier the deeds. This understanding avoids many aspects commonly assumed in the discussion of 'miracles', which is a relatively modern concept.

Jesus' response to the demand was to groan in sorrow or anger and to ask a question, 'Why does this generation seek a sign?' The claims implied by his mission provide an adequate answer to this question. But then involved in the mission were numerous notable works which could have been construed as validating signs. In Mark, as in John (6.30), a demand for a sign follows a feeding 'miracle'. This means that those who objected to Jesus failed to see his mighty works as the sign they demanded. For such a generation no sign would be given. Consequently, Jesus was not able to respond to the objection to the satisfaction of the Pharisees. There was nothing for him to do but to withdraw, which he did by embarking and journeying by boat to the other side. In due course it is revealed that this is a journey to the north-east, to Bethsaida. On this occasion, however, the journey is not just the means to get Jesus from A to B.

## +'BEWARE OF THE LEAVEN OF THE PHARISEES AND THE LEAVEN OF HEROD', 8.14–21

In this correction story the journey announced in 8.13 is described in 8.14–21. This is the third detailed account of a sea crossing by Jesus and the disciples (4.35–41; 6.45–52; 8.14–21). In none of these situations do the disciples fare well; fearful and faithless in the face of the storm and fearful and ignorant in response to Jesus' power; fearful in the presence of Jesus at night on the sea. Now (as in 6.45–52) they show themselves to be blind and deaf, without understanding and hard of heart. The imagery of 4.10–12, drawn from Isaiah 6.9–10, is thicker in use here of the disciples than in relation to the crowd in Mark 4.

The scene is set by the indication that Jesus embarked and went to the other side, 8.13. Here, as in 8.27, the journey is reported before turning back to say what happened on the way. The narrative indicates that the disciples forgot to take bread, which is then qualified, except for one loaf. Against this background Mark reports Jesus' command to the disciples, '*See* that you *beware* of the leaven of the Pharisees and the leaven of Herod'. The leaven of the Pharisees fits naturally here in an incident that follows the Pharisees' demand for a sign, although Jesus had just performed a notable feeding miracle. The dispute amongst the disciples over bread is equally blind to the demonstrated ability of Jesus to provide bread. The leaven of the Pharisees is their corrupting power and the disciples show themselves to be infected. The leaven of Herod is Herod's evaluation of Jesus as John risen from the dead, which underestimated the significance of Jesus, as the disciples now did also.

From a narrative point of view the disciples have been set up. In a context of a shortage of bread a symbolic use of 'leaven' is almost inevitably misunderstood. Or is it that in their concern for bread the disciples failed to hear Jesus' question about the leaven of the Pharisees and of Herod? Either way of reading makes sense of Jesus' question, 'Why are you discussing the fact that you have no bread?' This could mean that they thought Jesus was talking about bread or that, because of their own concern for bread, they didn't even hear his question. Jesus concluded, though this is expressed in a series of questions, that the disciples are without understanding, have hard hearts, cannot see, cannot hear, do not remember (and cannot grasp the implications of) the feeding of the five thousand or the feeding of the four thousand, do not yet understand. This is an extremely heavy stress on the lack of perception and understanding of the disciples. No relief is in sight as far as they are concerned.

## +HEALING A BLIND MAN AT BETHSAIDA, 8.22–26

This modified quest story commences with the arrival of Jesus and the disciples at Bethsaida, where an anonymous 'they' *bring* a blind man to Jesus and implore Jesus to touch him. What follows is an unusual healing miracle story. First, there are unusual secrecy motifs which do not fit any previous incident. Then there is an unusual emphasis on the physical means of healing and the gradual process produced by Jesus' actions. Jesus speaks no healing word, though he does ask the man if he can see anything.

1 The secrecy motifs include 'bringing' (same verb) the man out of the village, presumably away from the crowds. Then, when the man was healed, Jesus 'sent' him home, telling him not even to enter the town (compare 5.19–20). This assumes that the man lived outside the town. Unlike 5.19–20, nothing is said of what the man actually did. No doubt the expectation, raised by other parts of

Mark, has led to textual variants in which the man is instructed not to report what had happened. At the end of the episode, Jesus and his disciples left Bethsaida and went to Caesarea Philippi, 8.27.

2 Jesus performed the healing by spitting in the man's eyes and laying his hands on him. Yet this act produced only indistinct vision of men as if they were trees walking. Consequently a second act of healing was necessary, and Jesus again laid his hands on the man. It is now made explicit that he laid his hands on the man's eyes. Only then did he see clearly.

3 Only Mark records this healing story and the healing of the deaf and dumb man of 7.31–37. The similarity between the practice of Jesus and other healers of the day is apparent and might have discouraged the use of these stories. Both are crudely physical in that Jesus uses his spit in the process of healing and the power of touch goes beyond simply laying his hands on the sick. In the present story there is also the seeming failure of Jesus, or at least partial success in his first attempt. Mark was sensitive to none of these problems.

4 Mark might have wished the healing of the blind man to have been understood in a parabolic sense. This story follows the narrative of the sea crossing, in which the blindness and insensitivity of the disciples were uncovered. That episode concluded with Jesus' question to them, 'Do you not yet understand?' The obvious answer implied is that they did not understand. This story of the gradual restoration of sight perhaps provided some hope that they might yet see clearly. Jesus had laid his hands on them and they now saw indistinctly. If they continued with Jesus they might yet see clearly.

## +PETER'S CONFESSION: A GLIMMER OF SIGHT?, 8.27–30

A new episode is indicated by the *movement* of Jesus with his disciples from Bethsaida to the villages of Caesarea Philippi in the territory of Gaulanitis. The important dialogue between Jesus and his disciples took place on the way there. Compare 8.27 with the way the journey is first indicated in 8.13 before the narration of what happened on the way in 8.14–21. The incident 'on the way' to the villages of Caesarea Philippi is often seen to be a turning-point in Mark. If so, it is an ambiguous turning-point.

What follows is an inquiry story in which Jesus asked two questions. Inquiry stories function to focus attention on the answer or answers given. Thus neither Jesus as the questioner nor the disciples as respondents are central in this story. Jesus' questions provide the opportunity for the answers to be given. He first asked the disciples whom people were saying he was. The answer given corresponds to what Herod heard of Jesus (6.14–15). Here the disciples reiterate what 'everyone' was saying and Jesus' question was simply another opportunity to make this known. Jesus then pressed the disciples for their opinions. Either that they must choose between these options or press on themselves to the truth that remained hidden. Here this episode takes the reader beyond the views reported to Herod. Peter, speaking for the disciples, replied, 'You are the Christ'. Because his confession uses a title corresponding to the opening of the Gospel, the reader recognises that the disciples have progressed. The reader has possessed this insight from the beginning. This can be viewed as a turning-point *for the disciples*. Yet serious complications arise from the following scene (8.31–33) and the conclusion of this one, where any advance is put in question. Jesus *charged* the disciples to say nothing concerning him to anyone. The same term is used to describe Jesus silencing the unclean spirits (1.25; 3.12). Peter's confession struck the truth, but they cannot proclaim Jesus as the Christ until they know what this means *for him and for them*. Just when it seems that the disciples have grasped the truth their words are shown to cover their continuing ignorance. Thinking that they know when they do not is no advance on an awe-inspired ignorance: 'Who is this, that the wind and the waves obey him?' (see 4.41).

## +THE SUFFERING AND RISING SON OF MAN I: PETER: FROM SIGHT TO BLINDNESS, 8.31–33

The new episode can be understood as a correction story. Having silenced the disciples, Jesus now *began* to teach them. But this is not just the beginning of another teaching session. It is a turning-point, the beginning of a new phase of teaching, a new theme, a new teaching. The focus is on the Son of Man, which is a change from Peter's confession of the Christ. Jesus had spoken of the Son of Man before (see 2.10, 28), so that is not the new element. Nor does the Markan Jesus simply replace 'Christ' with 'Son of Man'. Rather, 'Christ' is being redefined by what the Markan Jesus says *about* the Son of Man. This constitutes the new teaching correcting Peter's confession. Sayings predicting the suffering and death of the Son of Man are peculiar to Mark and are known in other Gospels where they have made use of Mark.

Given that this is the first of a series of 'passion predictions' (8.31; 9.9, 12, 31; 10.33–34, 45), it is worth noting precisely what the Markan Jesus said.

> The Son of Man *must* suffer much [or many things] and be rejected by the elders and the chief priests and the scribes and be put to death and after three days to rise again.

The response of the Markan Jesus to the scandal of the rejection and crucifixion of the Christ was to affirm that his suffering and death were *necessary*, predicted in the Scriptures and an expression of the will and purpose of God. Just how this could be will be clarified to some extent in successive predictions.

In this prediction the opponents of Jesus are identified with the groups that made up the Sanhedrin: the elders were leading laymen; the chief priests were from the leading priestly families from which the high priest was chosen; the scribes were an influential scholarly class. They reappear in 11.27, after the 'cleansing of the temple', to challenge the authority of Jesus. In Mark, unlike Matthew, the Pharisees do not play a leading role as protagonists of Jesus.

The Markan Jesus also predicted his vindication, and in precise terms, from the first instance. He will rise again after three days, a formula with no different meaning than 'on the third day', which was preferred by Paul (1 Corinthians 15.4) as well as Matthew and Luke. This, the first of three predictions of resurrection vindication (8.31), is set in the villages of Caesarea Philippi. The second is set on the journey through Galilee (9.31), and the third on the journey to Jerusalem (10.34).

In summary Mark says that 'He spoke the word openly' (8.32, compare 4.33). The notion of 'the word' has a sense of 'gospel' about it and this implies that Mark's understanding of the gospel is centred on the passion of Jesus. 'Openly' here has the sense of 'plainly', 'clearly'. Thus Mark leaves no room to justify any misunderstanding or inappropriate response to Jesus' words.

If Jesus had begun to teach the necessity of the suffering of the Son of Man, Peter now *began* to *charge/rebuke* him. The term that described Jesus' response to the demonic and the storm, and most recently to the disciples in *charging* them to say nothing about him (8.30), is now used by Peter in relation to Jesus. This is hardly consistent with the words of his recent confession. Jesus' response was first to turn. He saw the disciples. Why Mark finds these actions significant is unclear. Perhaps it is implied that Jesus responded to the words of Peter who was, as in 8.29, the spokesman for the disciples. Jesus then *rebuked* Peter, 'Get behind me'. Peter's assertion of authority in relation to Jesus was inappropriate for a disciple. He had to become a 'follower' once more, to follow after Jesus (see 8.34). He is called Satan because of his rejection of the way which God had called Jesus to fulfil. His thoughts did not comply with the will of God but with human aspirations dominated by Satanic values. The kingdom of God was again in conflict with the power of evil.

## +DISCIPLESHIP: THE CALL TO THE CROWD WITH THE DISCIPLES, 8.34–38

A new episode widened the context of Jesus' teaching. Jesus *called* the crowd to him so that they joined the disciples to form the audience. Even so, Jesus maintained an open form of teaching in which the consequences of the vocation of the suffering Son of Man for those who *follow* him are made clear. It may be that Mark implies that the reader should think that the series of sayings would be clear only to the disciples (see 4.10–12, 33–34) because the crowd did not have the benefit of Jesus' passion prediction (8.31–33). But that would imply that Mark thought that Jesus called the crowd with the intention of confounding them. Rather it seems that, speaking through Peter, the disciples have shown themselves to be in no advance of the crowd that followed Jesus. Thus to both groups, and to the reader, Jesus now makes clear the implications of following him. Six independent sayings related to the theme of following Jesus are gathered here.

In the first saying (8.34), some scribe has found the expression 'follow *after* me' strange and made redundant by the direction at the end, 'let him follow me', and has introduced instead at the beginning 'If anyone wishes to come after me . . . let him follow me'. Certainly Mark uses 'to come after' and 'to follow' as synonyms (see 1.17–18, 20), but following was the original reading. The redundant 'after' was used to re-emphasise the subordinate place of the follower. The second use of following is not, however, tautologous because, in between the first and second use, it has been made clear what following involves. First, it involves self-denial, that is, to renounce oneself for the sake of the one followed. Instead, we will learn that Peter denied Jesus to save his own face (14.30–31, 72). Second, Jesus has spoken of the suffering and death of the Son of Man, which Peter understood, and Mark intends the reader to understand as a reference to Jesus' own death (8.31). It now becomes clear by what means he is to die because the follower is also to take up his cross. Mark intended readers to take the threat of crucifixion seriously.

The second saying (8.35a) is more general. It is philosophical in stating that in the will to life, life is lost. This sounds like a proverbial saying in which the life that is lost is a quality of life. In the Markan interpretation we should understand this primarily as the loss of eternal life at the judgement, as the following and final sayings make clear.

In the third saying (8.35b), a characteristically Markan perspective associates Jesus with the 'gospel' understood as the ongoing cause of Jesus. Those who lose their lives now in the service of Jesus and the gospel will be 'saved' at the judgement.

The fourth (8.36) and fifth sayings (8.37) have a philosophical ring about them, making clear, in the form of two questions, that no thing, not even all things, is more valuable than life. While this is a worldly truth that people do not always acknowledge in their lives, this is hardly Mark's point.

The final saying (8.38) brings the matter to utter clarity. It deals with those who are ashamed of Jesus and his words in 'this adulterous and sinful generation', the description of the world as Mark perceived it to be until the judgement. It was the world dominated by the powers of evil. Of these the Son of Man would be ashamed when he came in the glory of his father and with the holy angels. Peter's denial of Jesus (14.66–72) can be seen as an expression of shame. Although in the saying the first part concerns Jesus and his words, and the second concerns the Son of Man, there is no doubt that Mark understood the latter as a self-reference by Jesus. Here the title Son of Man is used because of the tradition of interpreting Daniel 7.13–14, which associated the coming Son of Man with the judgement. Perhaps the heavenly setting of Daniel 7 also explains the association of the Son of Man with glory and angels. But the reference to 'the glory of *his father*' is a consequence of the early Christian assimilation of titles in understanding Jesus as the Christ. For Mark, as for the early Christians generally, Jesus was Son of Man and Son of God.

## +THE TRANSFIGURATION (*INCLUSIO*, THE BAPTISM, 1.9–11), 9.1–13

The transfiguration is made up of a number of associated scenes 9.1 provides an introductory 'prelude' connected to the transfiguration by one of only two explicit time notes made in Mark, 'After six days'. Then there is the narrative of the transfiguration itself (9.2–8), followed by the account of the dialogue between Jesus and the disciples on the descent from the mountain (9.9–13).

### +Introductory saying, 9.1

Mark has placed 9.1 immediately before the account of the transfiguration, suggesting that the reader should relate the saying of Jesus to the account of the transfiguration. Because no new audience or location is mentioned, we assume that the saying was spoken to the crowd with the disciples (8.34). The saying seems clear, but is puzzling in retrospect. 'Truly I say to you, there are some standing here who will *certainly not* taste of death until they see the kingdom of God come with power.' The use of 'Truly' introduces solemn and important sayings of Jesus (see 3.28; 9.1, 41; 10.15, 29; 11.23; 12.43; 13.30; 14.9, 18, 25, 30) and the double negative (translated 'certainly not') expresses strong negation. The Semitic metaphorical use of 'to taste' has the meaning of 'to experience'. In the Markan framework 'the kingdom of God come with power' sounds like a prediction of the end of the age and the coming of the Son of Man in judgement. Not only did this not happen in the first century, it has not happened yet. The saying in Mark can be read as an attempt to rekindle the fervour of expectation as the decades passed without the return of the Son of Man. But this interpretation does not make sense of the placement of the saying immediately before the account of the transfiguration.

### +Transfiguration narrative (*inclusio*, the baptism, 1.9–11), 9.2–8

This correction story begins with the unusual (for Mark, see 14.1) indication of time-relatedness, suggesting that the new scene is related to the saying. The new scene involves Jesus with a more restricted audience and a lonely place identified as a high mountain, both of which he chose. While a restricted audience suggests the principle enunciated in 4.33–34, it may be that the failure of teaching the disciples as a group has now led Jesus to restrict this group to just Peter, James and John. The high mountain was obviously a lonely place. But there is more to it in this context. The mountain is not named but symbolises the place of revelation, the place where God spoke to Moses and revealed himself to Elijah. The events on the mountain are expressed in four scenes.

1 On the mountain Jesus was 'transfigured' *before them.* It is implied that the events took place for the sake of Peter, James and John. What happened was that Jesus was 'transfigured'. This term, from which we derive the term *metamorphosis,* in Hellenistic religious traditions carried the sense of divinisation, of a human being becoming a God. Obviously, Mark has not used the term in this way and has clarified his meaning by describing the way Jesus' clothing became radiantly white, whiter than any ordinary clothes. There is an influence from the description of Moses on the mountain. Jesus reflected the divine glory.

Elijah was seen with Moses, talking to Jesus. Although Elijah is mentioned before Moses he is not given priority because it is said that he was *with* Moses. Nor are they given priority over Jesus, who is mentioned third, because it is said that they were conversing *with* Jesus. According to 2 Kings 2.1–12, Elijah did not die but was carried up to heaven in a fiery chariot. In tradition known to Josephus (*Antiquities*, 4.8.48), Moses did not die either. Hence two notable figures who did not die reappear with Jesus. Perhaps they represent the revelation of God in the past. Elijah also was expected to return as a forerunner of the day of the Lord (Malachi 3.1; 4.5–6), an idea expressed in the surrounding dialogue, 9.11–13.

2 Peter's response here, as in 8.29, is *representative* of the three. According to the narrator it was an expression of ignorance. Peter did not know how to respond. The response was an expression of fear. They were scared witless. Peter called Jesus 'Rabbi', showing no awareness of the implications of what had taken place. He affirmed 'it is good *for us* to be here', which probably means that the three recognised that the experience had been good for them. He proposed making three tabernacles as shrines commemorating the occasion as if to freeze it in time. It is as if Peter has groped for a position which at last admits Jesus to the same level as Moses and Elijah. But this was mistaken. Even after a special revelation to the three, they had made no progress.

3 Then a cloud overshadowed *them*. The cloud was a manifestation of the divine glory, like the pillar of cloud that led the Israelites in the Exodus. Not the disciples, but Jesus, Moses and Elijah, were overshadowed. They had no need for 'tabernacles' because the divine glory provided their dwelling. The voice came from the cloud, which symbolised the divine presence as in Exodus 24.16; 34.5. The words spoken were not addressed to Jesus, as were the almost identical words at his baptism (1.11). Nor is it likely that they were spoken to Moses and Elijah. The words were spoken to the three disciples to *correct* their faulty view. They were alerted to the true status of Jesus, 'This is my beloved son', and they were instructed, 'listen to him'. Peter's confession of Jesus as the Christ was modified by Jesus' words about the Son of Man. Now Mark portrays modification by the voice of God (*bat qol*). See 1.11 above.

4 Then suddenly the experience was over. They could no longer see anyone except Jesus alone. Two points are made here. First, such experiences are of limited duration and should not be overvalued. Second, the real point of the appearance of Elijah and Moses was to make clear the significance of Jesus. Thus their disappearance, suddenly, leaving the disciples alone with Jesus, was to make clear that Jesus was peerless, he stood alone.

### +The suffering and rising Son of Man II: Peter, James and John remain mystified, 9.9–13

An inquiry/correction story concludes the transfiguration complex. The transfiguration can be interpreted as a secret revelation, restricted by Jesus to Peter, James and John. The sense of secrecy is reinforced by Jesus' command that they tell no one what they saw until the Son of Man was risen from the dead, presupposing his teaching 8.31–33. Peter's confession of Jesus as the Christ needed to be clarified by Jesus' teaching about the suffering, dying and rising Son of Man. So also did the revelation of the sonship of Jesus on the mountain. Just as Peter had failed to grasp the teaching in 8.32–33, so Peter, James and John failed to grasp it here (9.10). Mark says that 'they took hold of this saying' only to dispute among themselves about what it meant (for the Son of Man) to rise from the dead. Thus Mark shows that the disciples had made no progress. They remained as lacking in understanding and *insight* as the crowds (see 4.10–12; 6.52; 8.16–21).

It was not the perplexing question of the resurrection that the disciples raised with Jesus. The group (no spokesperson is named) quoted the scribes as saying 'Elijah must come *first*', probably referring to the interpretation of Malachi 3.1; 4.5–6, in which Elijah was understood to be the forerunner of the day of the Lord which Mark has interpreted in terms of the kingdom of God. Now, in response to Jesus' assertion that some of those referred to in 9.1 would see the kingdom of God come in power, that is, the day of the Lord, they ask, 'Must not Elijah come first? as the scribes say'. This is surprising in the light of the appearance of Elijah with Moses in the revelation on the mountain. The question allows Jesus to elaborate the theme of the coming of Elijah in a direction not yet known *to the disciples*. The reader has already been alerted to it in the opening account of the mission of John (1.4–8, especially 1.6).

Jesus concurred, Elijah must come first. Referring to the fate of John the Baptist (6.14–29), Jesus affirmed that he had come and they did to him as they wished, as the scriptures said. Perhaps the scriptures referred to are an allegorical reading of 1 Kings 19.1–3, so that Herodias succeeded in doing what Jezebel failed to achieve. Even so, Jesus affirms that John (Elijah) has 'put everything in order'. He successfully performed the role of the forerunner. Sandwiched in these sayings is Jesus' reiteration of how it is written (in scripture) that the Son of Man is to suffer many things and be treated with contempt. We know of no such saying in the scriptures *concerning the Son of Man*. But the early Christian method of interpretation brought together a variety of traditions which were regarded as messianic *in the light of Jesus' mission* (life, death and resurrection). These were applied to Jesus in relation to various titles. In Mark the suffering is linked specifically with the Son of Man title, but the texts which speak of suffering do not mention the Son of Man. Rather, they deal with the suffering righteous one (Psalm 22.6 [LXX 21.7]) and the suffering servant of Isaiah (especially 52.13–53.12). Thus, although the disciples' question ignored any reference to the resurrection of the Son of Man, asking instead about Elijah, Jesus' answer reintroduced the Son of Man while dealing with and correcting the assumptions entailed in the question concerning Elijah. Just as John came preaching and was rejected and killed, so now Jesus came preaching and would be rejected and killed, and all of this was in the fulfilment of the scriptures. Having first spoken of the resurrection of the Son of Man (9.9), this dialogue concludes with Jesus' words about the suffering and rejection of the Son of Man and the implied death of Elijah (John).

## +A MIRACLE QUEST STORY AND THE FAILURE OF THE DISCIPLES, 9.14–29

This hybrid miracle quest/correction story is connected to the previous scene by the indication that *they* (presumably Jesus, Peter, James and John) came down the mountain to the disciples (presumably the other nine) and saw them with a great crowd around them and scribes disputing with them. The story is complex in that the *quest* of the father to have his son healed is intertwined with the story of the failure and *correction* of the disciples, which is in focus at the beginning and the end of the story. In the middle Jesus heals the boy.

1 Jesus and the three came to the disciples and saw the great crowd and the scribes 'disputing *with them*'. Mention of the scribes in 9.14 is puzzling and occurs only in the first mention of the 'dispute'. Grammatically, it is possible that the scribes were disputing with the crowd or with the disciples. Since 3.22 the scribes have been established as opponents of Jesus. Mention of them implies an *adversarial* role in relation to the disciples and thus to Jesus, also thus implying the sense of 'disputing' or 'arguing' rather than 'discussing' in 9.14. The disappearance of the scribes from the story, without playing any significant role, suggests that Mark might have adapted a controversy story to make it a correction story in relation to the disciples.
2 When the crowd saw Jesus they were amazed and ran to greet him, 9.15. What amazed them is unclear. Mark might imply that, just as the appearance of Moses was affected by his experience on the mountain, so was the appearance of Jesus, see 9.2.
3 Jesus asked (the crowd is the implied audience) what they were 'discussing' *with them* (9.16). The same term translated as 'arguing' in 9.14 is used here. Because the scribes have vanished, a discussion between the crowd and the disciples is implied. The question was answered, on behalf of the crowd, by the boy's father. His answer confirms this reading.
4 The father reported, 'Teacher, I brought my son to you, possessed by a dumb spirit'. The man addressed Jesus as 'Teacher', which is the Greek equivalent of the Jewish 'Rabbi'.

5 The severe and destructive character of the possession was described.

6 Yet it becomes apparent that Jesus was absent because the man goes on to say, 'I asked your disciples that they should cast it out and they were not able'. So far the story reads like a failed quest story. The man brought his son to Jesus for exorcism and the disciples, having been sent out earlier on a mission with authority to cast out demons (6.7–13), assumed responsibility but failed. The man's report implies that the failure of the disciples is the failure of Jesus also. Yet he persisted in spite of that difficulty.

7 Jesus *rebuked* them (the disciples). This sounds a dismal note for the nine who had been left behind. While the three failed on the mountain, the nine were doing no better. The rebuke was also a signal of hope for the boy's father. Could Jesus do better than his disciples? Jesus called for the boy to be brought to him. This was done.

8 The reaction of the spirit on seeing Jesus is described. Because it was a dumb spirit, no words of recognition were spoken (contrast 1.24, 34; 5.7), but it threw the boy to the ground in a seizure.

9 Jesus asked the father how long his son had had this affliction and was told, since he was a little boy, thus reinforcing the long-standing and serious nature of the problem, which had been outlined in 9.18 and is further elaborated in 9.22.

10 Having failed in his appeal to the disciples, the man then appealed to Jesus, 'If you are *able* have compassion on us, help us'. This request shows that the man, however uncertainly and misguidedly, overcame this obstacle and did not abandon his quest for the healing of his son.

11 Jesus' response was in the form of a rebuke; 'What is this "If you are able"? All things are possible to the one who believes.' This response exposes the flaw in the reiterated request. 'If *you* are able' shows that the man, in his desperation, was willing to allow that, although his disciples had failed, Jesus *might* be able to do something. Jesus' response was in terms of a memorable pronouncement, 'All things are possible to the one who believes'. This now becomes the crux in the story. Certainly, the man had not previously demonstrated faith in his tentative request to Jesus.

12 At this the father cried out, 'I believe, help me with my unbelief'. This response is to be seen as the overcoming of the

objection raised by Jesus with his notable pronouncement. It makes a significant contribution to Mark's understanding of the role of faith in healing and salvation. The man's imperfect response made the success of his quest possible.

13 Strangely, it is noted that Jesus now saw the crowd gathering (9.25), yet they had greeted him in 9.15. This may be another indication of Mark working with tradition, though we need to look for the way the completed Gospel tells the story. Perhaps the point is that the crowd began to gather at 9.15 and, as it grew, this became a reason for Jesus to act quickly.

14 Jesus *rebuked* the 'unclean spirit', saying 'I command you to come out of him and no longer enter into him'. Here, unlike other healing stories, the act of exorcism was by word only. In the face of the failure of the disciples and the tentative overcoming of the obstacles by the boy's father, the word of Jesus emphasises his supreme authority over unclean spirits.

15 The reaction was that the spirit cried out, and having convulsed the boy greatly, came out of him, leaving him prostrate like a dead person. Many thought that he was dead. But Jesus took him by the hand and raised him up. This act should not be seen as part of the exorcism but as Mark's attempt to provide evidence of the cure.

The story bears all the marks of a miracle story. The situation of the boy is briefly and dramatically described, making clear the serious nature of his condition. The failure of the disciples reinforces this. The means of exorcism is briefly and clearly outlined. Evidence of the exorcism is provided. What makes this miracle story into a miracle quest story is (1) the request made by the father; (2) the obstacles the father confronted and overcame in fulfilling his quest; (3) the clear indication of the success of the quest; (4) there is also the memorable pronouncement of Jesus.

This miracle quest story has been set in the context of the theme of the failure of the disciples to grasp the nature of Jesus' vocation and the implications for their own lives and mission. The exorcism successfully completed by Jesus, the disciples could now privately, in a house, deal with the question of their failure. Why were they unable to cast out the unclean spirit? Jesus' answer is, 'This kind does not come out except by prayer'. Some texts add 'and fasting', but this is obviously a scribal addition. Jesus' criticism implies that the disciples had not used prayer, suggesting that the disciples, having returned from a successful mission, assumed that *they* had the authority to cast out unclean spirits. By turning their attention to prayer Jesus directed the disciples to the need for dependence on God. But what is meant by 'This kind', which suggests a particularly critical problem? It seems more likely that Mark sees the event as a general failure of the disciples rather than failure in the face of a more than usually difficult case. This is confirmed by the three incidents that Mark has placed immediately following, in which the disciples appear in a negative light.

## +PREDICTION OF THE DEATH AND RESURRECTION OF THE SON OF MAN III, 9.30–32

From the villages of Caesarea Philippi (8.27) the itinerary of Jesus and his disciples has been vague. In 9.2 a change of location is indicated, but the mountain in question is not named and we are none the wiser about the location when we are told that they came down from the mountain (9.9). Wherever that was – it may still have been in Gaulanitis (see 8.27) – we now learn that *they* left that location and journeyed through Galilee. This again appears to be a case of first indicating the journey before describing what happened on the way (see 8.13–21; 8.27–9.1). Although unclear, it now seems that Jesus did not wish the journey to be known because he wished to be alone with the disciples. This interpretation is supported by 'for he was teaching his disciples' (9.31), providing another instance of the division of Jesus' teaching activity between the crowds and the disciples. His teaching reiterates the new teaching begun in 8.31; 9.9, 12, and, like 8.31 and 10.34, also deals with resurrection vindication after three days (see on 8.31 above).

This passion prediction differs in two important ways from its parallels. First, Mark does not here speak of the specific opponents of Jesus (elders, chief priests, scribes), but simply of 'men'. Second, the description of being '*delivered* or *betrayed* into the *hands* of men' alerts even the first-time reader to the fact that Judas Iscariot, one of the twelve, *betrayed* Jesus (3.19). The following detailed prediction and account (14.18–21, 41–46) reinforces this interpretation. For example, in 14.41 Jesus says, 'Behold the Son of Man is *betrayed* into the *hands* of sinners'. The context of 14.18–21, 41–46 leaves no doubt that the betrayer is Judas. Already in this passion prediction a shadow has fallen over the twelve in that one of their number is to betray Jesus. Progressively there *will be* more bad news. They will all flee in terror and Peter will deny Jesus. For the present the narrator informs the reader that the disciples did not understand this teaching (cf. 9.32 with 8.32). Yet this is already the third occasion upon which Jesus had spoken to them on this subject. Further, they were *afraid* to ask Jesus about the teaching. This is not awe in response to the divine, but fear of acknowledging their ignorance. Possibly they had not changed their views, which were expressed by Peter in 8.32 and, in the light of the way Jesus responded to him there, they were afraid to raise the subject again. In the light of 9.33–35 this conclusion is likely. It is not surprising that they were afraid to ask.

## JESUS AS THE TEACHER OF UNRESPONSIVE DISCIPLES, 9.33–50

A series of sayings follows (9.35b–50), set in a context that is described in both geographical and circumstantial terms (9.33–35a). For the first time since 8.27 (Caesarea Philippi) the itinerary of Jesus is specifically noted.

### +The context, 9.33–34

The new scene indicates the arrival of Jesus and the disciples at Capernaum, where they entered the house. The house is not identified but again illustrates the importance of hospitality in Mark's account of the mission of Jesus. Yet the connection with the previous subject is made by Jesus' question concerning what they were *discussing* or *arguing* about on the way (9.33). The dispute on the way is doubly emphasised by the narrator, who first notes that the disciples *were silent* (again, see 9.32). Although they were silent, the narrator knows the answer and informs the reader that they were silent 'because on the way they were *disputing*, "Who is greatest?"' (9.34). The reader will be aware that Jesus, although he has not been told, also knows and, indeed, that was why he asked. The disciples were unwilling to admit the subject. Again they were silent.

On the way, while Jesus spoke to them of the betrayal, death and vindication of the Son of Man, they were disputing 'Who [which of them] is greatest?' This should not be understood as an 'academic' debate about facts. Rather, it is an expression of the will, the desire to be first, to be the greatest. Just as Peter's rebuke of Jesus followed the first passion prediction, so now the dispute concerning which of them is greatest follows this prediction. In due course we will see how the passion and resurrection prediction of 10.33–34 is followed by the request of James and John to sit one on the right and the other on the left of Jesus in his glory, 10.35–45. This arrangement can be no accident. In each case, just when the Markan Jesus has made his most profound and revealing teaching to his disciples, they show themselves to be blind and devoid of any understanding of Jesus' vocation as Son of Man and how this should involve them.

### +Jesus' response to the disciples' dispute, 'Who is greatest?', 9.35

A correction story follows in which the behaviour of the disciples provides the basis for the correcting teaching of Jesus. Jesus' response to the silence (9.34) was to sit down. Sitting was the traditional posture for the teacher. Thus he sat down to teach. Having done so he called the twelve. Thus Jesus is seated (9.35) in the house (9.33) teaching *the twelve* (9.35). On the way (8.31) he had taught his *disciples*. With no indication of any change of audience we must suppose that his question, 'What were you discussing on the way?', was also addressed to his disciples. It makes no sense to suggest that the twelve are a more restricted group than the disciples mentioned in 8.31, whose presence is assumed in 8.33–34. Thus the reference to Jesus sitting and calling the twelve is not to indicate a changed audience but a changed situation. From the informal question of 8.33 Mark indicates a formal teaching situation. If there were doubts that Mark intended the reader to think that Jesus already knew the answer to his question when he asked it, these doubts are now swept away.

The subject of the teaching concerns the person who wishes to be *first*, a variation on greatest. Such a person will be last of all, a variation on 'least', and *servant* of all. Here an important term is introduced, and it will be developed in terms of the mission and vocation of the Son of Man in 10.45 in a saying which completely undermines and *corrects* the disciples' quest for greatness.

### +Receiving the humble in Jesus' name, 9.36–37

Mark 9.36–37 does not fit neatly at this point, perhaps because Mark has introduced an independent tradition. It is only generally relevant to the present theme. The child placed in the midst of the disciples, received by Jesus, who put his arms around it, becomes a lesson about receiving the humble in Jesus' name. To receive such is to receive Jesus and to receive Jesus is to receive 'the one who sent me'. This phrase is important because it signals Jesus' awareness of mission. In the Gospel of John the evangelist has developed this formula to explore the character of God as sender and the authority of Jesus as the one sent (see John 4.34; 5.23, 24, 30, 37; 6.38, 39, 44 and many other references).

### *Accepting others working in Jesus' name, 9.38–41

The acceptance of others is the subject of this section, which is also a correction story. A new beginning in the teaching situation is signalled by an intervention by John, presumably the brother of James. The brothers appear again in 10.35–45, where they request places of privilege with Jesus in his glory. In this incident John reports forbidding ('We forbade him') a certain exorcist from casting out demons in Jesus' name because 'he was not following us'. The success of the unnamed exorcist stands in stark contrast to the failure of the disciples in their attempt to exorcise the boy, 9.14–29. Placed here, this report indicates the concern of the disciples to protect their exclusive privileges. Jesus' response was a clear counter-*command* and *correction*, 'Do not forbid him!' The disciples have again got it wrong. They do not constitute an exclusive club with all its privileges. Those acting in his name are not against him. Naturally, this formulation presupposes that they are acting in a way consistent with his mission, that is, as an extension of his mission. No doubt this saying was important for the Markan community in its relation to other Christian communities.

### +Associated teachings, 9.42–50

1 Teaching concerning 'the little ones' (9.42) is thematically closer to Jesus' words about children in 9.36–37 than the preceding discussion (9.38–41), which could thus be considered an interruption. But what follows suggests that the teaching themes have been loosely strung together. Yet there is a verbal connection between 9.37 and 9.42. In the first Jesus spoke of *whoever* receives *one of these* children. In the second he spoke of *whoever* causes *one of these* little ones who believe to *stumble*. Receiving has its blessing, but causing such a one to stumble has a fate worse than death.

Just how is not spelt out, but probably implies terrible punishment at the judgement (see 9.47–49).

2 The sayings of the next series (9.43–48) are connected by the catch word 'to cause to *stumble*'. This is not about causing others to stumble, but about some member of the physical body causing the individual to stumble. Whether it is a hand, foot or eye, if it causes stumbling it should be removed because it is better to enter 'life', the kingdom of God, with one hand, one foot or one eye, than with a whole body to be cast into Gehenna. Gehenna is a valley near Jerusalem where human sacrifices had been offered to the god Moloch. It became a rubbish dump which was always burning, a symbol of the place of eternal punishment, and in this sense is used here. There is some evidence that certain crimes were punished by the loss of a limb or eyes. If the practice were known in Mark's time it would make this teaching more forceful. But the urgent meaning is clear. A whole body in Gehenna is worthless and a maimed body in the kingdom of God is by far to be preferred. We may suspect hyperbole in the service of forceful teaching about the priorities involving the kingdom of God. The punishment of Gehenna is described in terms of unquenchable *fire*. Thus fire becomes the new catch word.

3 'For everyone will be *salted* with fire', 9.49. The meaning of the saying is obscure. It cannot mean that all will be burnt with the fire of Gehenna because the action proposed in 9.43–48 was precisely to avoid this. Perhaps some alternative cleansing is in view (1 Corinthians 3.10–15). In this context it might have been clearer if the expression had been 'all will be burnt by salt'. However we understand this saying, 'salt' now becomes the catch word. It has a positive sense of cleansing and preserving without being clearly defined.

4 'Salt is good' as long as it retains its salty quality. This is a saying of 'conventional wisdom' and has to be contextualised to take on its precise meaning. The agent of cleansing must be active. In this context the next saying is reasonably clear.

5 'Have salt amongst yourselves!' Cleansing and preserving powers are needed in the community. 'Be at peace amongst yourselves!' may be intended as an explanation, suggesting that rivalry amongst the disciples, in which each sought to be first, was that from which they needed to be cleansed. Such rivalry was corrupting and destructive. Only when purified of this would they be at peace with one another.

## +DIVORCE: A JUDAEAN CONTROVERSY WITH THE PHARISEES, 10.1–12

A new scene, which can be described as a testing inquiry or an objection story, is introduced, indicating that Jesus moved to the regions of Judaea beyond the Jordan, that is, Peraea, which is not part of Judaea. Perhaps Mark has first named the destination (Judaea) before naming the route (via Peraea), see 11.1 below. This confusion has given rise to textual variants.

There is no mention of the disciples at the beginning, but the scene ends with Jesus in 'the house' with his disciples (10.10). Mark intends the reader to conclude that the disciples travelled with Jesus even when they are not specifically mentioned. The concluding focus on the disciples shows that although this incident commences as an example of Jesus' *customary* teaching practice with the crowd (10.1), leading to a testing inquiry by the Pharisees (10.2), it is the disciples who are given the clearest explanation of Jesus' teaching (10.10–12).

The incident assumes that Jesus' movements were known, so that his presence led to the coming together again of the crowd. His *customary* practice of teaching the crowd is the context for this incident, though no indication is given of what he taught them. For Mark, Jesus is 'the teacher', although comparatively little of his teaching is recorded. The teaching activity of Jesus is the context of the putting of a testing inquiry to him. Although there are textual variants, it is clear that it was the Pharisees who questioned him, seeking *to test* him. It is implied that they sought to lead Jesus into a contradiction of the law. Mark does not explicitly indicate that Jesus had given grounds for some expectation of this kind, though Jesus' answer suggests that his teaching provided grounds for the suspicion that he rejected the legitimacy of divorce. This seems to put him at odds with the law.

Jesus turned the question, 'Is it lawful for a man to divorce his wife?', back on the Pharisees. He asked, 'What did Moses command you?' The assumption that Moses wrote Deuteronomy 24.1, 3 was accepted by all. Thus the answer was simple. But the *meaning* of *what* Moses wrote is dependent, to some extent, on *why* it was written. The provision of a bill of divorce was a legal protection for a woman who might otherwise simply be abandoned by her husband. Nevertheless, this provision allowed a man to divorce his wife if she failed to please him. The debate in Jesus' day concerned whether divorce was permitted 'for any cause', which was supported by Hillel, or only in a case of adultery, being the position of Shammai. The Jewish position of the time recognised adultery only in the case of a married woman and the man in relation to her. Jesus' teaching in Mark does not fit either of the major positions noted. Indeed, he appears to express two quite different, but not necessarily contradictory, positions.

First, in dialogue with the Pharisees, he agreed with their answer to his question about *what* Moses wrote. This was his way of dealing with the legal question. Is it lawful? His implied answer is 'Yes, it is lawful!'

Second, his ensuing argument qualifies this by arguing that the lawful provision took account of the actualities of the human situation, which involved the hardness of human hearts. While the wording is, 'the hardness of your hearts', the Markan Jesus cannot mean to restrict this condition to his hearers because they were discussing an age-old provision sanctioned by Moses. The legal provision was to deal with the condition of 'a hard heart' (sclerosis of the heart), which, like the alternative description of 'the heart without feeling', is part of the description of those who are insensitive to God and Jesus, who are blind to his action and deaf to his word (see Isaiah 6.9–10; Mark 4.10–12; 6.52; 8.15–18). Over against this Jesus set the ideal, which is rooted in the beginning of the creation as set out in Genesis (see 1.27; 2.24; 5.2). There the creation of male and female is attested, as is the principle of a man leaving his father and mother and becoming one flesh with his wife. The resultant unity out of the union between the man and the woman is strongly stressed in that Jesus not only quotes from Genesis, but repeats the point in his own words, both positively, 'one flesh', and negatively, 'they are no longer two'. Clearly, Jesus' statement of the original ideal in creation leaves no room, for those sensitive to the will and purpose of God, for an approach to marriage lightly entered into and easily broken.

Thus, having given the legal answer, Jesus then expressed the principle enshrined in creation, which led to a concluding statement. 'What God has yoked together let [a] man not separate!' The term used here for 'separate' is used in the Hellenistic papyri to mean 'to divorce'. Thus the concluding direction is to the *man* who would divorce his wife. This reaffirms that divorce is not in the will and purpose of God. There is no advice here on how the legal provision and the divine ideal might be held together. Rather, it seems that divorce is to be excluded by those sensitive to God's will and purpose, though it remained a legal provision for those insensitive to his will. If the direction of 10.9 is given to the *man* who would divorce his wife, it reflects the Jewish legal situation. But 10.12 allows for the wife to divorce her husband. It may be that in 10.9 'man' is understood generically as 'person', at least in the final text of Mark.

Following the public teaching and dispute with the Pharisees Jesus withdrew into the house, 10.10. There can be no suggestion that this is Jesus' home. Rather, it is again confirmation of the principle of hospitality utilised by Jesus' mission. The house is the private situation where Jesus talked with his disciples alone. The disciples questioned Jesus concerning this teaching. The teaching of 10.3–9 can hardly be considered parabolic, but 10.11–12 is an example of Jesus explaining all things to his disciples in private (4.34). The explanation (10.11–12) assumes a Roman legal situation, where a woman could also divorce her husband. Also different from the Jewish legal position, Jesus asserted that a husband could commit adultery as well as a wife and under the same conditions. The most radical point of departure was the assertion that a husband or wife who divorced his or her spouse and remarried, committed adultery with the new spouse. Given that a bill of divorce was precisely to legitimise a subsequent marriage, holding together Jesus' public teaching to the Pharisees with his teaching to the disciples is difficult. It suggests the recognition of divorce but the rejection of remarriage. Alternatively, it might be understood that Jesus' teaching to the disciples develops the teaching about the ideal rather than the legal position, though discussion of adultery appears to introduce the legal situation.

Jesus' answer to the Pharisees avoided the pitfall of teaching a position contrary to the law, thus negotiating successfully their testing inquiry. The teaching given to the disciples alone complicates the issue. Given that it reflects a Roman rather than Jewish perspective on divorce, it is Mark's application of the teaching of Jesus to his own time. That being the case, Jesus can be understood as setting the ideal, embodied in creation, over against the legal position, which reflected the contingencies of human life.

## +JESUS, THE DISCIPLES AND THE CHILDREN, 10.13–16

A hybrid quest/correction/commendation story follows in which the disciples, again shown to be hard of heart and lacking in understanding, were corrected by Jesus. It is also a quest story in which those who brought children to Jesus faced the obstacle posed by the disciples. When this was overcome they achieved their goal. If the disciples were reprimanded then the children were commended. Correction and commendation often appear side by side.

No change of location is indicated, but the situation is changed from private to public by children being brought to Jesus for him to touch them. The kind of 'touch' in view was a 'blessing' (10.16). But the disciples *rebuked* (see 1.25; 8.30, 32, 33) them, probably meaning those who brought the children rather than the children themselves. The disciples did not remember the lesson about receiving the little children in Jesus' name (9.36–37). Not only is there reference to children in both passages, Mark describes Jesus putting his arms around the child/children (9.36; 10.16). As well as indignantly correcting the behaviour of the disciples Jesus told them, in a saying that has become a well-known pronouncement, 'Permit the children to come to me, do not forbid them, for of such is the kingdom of God'. Jesus concluded with a solemn 'Amen . . .' saying in which the children were used as the model for those who would enter the kingdom of God. Thus those commended become role models, while those corrected become warnings.

Just what aspect of a child's behaviour is the model is unclear. It is often taken to be the trusting attitude of the child. The story concludes with the indication that Jesus took the children in his arms, laid [his] hands upon them and blessed them. Thus his final action was at once a correction of the disciples, a commendation of the children, and the fulfilment of the quest of those who had brought the children to Jesus.

## +THE COST OF DISCIPLESHIP, 10.17–31

A new scene is indicated by Jesus commencing a journey, presumably from the house mentioned in 9.33. Although the disciples are not mentioned at this point, it becomes obvious that they were present, 10.23. The explicit mention of the disciples signals a transition from the public aspect of the story to Jesus' private discussion with them concerning the implications for them. This discussion takes its point of departure from the theme with which the preceding story ends, but moves on to other related themes.

### +The failure of the rich man's quest for eternal life, 10.17–22

The opening is a failed quest story embodying the perennial quest for eternal life. The quest is dramatically portrayed through the description of a man urgently *running* to Jesus as he journeyed on the way, *kneeling* before him and asking, 'Good teacher, what must I do to inherit eternal life?' Given that the man asked a question rather than making a request, this seems to be an inquiry story. It is a quest story because the question gave expression to a genuine quest for eternal life. Jesus' answer posed a problem which the man failed to overcome, so that his quest failed.

That the man addressed Jesus as *teacher* is appropriate to the story. The man expected Jesus to answer his urgent question. But what is meant by '*Good* teacher'? And why did Jesus question 'Why do you call me good?', affirming 'No one is good except one, namely, God'? The Markan Jesus did not repudiate this ascription, but raises the question as to why it had been applied to him in the light of the exclusive goodness of God. That this question is addressed to the reader is implied by the absence of any opportunity for the quester to make a response. Mark challenges the reader to see that the goodness of Jesus points to his relationship with God.

Jesus' answer was to remind the man of the commandments, but in listing them he omits any reference to the first four, which relate to God directly. This implies that the challenge for this man lay at the social level. The last six commandments are listed in the order six to ten and, finally, five. The tenth commandment is modified from 'Do not covet' to 'Do not defraud'. There is no apparent reason for these changes. The man's response suggests no awareness of a special interpretation of the commandments. He affirmed that he had kept these commandments from his youth. Mark records that Jesus then looked at him and loved him, implying that the man's affirmation was sincere and true. Nevertheless, the call to discipleship, which is here identified with entry to the kingdom of God or entry into life, demands a higher righteousness.

At this point Jesus introduced the objection which the man had to overcome if his quest was to be successful. He demanded a total commitment which, in this story, exposed the man's attachment to his possessions. The reader knows that Jesus taught that any cause of stumbling which might prevent a person from entering life, the kingdom of God, should be cast off, even an eye, hand or foot (9.43–48). Here the man's wealth stood between him and discipleship, between him and eternal life. He was unwilling to sell his possessions and give the proceeds to the poor and to follow Jesus (compare 8.34). Nevertheless, the man was torn by his wish to have eternal life and his attachment to his possessions. For this reason Jesus' answer was a cause of grief for him, and his quest for eternal life failed.

Jesus exposed a serious flaw in the man's response to the commandments, which had remained hidden throughout the discussion of the last six commandments. He failed to keep the first and great command expressed in the Shema (Deuteronomy 6.4–5). Riches came between him and God, between him and eternal life.

### +Riches as an impediment to entering the kingdom of God, 10.23–27

The new scene turns attention to the disciples, who were not mentioned in 10.17–22. Now, on each occasion when Jesus speaks to the disciples, it is first noted that he looked at them, emphasising the solemnity of what he says to them concerning the difficulty of entering the kingdom of God and, in particular, the difficulty caused by possessions or riches. In this teaching Jesus used a *parable* (not named as such), which asserts that it is easier for a camel to pass through the eye of a needle than for a rich man to enter the kingdom of God. The disciples, amazed and perplexed by this, questioned, 'Who then can be saved?' Without wishing to diminish the difficulty, Jesus replied that, though not humanly possible, it was possible for God to save even the rich. The imagery of the parable depends on hyperbole or gross exaggeration for its force. In this way the extreme difficulty is made apparent.

### *Peter's claim on behalf of the disciples, 10.28–30

Peter is now named as spokesperson for the disciples (see 8.29, 32; 9.5 and cf. John in 9.38). Whatever demands Jesus had made of the rich man, Peter now affirms that he and the other disciples have fulfilled them. Formally this claim appears to be beyond dispute (see 1.16–20), though it has a ring of self-righteousness about it. Jesus' reply also seems to qualify and correct the tone of the claim. It is introduced by a solemn 'Truly', and affirms that no one has left anything (specifying house, brothers, sisters, mother, father, children, fields) for his and the gospel's sake who will not receive in kind in this age one hundredfold. This may be a reference to the new and enlarged family of believers referred to in 3.35 and all the houses which made possible the success of the mission. But there is more, 'with persecutions'. This does not fit easily with the rest of the statement, but certainly made sense of the life of the community for which Mark wrote. Given the question asked at the beginning of the story upon which this discussion is based (10.17), the concluding remark is essential, 'and in the age to come, eternal life'. While the call to become part of Jesus' group of disciples seems, at times, to be a call to be part of his mission, here it also seems to be an essential condition for eternal life.

### *Reversal, 10.31

What appears to be an independent saying has been placed here by Mark. With the disciples' dispute about who is greatest (9.34) in mind, this saying seems to put a qualification over Peter's claim to have forsaken all to follow Jesus. Peter's affirmation, 'We have left everything to follow you', was a claim to the priority of the twelve. In this context, 'Many first will be last and last first' makes sense. If the aim of the twelve in following Jesus was to be first, then they have missed the point of his teaching (9.35). Claims to priority and greatness amongst the twelve have not been left behind, as will soon be confirmed, 10.35–45.

## *PREDICTION OF THE DEATH AND RESURRECTION OF THE SON OF MAN IV, 10.32–34

Given the continuous programme of travelling (from 7.24), it might be coincidental that Jesus' teaching to his disciples concerning the death and resurrection of the Son of Man always took place on a journey; for the first time on the journey to Caesarea Philippi, which was a turning-point *in the teaching of Jesus*. That the teaching occurred on the journey is carefully noted by Mark using the words 'on the way', 8.27. The second occasion was *coming down* from the mountain of transfiguration (9.9, 12). The third was journeying through

Galilee (9.30) and the fourth 'on the way' going up to Jerusalem (10.32). The journey motif expresses the acceptance of suffering and death as the fulfilment of the will and purpose of God.

The scene of 10.32 is not altogether clear. Certainly, Mark places Jesus out in front 'leading' (see 14.28; 16.7). Others are described as being amazed or shocked, while those who *followed* were afraid. The twelve were there because Mark notes that Jesus took them aside, apparently from the crowd. On such a reading the twelve might be amazed or shocked while the crowd was afraid. What was it that produced these responses? Mark implies a premonition of disaster that awaited them in Jerusalem and towards which Jesus rushed on relentlessly. But Jesus had not yet begun to speak of the events that were about to overtake him. This he now did, speaking in more detail of the betrayal of the Son of Man to chief priests and the scribes, who condemn him to death and hand him over (betray him) to the Gentiles (Romans), who mock, spit upon, scourge and kill him, and after three days he will rise (10.33–34). This is an accurate summary of what Mark later describes as befalling Jesus in Jerusalem; betrayed by Judas (14.10–11, 43–45) to the chief priests and scribes (14.1–2, 10–11, 53) who condemned him to death (14.64) and handed him over (betrayed him) to the Gentiles (Pilate), (15.1), who mocked him (15.16–20, 25–32), spat upon him (15.19), scourged him (15.15), killed (crucified) him (15.24–25, 37), and he rose after three days (16.1–8). In the light of this teaching the urgent hurry of Jesus to reach Jerusalem is truly awesome and frightening. Nevertheless, the picture of Jesus striding along out in front, with the disciples following along behind marvelling and fearful, is something of an ideal picture and one that the disciples failed to achieve at the end of the Gospel, 16.7–8.

## THE QUEST FOR GREATNESS CONTINUED, 10.35–45

Each of the passion and resurrection predictions is followed by an account of the failure of the disciples: Peter's rebuke of Jesus (8.32), the failure of the disciples in the attempt to exorcise the boy (9.18), their dispute over which of them was greatest (9.34), and now the request of James and John to sit on the right and left of Jesus in his glory (10.37). In this way, the failure of the twelve (disciples) is dramatised and stands out starkly against the background of the teaching of Jesus to them. This incident is in two scenes. In the first, James and John make requests of Jesus, to which he responds. In the second, the other (ten) disciples react to their request and Jesus further develops his teaching on the nature of discipleship, based on the model of his own vocation.

### +The requests of James and John, 10.35–40

In this failed quest story /correction story James and John came to Jesus with a request. They addressed him as 'Teacher' which, though appropriate, is inconsistent with the request they made of him. Their request was in two parts. In the first they masked their request and sought to get Jesus to agree to do whatever they were about to ask him. The form of this question implies that those who asked thought they had some claim on Jesus, but because they could predict the answer Jesus would give (see 9.35) they masked the actual question.

Instead of agreeing to the unspecified 'favour', Jesus asked what it was that they wished him to do for them. Ambition unmasked, they asked Jesus to give them [the right] to sit one on his right and one on his left in his glory. In the present context, 'in your glory' probably means 'in your kingdom', which they understood to be the reality that Jesus now urgently sought to establish on his arrival in Jerusalem, thus explaining why he strode out in front of all in his impatience to be there (10.32). Because this is presented as a joint request, which of the two should be given priority (on the right side) was left for Jesus to decide.

Jesus made a twofold response. He told them, 'You do not know what it is that you ask'. Of course, in one sense they did know. This is a re-run of the quest to be greatest (9.34). At a deeper level, they did not know what they were asking. This ignorance is not simply about what was involved, that is, the cup that Jesus was to drink and the baptism he was to undergo. The cup is a metaphor drawn from scripture (Psalm 75.8), used by Jesus of his imminent suffering in the agony in the garden of Gethsemane (14.36). Baptism is also used as a metaphor of suffering and testing. Without knowing what these metaphors involved, James and John affirmed they were able to undertake them. A degree of ignorant commitment is implied here. More significantly, they did not know that what they asked of Jesus was not his to give but belonged to those for whom it was prepared.

Two things of importance emerge here. Mark was not sensitive to statements that limited Jesus' authority. This matter was not in his gift, not in his power. Then, by asserting that these positions already belonged to those for whom they were prepared, Jesus placed the question of priority outside the legitimate area of their concern. Clearly, their quest for greatness had failed and Jesus had cast a question mark over their ambition.

### +The consternation of the ten, 10.41–45

This correction story commences with the report that when the ten heard of the request of James and John, they began to be angry. Jesus' response suggests that Mark intends the reader to suppose that what angered them was that James and John had unfairly sought an advantage, asking what each of the twelve would like to have asked. The *correction* is given in the teaching of Jesus, presumably to the twelve, concerning the reversal of values. Amongst the nations the great and powerful lord it over their subjects. But Jesus asserts that this is not the way it will be amongst his disciples. Amongst them, whoever wishes to be 'great' will be 'servant' of all and whoever wishes to be 'first' will be 'slave' of all. In all probability, the terms used for *servant* and *slave* are synonyms, with no difference of meaning. This is important for the interpretation of 10.45.

Although 10.43–44 is addressed to the problem of reversing the values of the twelve (and the reader), it is possible to read these verses as a new strategy for 'greatness' and 'priority'. But greatness and priority have here been redefined by relating the behaviour of the disciples to the vocation of Jesus. This is done in 10.45, which is introduced by 'For', giving the reason for the reversal stated in 10.43–44.

Given that the Son of Man of Daniel 7 had by the time of Jesus come to be understood as an imperious heavenly messianic figure (in 1 Enoch, 4 Ezra, 2 Baruch), and that the Markan Jesus used Son of Man as a figure of authority acting in relation to the law (2.10, 28), the move to speak of his suffering and death appears to have been somewhat confusing (see 8.31; 9.12, 31; 10.33–34). There he spoke of what *will be done to* the Son of Man, making this the basis for his teaching on discipleship (8.34–38), asserting that his disciples would face the same fate as the Son of Man. This falls short of rooting the vocation of the disciple in the model of the *vocation* of the Son of Man. The vocation concerns not just what happens to the Son of Man, but the very purpose of his coming. Thus 10.45 is not simply a restatement of the earlier predictions because: (1) it goes beyond speaking of what was done to Jesus to speak of the very purpose of his coming; (2) that purpose is shown to culminate in *giving* his life as a *ransom* for *many*; (3) there is no reference here to resurrection after three days because the focus is on the reversal of values in a vocation of serving epitomised by the giving of his life.

Reinforcing the reversal of values, the purpose of his coming is stated both negatively, 'not to be served', and positively, 'but to serve'. This term links Jesus' vocation linguistically with the 'servant' ideal for the disciples outlined in 10.43. The use of this language is sometimes taken as an argument against the recognition of the influence of the tradition of the 'suffering servant' of Isaiah (especially 52.13–53.12) on this Son of Man saying because the natural translation of *ebed* would be *pais* or *doulos* (slave). But in this context in Mark, *servant* and *slave* are synonyms (10.43–44) and the verb *to serve* is appropriately used in 10.45. The servant songs of Isaiah (normally recognised in 42.1–9; 49.1–13; 50.4–9; 52.13–53.12 and perhaps 61.1–3) are the most notable body of tradition on the theme and certainly the early Christians found the association inescapable (see Acts 8.26–40, especially 32–35). Thus, while the language of Mark cannot be derived exactly from Isaiah, the outline of the servant's suffering, bearing the sin of *many* and pouring out his life to death, seems to have shaped the Markan saying. Further, the theme of the *redemption* of Israel by God surrounds the servant songs in Isaiah 41.14; 43.1, 14; 44.22–24; 52.3. What is distinctive is Mark's interpretation of the vocation of *the Son of Man* in terms of the role of the suffering servant. We may see this as an example of the assimilation of expectations and titles in the interpretation of Jesus, but in a distinctively Markan fashion. Mark 10.45 is not just a repetition of the predictions of the suffering of the Son of Man; it is the culminating statement of this theme, which makes as clear as Mark is able, the nature and purpose of the service of the Son of Man in the giving of his life. In this way, too, the service of the Son of Man has become a more adequate basis and model for the vocation of the disciples.

## +BARTIMAEUS: THE BLIND MAN SEES AND FOLLOWS ON THE WAY, 10.46–52

A miracle quest story begins by noting the next stage in the journey. Arrival at Jericho, only about fifteen miles from Jerusalem, heightens the sense of the anticipated destination. Given the proximity of Jericho to the Jordan, the reader must wonder where Jesus has been since arriving in the regions of Judaea and Peraea (10.1, see 10.17, 32). This is the first specific identification of place since they came to Capernaum in 9.33. Who is included in 'they' is probably clarified by the description of Jesus' departure, 10.46. Jesus departed from Jericho with his disciples and a large crowd. It may be that the crowd was attracted to Jesus as he passed through Jericho, though some may have been travelling with him (see 11.9). Jesus' journey through Jericho was the opportunity for a blind man who sat beside *the way* (road). He is identified as 'the son of Timaeus', which is a translation of the Aramaic Bartimaeus.

The scene is now set for a miracle quest story. Jesus' visit to Jericho was grasped by Bartimaeus as his opportunity. Hearing of the presence of 'Jesus the Nazarene', he began to cry out. The narrator identified Jesus as 'the Nazarene', indicating that Jesus was from Nazareth (1.9 and see 1.24; 14.67; 16.6). Bartimaeus did not refer to the Nazarene. He called out, 'Son of David, Jesus, have mercy on me'. Son of David is a designation for the messianic king. Associated with the cry, 'have mercy on me', it is not interpreted in the militaristic sense of the Psalms of Solomon 17–18 etc. Rather, it implies one whose works of mercy are expressed in healing and deliverance (see Isaiah 29.18; 32.1–3; 35.1–10; 61.1–4). For Mark there is something more mysterious about Jesus as son of David than was commonly thought (see 12.35–37). Given that Bartimaeus called for the son of David to have mercy on him, the reputation of Jesus must have impacted on his understanding of the Messiah.

The initiative of Bartimaeus is clear, as are the obstacles to be overcome if he was to succeed. First, there was the impediment of his blindness. Then there was the crowd that stood between him and Jesus. Further, the crowd sought to suppress his attempt to reach Jesus by sternly *charging* (see 1.25; 4.39; 8.30, 32) him to be quiet. These seem to be insuperable odds to overcome. Nevertheless, he cried out the more, 'Son of David, Jesus, have mercy on me'.

Because Bartimaeus persisted against all odds, Jesus instructed the crowd to *call* him. That Jesus 'called' Bartimaeus is given a threefold emphasis in 10.50 where Jesus instructed the crowd to *call* him, his *calling* by the crowd, and the report to him, 'Be of good cheer, get up, he *calls* you'. Thus, at the conclusion of a section of Mark in which Jesus has taught the disciples concerning the vocation of the Son of Man and the implications of this for discipleship, Jesus *called* Bartimaeus.

The fishermen had left their nets, boats and families to follow Jesus (1.18, 20). Now Bartimaeus cast aside his cloak, sprang up and came to Jesus. This is not simply an action which expresses the overcoming of the obstacle to his quest for sight. The action of leaving his beggar's cloak, which was spread on the ground to receive alms, signified the leaving of his possessions. In due course Mark makes clear that, unlike the rich man of 10.17–22, but like the fishermen (10.28), Bartimaeus left all to follow Jesus. Another level of reading suggests that Bartimaeus left the beggar's cloak with the conviction that he would no longer need it. Jesus would heal him.

In due course he came to Jesus, who asked him, 'What do you wish me to do for you?' (10.51). The question is identical to the one asked of James and John (10.36). The story of Bartimaeus is being told as a conscious comparison with the story of the disciples. James and John addressed Jesus as 'Teacher', and asked to sit one on the right and one on the left of Jesus in his glory. This was shown to be an inappropriate request. Bartimaeus asked, '*Rabouni*, that I may see again'. *Rabouni*, 'my Rabbi' (my teacher), is a more solemn form of address than 'Rabbi' or 'Teacher'. The request shows that Bartimaeus had come to understand the son of David as one who could open the eyes of the blind (see Isaiah 35.4–5; 61.1–4). Jesus responded, 'Go, your faith has saved you'. Thus Jesus interpreted as saving faith the persistent tenacity of Bartimaeus in believing that Jesus could give him his sight, and asking him to do this. To be saved is, in the first instance, to see again. Immediately, Bartimaeus saw again. But sight is also a metaphor of salvation.

In another sense, it was the blind man who could see and not the disciples. It is interesting that, after the initial identification of the blind beggar as Bartimaeus (10.46), in the subsequent story he is called the blind man (10.49, 51) and his name is not used again. The irony is that, in the midst of the crowd, the one who is identified as the blind man is the one who could see. He identified Jesus as the son of David and called on him to 'have mercy on me'.

He came to Jesus, who restored his sight. Although Jesus told the man to 'Go!', 'he *followed* him on the way'. There is no sign that Jesus sought to dissuade him from *following* him. Here, 'Go!' is not to be understood as a rejection. Rather, 'Go! Your faith has saved you' affirms the granting of the request. This is confirmed by the narrator, who says, 'immediately he saw again'. Further confirmation is provided: 'and he followed him in the way.' These words are pregnant with the Markan understanding of discipleship. Bartimaeus, rather than the twelve, has become the image of the true disciple. It was no accident that Mark portrays a blind man as the first person to perceive that Jesus was the son of David. His persistent (double) confession of Jesus as such is the first use of the title in the Gospel, preparing the way for the interpretation of this title in the next incident (11.9–10).

# Chapter 6

# Jerusalem, 11.1—16.8

## THE LORD COMES TO HIS TEMPLE, 11.1–13.37

### +The coming of the king, 11.1–11

Mark announces that they drew near to Jerusalem, naming the place 'Bethphage and Bethany near the Mount of Olives'. Both villages are on the slopes of the Mount of Olives. Coming from Jericho, Jesus would first have come to Bethany, about two miles from Jerusalem, and then Bethphage, a bit more than a mile closer in. The geographical order Jerusalem, Bethphage, Bethany, Mount of Olives is a bit puzzling. Perhaps the logic of it is that Jerusalem is stated first as the destination of the journey, Bethphage next as the point at which the party had actually arrived, Bethany as the previous village, perhaps better known than Bethphage and named because Jesus and his party would return there (not to Bethphage) after their initial visit to Jerusalem and the temple (11.11). Reference to the Mount of Olives provides more recognisable geographical bearings for the reader, though a theological meaning based on Zechariah 14.4 cannot be ruled out. There it is prophesied that the Lord will stand on the Mount of Olives in the day of judgement. Though the prophet was referring to God, Mark, like the early Christians generally, applied this title to Jesus.

The scene is set geographically at Bethphage. Mark then makes clear that the 'they' who had arrived are Jesus and his disciples, because he sent 'two of his disciples' to the adjacent village (11.1–2 and compare 14.13), probably understood as Bethphage. The group of disciples is identified as the twelve when they return with Jesus to Bethany at the end of the incident (11.11). Mark does not identify the two sent on this mission. The important details concern their mission. On entering the village they will find an unbroken colt (young donkey), which they are to bring to Jesus, and in the event of any objection they are to say, 'The Lord has need of it and will return it here'. This all happened as Jesus had instructed. Mark's understanding of this sequence is not altogether clear. There is no indication that Mark takes this to be a pre-arrangement made by Jesus or as evidence of his supernatural knowledge. Perhaps it is to be understood as the working out of the divine plan. More likely, in the context of this incident and remembering the confession of Jesus as son of David, a kingly ascription, Jesus is here recognised as king with the right to requisition the colt for his entry into Jerusalem. This is the point of the statement, 'The Lord has need of it'. Following the Mishnaic laws of borrowing, as soon as the need was satisfied, the colt was returned to the place from which it had been taken.

Given that Jesus' itinerant mission had been conducted on foot, it is an important occasion when he chooses to ride on a colt. The reader is not permitted to miss the point because Mark describes the elaborate arrangements made by Jesus. That it was an unbroken colt made it notable, too, in that Jesus rode it without resistance. It was an animal waiting and ready to fulfil its sacred purpose. According to M.Sanh. 2.5, no one should ride a king's horse. The horse was a mount for war. The colt Jesus rode was a young donkey, which makes no polemical statement or threat to the city he was entering. Nevertheless, it was unusual for a pilgrim to enter the city mounted rather than walking.

Mark describes Jesus entering the city seated on the colt upon which 'they' had placed their outer garments. 'They' probably refers to the two disciples. The following narrative is less than clear. No specific mention has been made of any crowd since 10.46. It may be implied that the crowd went with Jesus and the disciples, as we are told Bartimaeus did (10.52). Alternatively, Mark may imply that a crowd of pilgrims gathered around Jesus as he approached Jerusalem. However this is understood, Mark says that 'many spread their garments on the road [way]', forming a carpet. The picture of a large crowd going in front of him and following behind him, with Jesus riding the colt in the centre, has all the marks of a royal procession. The words of the pilgrims remove any doubt about what was perceived to be happening. They *were crying out*. Here the imperfect must be given weight as meaning that they were crying out over and over again. The words were partly taken from and partly based on Psalm 118.25–26. The word 'Hosanna' strictly means 'Lord save', but here it is a shout of praise to God, as is clear in the concluding words, 'Hosanna in the highest'. Mark has understood the words of blessing to refer not only to the pilgrim who comes to the festival, but a special blessing to the one whose coming is associated with the coming kingdom of David. This is not only a recognition of the kingly status of Jesus. It is a confession of his messiahship. Coming swiftly after the confession of Bartimaeus, Mark's narrative confirms that Jesus accepted these confessions as he approached Jerusalem and that he made no attempt to silence them. Not only Bartimaeus but also the crowd seem to be more perceptive than the twelve. Mark, however, makes no reference to Zechariah 9.9 (see Matthew 21.5 and John 12.15), appropriate as it would have been for his narrative.

Here, as elsewhere in Mark, the significant action took place on the journey. Given that the use of Malachi 3.1 in Mark 1.2 implies the climax of the Lord suddenly arriving at his temple (11.11), the actual arrival of Jesus in Jerusalem at the temple was an anti-climax. Nothing happened. By the time he arrived it was already evening, so that Jesus returned to Bethany with the twelve. Yet the reader has learned that the object of Jesus' journey to Jerusalem was the temple, to which he went immediately on arrival. This conclusion is confirmed when Jesus returned to the temple the next day. It should be noted that, although Mark implies that Jesus came up to Jerusalem at the time of a major festival and with other pilgrims, no particular festival is identified, nor is there any clear indication of a day-by-day itinerary. The events of 'the next day' (11.12) are an exception in the Markan narrative to make clear that Jesus, at the earliest possible opportunity, picked up his unfinished business with the temple.

## A tale within a tale: fig tree and temple, 11.12–25

### +*The cursing of the fig tree, 11.12–14*

The new scene begins with reference to 'the next day'. This scene is related to the previous day, taking up the business it was too late to complete on the previous day. The delay of a day leaves the reader in suspense, not knowing what Jesus came to the temple to do. In the same way, description of the incident with the fig tree delays his arrival at the temple again. This technique signals that an event of extreme significance for Mark's understanding of Jesus is imminent. But the fig tree incident is not just a delaying technique. Closely linked with the temple incident, it provides a symbolic framework within which the temple incident is to be understood.

Leaving Bethany for the temple in Jerusalem, it seems 'without breakfast', Jesus hungered. There was a fig tree, whose location is unspecified, with leaves but no figs. Mark (the narrator) informs the reader, 'It was not the season for figs'. On finding this Jesus said, 'Let no one eat fruit from you ever again'. The narrator again interjects, this time to tell us that the disciples heard him say this. That is as if to say that Jesus said this for their benefit. Although the narrator indicated only that Jesus hungered, it is clear that the disciples were with him.

The puzzling part of this is the narrator's interjection addressed to the reader, 'It was not the season for figs'. The question is, why did Mark wish the reader to know this? No specific time of year has been indicated, so that it is not a necessary adjustment to the seasonal reality of the story. It is a signal that the story is to be read for its symbolic meaning. Sandwiching the temple story within the story of the fig tree also suggests that the latter is to be used as an interpretative key for understanding Jesus' action in the temple.

*+A house of prayer for all nations, 11.15–19*

'And they came to Jerusalem.' Mark indicates that Jesus immediately went to Jerusalem to the temple. What follows is a correction story, in which the situation in the temple provokes the response of Jesus in action and word, which forms the correction. That the correction was ineffective is shown by the conclusion of the story.

The situation that provoked the correction is described in terms of the temple business, the sale of the sacrificial animals and the provision of temple money for that purpose. Jesus' action was to overthrow this system forcefully and to prevent any business from taking place in the temple, at least for that day. His words are introduced formally, 'he taught and said to them', to emphasise their importance. 'Is it not written, "my house shall be called a house of prayer for all the nations"? But you have made it a den of robbers.' The quotation is from Isaiah 56.7, but there is also an allusion to

Jeremiah's 'den of robbers' sermon, Jeremiah 7.11. Reference to the den of robbers implies that God was about to lay waste the temple, because Jeremiah's reference is in the context of the threat that what God had done to Shiloh was about to befall the temple, Jeremiah 7.14. Consequently, Mark intends the reader to understand Jesus' action as a sign of the impending destruction of the temple. A prophetic sign of impending destruction should be understood as a warning of disaster that may be averted by responding positively to the sign. The sign is then to be seen as a correction to the temple situation.

The sale of animals and changing of money took place in the court of the Gentiles. It was not so much that current practice was corrupt. It excluded Gentiles for whom the temple was also to be a house of prayer. Jesus' action was a correction to the current practice, an attempt to cleanse the temple to make it fulfil its true purpose. From Mark's viewpoint, Jesus' sign of correction was not heeded and the sign of destruction became reality. In Mark 13.1–2 Jesus was to speak of the destruction more directly.

If we ask who saw Jesus' action in the temple and who heard his words, Mark indicates only that the chief priests and scribes heard and as a result they sought to destroy him because they feared him. It is implied that the crowd also heard because it is said that they were amazed at his teaching. While the chief priests and scribes rejected the correction, the response of the crowd is probably positive. In the long run, the Markan story shows that the decision to destroy Jesus and to reject his correction and warning triumphed in his crucifixion. Given the context of the 'den of robbers' image in Jeremiah's warning of the desolation of the temple, Mark provides grounds for the interpretation of the destruction of Jerusalem and the temple as divine judgement for the crucifixion of Jesus, which is understood as a vivid symbol of the rejection of his teaching (see Eusebius, *History*, 3.7.7–9).

The incident is concluded by the indication that, at the end of the day, they (Jesus and the disciples) went out of the city. The incident begins with their arrival in Jerusalem and the temple (11.15), and concludes with their withdrawal. Yet, although it is assumed that they were with Jesus, the disciples played no part in the incident itself. Their continuing presence with Jesus is confirmed by specific reference to their presence on the journey, presumably back to Bethany.

*+The fig tree withered, 11.20–22*

The narrative takes Jesus and the disciples back to the fig tree which Jesus had 'cursed' (see 11.21). Although they left the city when evening came, Mark sets this scene early in the morning. In the sequence the reader must assume this to be the next morning. The narrator tells us that they saw the fig tree withered away to its roots. Then, to emphasise the point, it is reported that Peter remembered and said to Jesus, 'Rabbi, the fig tree that you cursed has withered'. The withering of the tree is doubly confirmed, by the narrator and an eyewitness. For the representative role of Peter in Mark see 8.29, 32; 9.5. In none of these instances does his leading intervention lead the reader to think well of Peter. Jesus' answer enigmatically now casts doubt on him. Jesus told him, 'Have faith in God', implying that Peter's observation gave expression to a lack of faith. An integral connection between the withering of the fig tree and the cleansing of the temple is confirmed by the sandwiching of the cleansing of the temple between the two parts of the fig tree story.

Three things strongly suggest that Mark regards the curse and withering of the fig tree as a parabolic action (*mashal*). Jesus' response to Peter, 'Have faith in God', suggests that something more alarming than the withering of a fig tree has occurred. In the scriptures the fig tree is an image often used of Israel (Jeremiah 8.13; Hosea 9.10; Micah 7.1). In these references Israel is also viewed as a vine (see also Mark 12.1–12), and the point is that the tree and vine failed to bear fruit. The following parable of the wicked tenants in the vineyard (12.1–12) confirms the *parabolic* nature of the action in the cursing and withering of the fig tree. It is the sign of the judgement of God, symbolically enacted on the temple in the 'cleansing' which threatened and warned of impending judgement. 'Have faith in God' is a word that points to the ongoing purpose of God. From the perspective of the narrative the way that purpose was to be fulfilled is mysteriously made clearer in the parable that is to follow. All of this would have been clear to Mark and his readers around 70 CE. The continuity of God's purpose was to be found in the mission to the nations, thus fulfilling the ideal that the temple should be a house of prayer for all of the nations.

**Catch word sayings connecting with 'faith', 11.23–25*

These sayings are introduced by a solemn '*Amen* I say to you [plural]'. They begin by stressing the effectiveness of unwavering *faith* which can move mountains. Whereas Jesus' response had been 'Have faith *in God*', this saying is about the *power* of faith. The link is then made to the role of *faith* in effective *prayer*, making *prayer* the new catch word. The next saying asserts that the one standing *praying* should forgive anyone whatever the grievance so that 'your heavenly father may forgive you your trespasses'. What appears as 11.26 in some manuscripts is an explanation of this saying taken from Matthew 6.15 and not original to Mark. Although these sayings divert attention from the larger theme being developed by Mark, they have been retained because they add something to the theme of faith which is important for Mark.

## Jesus' authority challenged in Jerusalem, 11.27–12.12

Jesus' return to the temple in Jerusalem is described but without any time reference. Whether this was a day or days later is not significant for Mark. What is important is made clear. Jesus has now run headlong into a conflict with Jewish authority.

*+'By what authority do you do these things?', 11.27–33*

Mark indicates that Jesus returned to Jerusalem where he was walking in the temple. What follows is narrated in the form of a testing inquiry story. In it the chief priests, scribes and elders (groups that constituted the Sanhedrin) came to Jesus. In the first passion prediction (8.31) Jesus said that he would be rejected by the elders and the chief priests and the scribes, naming the same groups, though placing the elders first instead of third. This story dramatically fulfils Jesus' prediction. Their coming to Jesus implies an official confrontation. The confrontation proceeds in dialogical fashion with (1) a challenge (testing inquiry) to Jesus' authority, (2) which he met with a counter-testing inquiry, (3) which they refused to answer, (4) and as a consequence, Jesus refused to answer their challenge.

Their objection was made in a question, which came in two forms. 'By what authority do you do these things? Or, who gave you this authority to do these things?' In this sequence there can be no doubt that the questions concern Jesus' actions in cleansing the temple. Obviously the Sanhedrin had not authorised him to do these things. Thus they objected to his actions and questioned his authority. Jesus' strategy was to ask them a question; if they would answer his question, he would answer theirs. His question concerned the baptism of John, whether it was from heaven or from men, a question that deliberately created a dilemma for his interrogators. Mark contextualises this question, reminding the readers that John was commonly held to be a prophet. Hence Jesus' opponents 'were afraid' to dismiss John's baptism. At the same time, they could not affirm its validity because they had not been baptised and, according to Mark, it had implications for the validity of the mission of Jesus. Consequently they declined to answer, saying 'We do not know'. Jesus took this as a refusal to answer, saying, 'Neither will I tell you by what authority I do these things'. This can be seen as a 'stand-off' in which there was no winner. Jesus had popular support while the Sanhedrin, with Rome's backing, held the reins of official power.

*+The wicked tenants in the vineyard, 12.1–12*

Mark introduces a new phase in the debate between Jesus and the chief priests, scribes and elders. No change of location, time or audience is indicated. Hence, when Mark says 'he spoke to them', he can only mean that Jesus spoke to the chief priests, scribes and elders. It is what he spoke to them that has changed. 'He began to speak to them in parables.' As in 4.2, only one parable follows at this point. The parable concerns a man who planted a vineyard, built a wall, winepress and tower, and then let it out to tenants. But when the man sent first one, then a second, and a third and many other servants to collect 'the rent', the tenants beat them shamefully or killed them. Last, he sent his 'beloved son', thinking 'at least they will honour him'. He too was killed and cast out of the vineyard. The parable is told with all the colour of a familiar story in which dialogues and actions are described in detail. With the story almost complete, the question was asked by Jesus, 'What will the owner of the vineyard do?' The question was rhetorical and answered by Jesus himself. 'He will come and destroy the tenants and give the vineyard to others.' The response of the chief priests, scribes and elders was an attempt to arrest Jesus because they knew he spoke the parable against them. But the attempt to arrest Jesus failed because they feared the crowd. The episode is concluded with a note indicating that Jesus departed.

There is no suggestion that this parable was anything but powerfully clear in its meaning to the chief priests, scribes and elders, against whom it was told. Although the parable had within it a warning to them, their response ensured that the threat of the parable would befall them. To understand this we need to understand first that the vineyard is a figure for Israel. See Jeremiah 8.13; Hosea 9.10; Micah 7.1 but especially Isaiah 5.1–7 in the LXX, with which the wording of the parable shares too much common language to be coincidental. That being the case, the tenants represent the leaders of Israel and God is to be understood as the owner. The servants represent the prophets, sent by God and abused and killed by Israel's leaders. Last of all the owner sent his beloved son. Mark understood him to be Jesus. Thus the parable reflects the rejection and execution of Jesus by Israel's leaders. God's action was to destroy them, and to give the vineyard (Israel) to others, that is, to other leaders. But Mark probably understood this to mean the vineyard was given to the nations, the Gentiles. The destruction of Jerusalem and the temple were seen as the judgement of God in response to the rejection and death of Jesus. See Eusebius, *History*, 3.7.7–9.

Mark also knew of the resurrection of Jesus. Thus Jesus asks, 'Have you never read this scripture?', quoting from Psalm 118.22–23. The early Christians used this text as a reference to the resurrection of Jesus. He is the stone rejected who became the head of the corner, the keystone. The Psalm goes on to pronounce this event as a marvellous paradox. The implacable opposition to Jesus by the Jewish authorities has now become set. At the same time Mark makes clear that Jesus remained popular with the crowd.

## Opponents and questions in Jerusalem, 12.13–37

Four questions follow, the first and second in the context of testing inquiry stories. A testing inquiry is a subtle variation on an objection story in which the inquiry is used in an attempt to elicit the grounds for an objection. The first inquiry came from the Pharisees and Herodians in an attempt to trap Jesus either into encouraging a 'crime' against Roman law or an indiscreet and unpopular policy. The second question was asked by the Sadducees in an attempt to show the absurdity of the teaching of the resurrection which Jesus affirmed. The third was a sincere and serious question asked by a scribe concerning which is the first commandment. Perhaps because this scribe asked a sincere and serious question, yet the scribes have appeared in the Gospel as opponents of Jesus (2.6–7, 16; 3.22; 7.1), Jesus himself posed the fourth question, based on what the scribes taught. In these questions the reader is brought in touch with the four groups opposed to Jesus in the Gospel. In addition to appearing in a coalition with the Herodians, the Pharisees often appear independently as opponents of Jesus or in coalition with other groups (see 2.16, 24; 7.1; 8.11; 10.2). The four questions place Jesus in conflict with the four groups that appear as his opponents in the Gospel. Because two groups appear in one question there is room for the scribes to be featured in two questions, once positively in a way that stands out against the negative tone of the other questions. This might suggest that Mark's criticism of the scribes is somewhat softer. This impression is dispelled by the final section of this episode of teaching, in which Jesus condemned the practice of the scribes in harsh terms (12.38–40).

Suggestions have been made concerning the arrangement of the four questions based on comparisons with the Rabbinic literature. While these are interesting, and might reflect Jewish practice in Jesus' day, it needs to be remembered that the written form of this material is centuries later than the time of Jesus and Mark, even though it could be based on earlier tradition. Perhaps the most interesting are the four questions found in Deuteronomy 6.20; Exodus 12.26; 13.8, 14, which were read in the Passover Haggadah and were supposedly put by the wise son, the wicked son, the pious son and the fourth son, who is instructed directly by the father. The usefulness of this and other Rabbinic traditions is that it shows awareness of four different kinds of question, about practice (12.13–17), mocking questions (12.18–27), questions about the law (12.28–34), and about apparent conflicts in scripture (12.35–37). On this see David Daube, *The New Testament and Rabbinic Judaism*, pp. 158–69.

*+Pharisees and Herodians: 'Is it lawful to pay tax to Caesar or not?', 12.13–17*

This testing inquiry story begins with the sending of certain Pharisees and Herodians to Jesus. The reader knows that the association of these two groups spells trouble for Jesus (see 3.6; 8.15). What follows is an attempt to *trap* him in a word. The trap was set by an insincere form of address which, nevertheless, ironically states the truth. Jesus is addressed as 'Teacher' (see 9.17), and it is affirmed, 'We know you are true, you do not seek favour from anyone; for you do not show partiality to anyone, but teach the way of God in truth'. The idea of partiality is expressed in terms of 'looking at [or 'taking account of'] the face'. Consequently, they imply that they should get a straight answer. Their question is, 'Is it lawful to pay tax to Caesar or not? Do we give or do we not give?' The poll-tax referred to here was a tax levied on every person. It was imposed by the Romans in 6 CE when Judaea, Samaria and Idumaea came directly under Roman rule. The trap was concealed in the question because to encourage or provoke the non-payment of Roman taxes was a crime against the Roman state. But to advocate the lawfulness of the tax would be to legitimise Roman government, with all the oppression involved, and worse, to deny Israel's freedom under God. Any answer seemed to lead to disastrous consequences. By addressing Jesus as one who fearlessly taught what was true, they challenged Jesus to answer, regardless of consequences.

Mark indicates that Jesus knew their hypocrisy, that is, that their words covered and hid their intentions. Thus he replied, 'Why do you test me?' He requested, 'Bring me a *denarius* [a Roman coin worth a daily wage] that I may see it'. Jesus did not have it himself. It was produced by his interrogators. He asked whose image and inscription appeared on the coin. Their answer, 'Caesar's'. His answer to their question was derived from this observation. 'Give to Caesar what belongs to Caesar and to God what belongs to God.' This pronouncement provides the climax to the story. It is formally a *clever* answer, one which seems to avoid a real answer because it does not specify what belongs to Caesar and what belongs to God. This decision is left for the hearers to make for themselves. But in the context of the production of the coin it is implied that the Roman coin belonged to Caesar and it is symbolic of all that Caesar provides. Those who make use of the benefits provided by Caesar must pay for them. What Jesus did was to challenge his opponents with the question of what belongs to God. Mark intends the reader to be aware of the masterful answer given by Jesus and to this end indicates its effect on his opponents. They marvelled at him. This is of course Mark's assessment. It means, in the first place, that Jesus had thwarted their plot against him. But Mark intended the reader to conclude more than this. Jesus' answer made even his opponents marvel. There is a hint of their awareness of the revelation of the divine in this response, which the telling of the story has highlighted powerfully.

*+Sadducees: 'In the resurrection whose wife will she be?' 12.18–27*

A second testing inquiry is introduced by reference to the coming of the Sadducees. Although they are mentioned only here in Mark, their influence is presupposed in the chief priests. But here the Sadducees are specifically mentioned because the question put by them to Jesus concerns a matter of their teaching, not an issue of their priestly office or political responsibility. Their question is a subtle attempt to expose grounds of *objection* to what they assumed was Jesus' belief in the resurrection.

The Sadducees, mentioned infrequently in the New Testament in the Gospels and Acts, probably take their name from Zadok, the high priest in the time of David whose family provided the high priest (see Ezekiel 40.45–46; 43.19; Ezra 7.2). Little can be gleaned about them from the New Testament and what we find there is unsympathetic to them. Josephus, also unsympathetic, provides us with our best source of information (see *War*, 2.8.14; 2.119; *Antiquities*, 13.5.9; 13.10.6; 18.1.4; 20.9.1; *Vita*). From his account it seems as if those described as 'chief priests' were the families from which the high priest was chosen. They were members of the wealthy aristocratic class, though not all members of this class were Sadducees. While they had been pervasively Hellenised, after the Maccabaean revolt they insisted on the freedom of temple worship. The law of Moses was authoritative for them and they were not bound by the prophets and the writings or the traditions acknowledged by the Pharisees. They came into conflict with Jesus over the teaching of the resurrection, which was not found in the law.

While the Sadducees addressed Jesus as 'Teacher', they did not respect him as such but sought to make him look silly on the assumption that he shared the Pharisaic teaching on the resurrection. The case outlined reads like a standard story used to disprove a case. The context is the provision outlined in Deuteronomy 25.5–10 (compare Genesis 38.8) to cover a man who dies without leaving children. Children born to the dead man's wife by his brother(s) were to bear the dead man's name. The story concerns seven brothers, each of whom married the same woman but died without leaving an heir. The story seemed to them to show how absurd ideas of resurrection were. In the resurrection, whose wife would she be? The absurdity of any solution proved the impossibility of the resurrection.

Jesus' answer came in three parts. First, he asserted that *they erred* because they did not know the scriptures or the power of God. His second and third points elaborate the first. Second, underestimating the power of God they failed to take account of the transformed nature of the resurrection life, in which there would be no marriage. Third, they failed to know the scripture upon which they claimed to base their beliefs. There in the law, the Pentateuch, it is written, 'I am the God of Abraham, the God of Isaac and the God of Jacob' (Exodus 3.6, 15, 16). Jesus concluded that God is not the God of the dead but of the living. From this he argued that the patriarchs were still alive (see 4 Maccabees 7.19; 16.25). His affirmation is based on a way of reading scripture that was understood in the Jewish groups of his time, but also on a conviction of the faithfulness of God. Thus both assumptions, that they do not know the scriptures and that they did not know the power of God, are present in the third point, though the particular form of the assumption about the power of God remains hidden and unexplained. Nevertheless, because of this, Jesus concluded as he had begun his answer, 'You greatly *err*'.

The objection raised by the Sadducees was resolved by the saying of Jesus. Resolution is for the reader rather than the Sadducees, therefore Mark takes no account of their response.

### +*A scribe: 'Which is the first commandment?'* 12.28–34

A new scene is introduced by indicating that one of the scribes came to Jesus when he heard that Jesus answered 'them' (the Sadducees) well. This might imply that the man was himself a Sadducee. The scribes were not confined to any one 'sect'. This is the first of three episodes featuring the scribes. What follows is an inquiry story in which the scribe questioned Jesus concerning which was the first commandment of all. A simple answer might have indicated the first of the ten commandments as found in Exodus 20.3. Jesus appealed rather to the form found in Deuteronomy 6.4–5, known as the Shema, which was recited daily by faithful Jews. Though asked for only the first commandment, his answer combined this with Leviticus 19.18 to provide a second. In answering in this way Jesus placed the two commandments above all others. This approach cut through all the details of commandments to what was really essential. Discussion of such principles is evidenced in the Rabbinic literature and attributed to Hillel and Akiba in the first and second centuries CE. The scribe approved of Jesus' answer. His response was largely a repetition of the texts appealed to by Jesus. He did, however, go beyond Jesus by specifically asserting the secondary nature of whole-burnt offering and sacrifice, a view clearly taught by some of the prophets (1 Samuel 15.22; Jeremiah 7.22; Hosea 6.6). This has been understood in two different ways. From one perspective, all of the detailed laws, of which there were over six hundred prohibitions and commands, were taken to be expressions of the way two principles of love towards God and neighbour were to be fulfilled. Alternatively, the two principles of love can be taken as the true meaning of all of the commandments. From this point of view the love principles become the test of the applicability of the numerous specific commandments. The latter seems to be the understanding advocated by Mark.

If the incident began with the scribe's acknowledgement that Jesus had answered well, it now concludes with Jesus' acknowledgement that the scribe had answered thoughtfully, which was expressed by telling him, 'You are not far from the kingdom of God'. This appears to be a *commendation* of this scribe's response to Jesus. Yet to be not far from the kingdom is nevertheless to fail to enter it. There was no further response from the scribe and the incident concludes with the indication that no one dared to ask Jesus anything. This conclusion tends to override the positive sense given by Jesus' concluding words. Jesus' words silenced their questions.

+*'How is it that the scribes say that the Christ is the Son of David?', 12.35–37*

Whereas the previous questions were asked by those in dialogue with Jesus, Jesus introduced a fourth question himself, attributing the substance of it to the scribes who dare not ask. The episode takes the form of a correction story in which Jesus corrects the assumptions of the scribes about the Messiah by asking his own question based on Psalm 110.1.

The incident is introduced by indicating that 'Jesus *answered* and said while he was teaching in the temple'. The temple location is a continuation from 11.27, but a new episode is signalled by this introductory quotation formula. The reference to formal teaching makes clear that this is a public situation, as is confirmed by reference to the crowd in 12.37. Jesus' question was, 'How is it that the scribes say that the Christ is the Son of David?' Mark is using 'Christ' as a translation of the Semitic 'Messiah'. The scribes, as the teachers of the law, were not alone in thinking of the Davidic descent of the Messiah. This was a widely accepted view amongst the Jews and early Christians from Paul (Romans 1.3; 15.12) to the Gospel writers, including Mark (10.47, 48; 11.9–10). Thus it is unlikely that Mark wished to repudiate this view. Attributing the view to the scribes gives weight to it as a view based on the scriptures.

In response Jesus quoted from Psalm 110.1. Assuming, as was common at the time, that David was the author, and asserting that in writing he was inspired by the Spirit, the quotation, 'The lord said to my Lord', is understood as meaning that God said to the Messiah (referred to as 'my Lord' by David), 'Sit at my right hand'. Although the early Christians used this text as a prophecy of the exaltation of the risen Jesus to the right hand of God (Acts 2.34–35), the only point made in this context is that David called the Messiah Lord. The question this raised was 'David called him Lord so how can he be his son?' Jesus did not reject the one on the basis of the other, but stated the matter in the form of a riddle. Romans 1.3–4 states of God's son that he was of the seed of David, according to the flesh, designated Son of God in power according to the Holy Spirit. But while Paul saw this designation or revelation in the resurrection, it seems that Mark understood that it took place at the baptism of Jesus, Mark 1.9–11.

Mark did not understand this correction as a repudiation of Davidic messiahship but exposes a mystery hidden in the affirmation. Son of David? Yes! But also son of God. Jesus raised the question in the form of a riddle which the crowd could not be expected to solve, but the reader is in a much better position to do so. Nevertheless the big crowd listened to him gladly, eagerly being drawn to the mystery of his teaching.

### +Denouncing the scribes, 12.38–40

This episode is a continuation of Jesus' teaching to the crowd in the temple. It is a warning in a correction story. It is linked to the previous episode via the scribes. The idiom in which the warning is expressed, 'Watch out for the scribes', suggests the term 'hypocrites' which, though not used, crystallises the details of the criticism. They seek public recognition and prominent places in synagogues and feasts, yet they devour the houses of widows and say long prayers. Certainly the seeking of prominence is opposed to the way Jesus set out for his disciples (see 8.34–38; 9.33–37; 10.35–45). Because widows were the epitome of helplessness, criticism of the exploitation of them was the more forceful and was supported by prophetic tradition. This criticism makes sense if the scribes from Jerusalem were mainly aristocratic and rich Sadducees infamous for their exploitation of the poor (see Josephus, *Antiquities*, 20.180–181, 205–207). Jesus' condemnation of them was forceful. 'They will receive greater condemnation.'

### +The widow's offering, 12.41–44

Linked to the previous episode by reference to widows (12.40), this commendation story is set opposite the treasury, which might indicate a special room in the temple but more likely indicates the chests that were placed in the court of the women. Jesus was seated watching those who made their gifts. The audience on this occasion was his disciples, whom he called to him (12.43). The subject for discussion was raised by what was going on in front of them where the people were making their gifts. Many rich people made large gifts and a poor widow donated two small coins, the smallest in circulation. But that was all that she had. The commendation of the widow is in stark contrast to the scribes, whose exploitation was condemned in the previous episode. It is implied that the disciples were impressed by the large sums of money donated by the rich. In this context Jesus made a startling pronouncement, 'This poor widow has cast in more than all of those casting into the treasury'. Jesus clarified his point by noting that the rich gave but a small proportion of their wealth, while the widow had given her whole livelihood, not even halving her 'wealth' by giving only one coin. Though these coins were worth very little, about one per cent of a *denarius*, which was the pay for a day labourer, it was all she had. Being a widow she had few if any ways of 'earning' any money. Thus she is *commended* for her generosity. This teaching, aimed at transforming the values of the disciples within the narrative, was also aimed at the reader.

## The temple and the Son of Man, 13.1–37

The temple was the focus of Jesus' action and teaching from the moment he entered Jerusalem, when the Lord came to his temple (Malachi 3.1). His coming was an act of judgement, first expressed in the 'cleansing' of the temple. He was now unequivocally to predict its destruction.

### +*The Lord abandons the temple and predicts its desolation, 13.1–2*

If Jesus' Jerusalem visit began with his *entry* into the temple (11.11), Mark now records his *exit* from the temple in the form of a correction story. His exit with his disciples was the opportunity for one of them to remark to him on the wonderful stones and buildings that constituted the temple. The comment drew Jesus' response in the form of a startling pronouncement, 'Do you see these great buildings? There will not be left here a stone upon a stone that is not thrown down.' Though expressed in negative terms, this prediction of the destruction of the temple is definite and certain. On this note the scene ends, but these words were to become the basis of the inquiry which constitutes the next scene.

The remainder of this chapter is taken up with the question that arose from Jesus' prediction and his complex set of answers.

### +*The inquiry*: +*'When will these things be?', 13.3–4*

The new scene is set on the Mount of Olives, on the eastern side of the old city overlooking the temple mount. Jesus was alone with Peter, James, John and Andrew, the four who were first called by Jesus, 1.16–20. The order of the four differs because Andrew has been displaced in the interest of naming together Peter, James and John (see 9.2; 14.33 and Eusebius, *History*, 2.1.3). The teaching response of Jesus in the remainder of the chapter is ostensibly addressed to these four, though it has a wider audience (13.14). Jesus did not withdraw from the crowd to teach the disciples. The four were alone with Jesus when they asked their question (cf. 4.10–12). Jesus made no comment about the esoteric nature of his teaching, though this might be implied by the restricted audience. No specific spokesperson is named. Characteristic of an inquiry story, the inquiry is important rather than the inquirer, who is not named. The inquiry is the pretext for the teaching given in this chapter.

The request, 'Tell us' asks two questions:

'When will *these things* be?'

'What is *the* sign that *all these things* are about to be fulfilled?'

The context in which Mark has set this question leaves no room to doubt that 'these things' concerned the destruction of the temple, which Jesus had recently predicted. Yet the double form of the question is overloaded if nothing more than this was intended. Reference to 'the fulfilment of all things' has about it a ring which suggests the end of the age. Matthew (24.3) certainly interpreted Mark in this sense. The term which is translated 'to be fulfilled' is the verb connected to 'the end'. The four disciples assumed that the destruction of the temple must be part and parcel of the events bringing in the end of the age. Consequently, Jesus was asked for a 'rundown' on his 'eschatology'. After all, the Lord who suddenly comes to his temple ushers in the day of the Lord, the day of judgement, Malachi 3.1–5.

The question, 'When?', was intended to include the end of the age. But this was not enough. They needed to know *the* unmistakable *sign* that signalled the end.

## Mark 13 and apocalyptic

This eschatological perspective is characteristic of apocalyptic writings. The term *apocalypse*, derived from the Greek word meaning 'uncovering', is frequently used in contexts relating to the uncovering of heavenly mysteries, that is, revelation. The word, used at the beginning of the last book in the New Testament, gives it its title, Revelation. Revelation has a close relationship to the discourse of Jesus in Mark 13, though closer to the form of Matthew 24, which was used to structure the book. Recognition of the apocalyptic genre is possible when it is noted that Revelation is closely related to a tradition of Jewish literature that became relatively common in the centuries immediately prior to the beginning of Christianity. While parts of Isaiah show a tendency in this direction, it is with the book of Daniel, especially chapters 7–12, that the literary development reaches something like a complete form. In the *Pseudepigrapha* a number of works are rightly recognised as apocalypses and some (see 1 Enoch; 4 Ezra; 2 Baruch), like Mark 13 and Revelation, show a literary dependence on Daniel. Apocalyptic literature reflects scribal activity as scriptures from the past are reworked to maintain relevance for the present. Not all works that do this are apocalyptic. Those that are interpret the scriptures in relation to the end.

In apocalyptic literature revelation takes place through vision (the dreams of Daniel 1–6 are a variation) or mediation by heavenly messengers (angels). In Mark Jesus functions as a heavenly messenger. The heavenly voice instructed Peter, James and John to 'Listen to him' (9.7). Another feature of apocalyptic is the pessimistic view of the world. Until God breaks in on the world dominated by evil, the righteous can expect only hardship and suffering and, indeed, a heightening of this as the end approaches. It is because the world is dominated by evil that the faithful look to God to intervene and save them. This is the perspective of Mark 13 (see especially 13.20).

Mark 13, like most apocalypses, is pseudonymous. Though not attributed to a notable figure from the *ancient* past like Adam, Enoch or one of the patriarchs, it is not an original unified discourse of Jesus but a composition by Mark and placed on the lips of Jesus. It speaks of events of the writers past and present as if they were future (from the perspective of Jesus). False prophets, false Messiahs and the elect are not mentioned in the rest of Mark and reflect the present struggle in which Mark found himself. Pseudonymity was a device for turning the narration of events past and present into fulfilled prophecy, providing assurance about the veracity of Jesus' word about the end.

Mark 13 is a sustained discourse unlike any other recorded in Mark. But although it lacks any reference to the kingdom of God, so characteristic of the preaching of Jesus, it seems likely that Jesus stood in a tradition of prophets who predicted the destruction of the temple (Jeremiah 7.1–5; 26.1–24; Micah 3.10–12). This is confirmed by charges brought against him at his trial (Mark 14.58; 15.29 and note Matthew 23.38; John 2.19). Although Jesus' response in Mark 13 appears to be composite there is no reason to posit a Jewish source. Its composite nature, like that of Mark 4, is also made up of a question by the disciples followed by Jesus' composite teaching response. As in apocalypses, there is a parable (of the fig tree, 13.28–31), and the bulk of the chapter is made up of prediction and warning. Jesus' answer from 13.5 to 27 is reasonably coherent, but 13.28–31, 32–37 are loosely connected by catch words. This method of constructing a discourse may seem strange to us. It was a readily recognised literary approach in Mark's day. Thus we should not expect a closely knit argument flowing throughout the discourse.

## Implications for dating Mark

The association of the destruction of the temple with the end of the age makes unlikely that Mark was written much later than the destruction of the temple in 70 CE. It soon became apparent that 'the end is not yet'.

### *Jesus' answer: 'Watch out, be alert', 13.5–37*

Jesus' answer is formally addressed to Peter, James, John and Andrew (13.3), but Mark clearly has the reader in mind and even addresses the reader directly, 'Let the reader understand' (13.14). This is a signal that this discourse incorporates the situation of Mark's readers and not just the situation of the four disciples named.

It has been likened to the farewell address of the testaments known to us in the farewell words of the patriarchs in Genesis, which became the basis of *The Testaments of the Twelve Patriarchs*. Jesus' discourse shares with these the warnings concerning the future, making the reader aware of issues that reach well beyond the passion story that follows. Nevertheless, the parallel breaks down because the discourse was given in response to a specific question and was not a farewell speech given on the night Jesus was betrayed.

From beginning to end it is a call to watchfulness, 13.5, 9, 23, 33, 34, 35, 37. But watchfulness has varied meanings which need to be noted carefully. Jesus' answer is introduced by a formula indicating that he began to say to them. This suggests an extended discourse and the warning that follows is in a number of discrete sections, the first two being introduced by 'Watch out', 13.5, 9. These two sections are followed by another two (13.14–20 and 13.21–23) dealing with the same themes as the first two but in the reverse order, so that it can be described as a chiastic structure where the themes are arranged in the order of $A^1$ (13.5–8), $B^1$ (13.9–13), $B^2$ (13.14–20), $A^2$ (13.21–23). The reprise of the theme is not a repetition but a restatement and development so that $A^2$ develops $A^1$ and $B^2$ develops $B^1$. At the conclusion of the four sections there is another call to watchfulness binding 13.5–23 together with an opening and closing use of 'Watch'.

A[1] Warning: 'Don't be led astray, the end is not yet', 13.5–8 (see 13.21–23)

The first warning, 'Watch out', concerns being led astray (13.5–6, cf. 13.22) and is given in the knowledge that many will be led astray by those who come 'in my name' claiming 'I am'. It is natural to understand this as 'in Jesus' name', see 9.38. But this makes little sense because the claim 'I am' implies impostors. Hence 'my name' must mean 'Christ' understood as a messianic claim. Josephus notes messianic claimants in the first century and in the lead up to the Jewish war, although the best known messianic claimant was Simeon Bar Kochba, who led the second great revolt against Rome in 132 CE. The warning that there will be many false Messiahs is supported by the specific reference to 'false Christs' in 13.22 when this theme is re-run. In addition they are warned that they will hear of wars and rumours of wars, all things that must take place. 'But the end is not yet', 13.7. Jesus was asked for '*the sign*' that heralds the end. He began by speaking of *signs* that signalled 'the end is *not* yet'. Wars are further elaborated in specific terms of nation against nation and kingdom against kingdom. Other disasters are also listed, widespread earthquakes and famines. While such events are common signs in apocalyptic literature, these too fall under the heading, 'the end is not yet'. These things are 'the beginning of the birth pangs' (13.8), which should be understood as those pains which must be endured before the birth of the messianic age. This leads naturally enough into the next section, which is a warning about the sufferings to follow.

B[1] Warning: 'You will be delivered up, betrayed', 13.9–13 (see 13.14–20)

A new theme is signalled by a second use of 'Watch out', 13.9, 'Watch out for yourselves'. The warning concerns what is to overtake the *followers* of Jesus and is reminiscent of the description of the fate of Jesus, betrayed, delivered to the Sanhedrin, beaten. Reference to being 'delivered' or 'betrayed' (13.9, 11, 12) to the Sanhedrin assumes the local Jewish courts, not the Great Sanhedrin of Jerusalem. The beatings mentioned were imposed by the courts but carried out in the synagogue, a fate Paul experienced five times (2 Corinthians 11.24). No one better fits the description of one who bore witness before kings and governors than Paul

(Acts 23.33; 25.6, 23). Reference to the necessity of proclaiming the gospel to all the nations makes good sense also in relation to the apostle to the nations (see Romans 9–11). Mark 13.10 asserts that the gospel must first be proclaimed to all the nations before the end comes. Thus again Mark has asserted, this time indirectly, the end is not yet.

Just as John the Baptist preached and was delivered up, Jesus preached and was delivered up, so also will the followers of Jesus preach and be delivered up. This patterning of history is characteristic of apocalyptic. Facing trial they are not to be anxious for they will give *testimony* (inspired by the Holy Spirit). The law court setting colours the notion of testimony, which is also understood as universal witness to the 'gospel' (13.9–11). The situation of trial is further elaborated by reference to pressures and threats which produce intrigue and betrayal even amongst close members of families, and the way families will be divided so that one member of the family delivers another up to death. There is also the implied division within families caused by the gospel. See Micah 7.6, which is quoted in the Q passage found in Matthew 10.34–39 which Mark presupposes. Jesus predicts that his followers will be hated by everyone for his name's sake, see 1 Peter 4.14. Hard times lie ahead, but those who endure to 'the end' will be saved (13.13) at the coming of the Son of Man in judgement, 13.7. Yet Mark does not deny that those who were faithful to death would be saved, though this issue remained unclarified (see 1 Thessalonians 4.13–18).

### B² Warning: 'Flee to the mountains', 13.14–20 (see 13.9–13)

The previous two sections were introduced by the atch word 'Watch out'. This section assumes that 'the abomination that makes desolate' will be seen and exhorts, 'Let the *reader* understand', noting the wider audience (than the four disciples) and explicitly marking out the words 'the abomination that makes desolate' from Daniel 12.11 (LXX), there referring to the altar to Zeus which Antiochus Epiphanes set up in the temple in 168 BCE (1 Maccabees 1.54, 59). This implies a repetition of that event like the action threatened by Caligula or perhaps fulfilled when Titus was proclaimed emperor in the temple precincts (see Josephus of War 6.6.1). Both Matthew and Luke have understood Mark to mean that the destruction of the temple was also involved and, for Luke, Jerusalem also (see Matthew 24.15 and 23.38 and Luke 21.20).

The sign of desolation, which the reader is called on to recognise *whenever* it occurs (and Mark is quite indefinite on this), is the moment for those in Judaea to take flight to the mountains. While Jerusalem was itself in the hills, this call was to escape to the desolate mountainous regions, confirming that the Jewish war is in view, with the terrible destruction of city and temple. While 13.14–17 read like a specific description of that situation, 13.18 introduces uncertainty with the call for prayer that the flight would not be in the winter. This 'affliction' is raised to an eschatological level by asserting that there had been nothing like it from the beginning of creation until now, nor would there be anything like it again, a theme which echoes Daniel 12.1. To heighten this further it is asserted that the affliction was so severe that no flesh would be saved unless the Lord shortened the time, which he did for the sake of the *elect*. The previous section ended with a call to endure to the end, 13.13. Now the elect, in the midst of terrible affliction, are assured that the Lord would shorten the time of affliction for their sake, 13.22. Although apocalyptic literature commonly presents a fixed plan for the last days, so disastrous is the affliction here that the Lord shortened the time.

### A$^2$ Warning: False Christs, false prophets, signs and wonders, 13.21–23 (see 13.5–8)

The next section beginning, 'Then' implies either the time of the great affliction or at its termination, and clarifies those who come 'in my name' asserting 'I am', 13.6. Thus the warning, 'If anyone comes saying "Behold, here is the Christ", or "Behold there", do not believe'. The warning goes on to tell of false Christs and false prophets giving signs and wonders, to lead astray, if it were possible, even the *elect*. The false prophets predict where and when the Christ was to appear, while the false Christs claimed 'I am'. Josephus draws attention to various figures commonly called 'sign prophets', who called people out into the desert promising them signs of deliverance (see *Antiquities*, 19.162; 20.167–172, 188; *War*, 2.258–263; 6.285–286). That these were messianic figures seems probable and they throw light on the situation referred to here. The warning asserts, 'Do not believe [them]'. Consequently, even their appearance is no more a sign of the end than the reports of wars and rumours of wars. The end is not yet.

This whole section (13.5–23) concludes as it began with a call to 'Watch out', here without any specific reference but covering all the warnings given to this point, with the assurance 'I have foretold all things to you'. The motto is 'forewarned is forearmed' as long as you 'watch out'.

## The end is the end, 13.24–27

The previous sections have been connected. A break is now signalled by 'But', introducing a scene situated in the days *after* that affliction. There is no clue as to how long the affliction was to be, only that it was not to be as long as it might have been. When that is brought to an end then 'the sun will be darkened, the moon will not give its light, the stars will fall from heaven, and the powers in the heavens will be shaken'. Such cosmic portents are commonly associated with the day of the Lord (see Isaiah 13.10; 34.4; Ezekiel 32.7–8; Joel 2.10, 31; 3.15; Revelation 6.12–14; 8.12). This should not be read as the signal warning of the end. *It is the end itself* which is concurrent with these portents, 'then they shall see the Son of Man coming with clouds' (see Daniel 7.13–14). The early Christian use of this text transformed 'one like a son of man' into 'the Son of Man', though it seems that this tendency was already to be found in the Jewish interpretation of the time. Naturally the identification of Jesus with this figure was exclusive to the early Christians. If the Son of Man was coming with clouds, was his destination to earth for judgement, or to God's throne in heaven? (See Daniel 7.9, 13–14.) The latter seems to be the case because he sends out the 'angels' to gather the elect from the four winds, from the borders of earth to the borders of heaven. This separation of the elect is to be seen as the first act of judgement in saving the elect. As in Daniel, the Son of Man is associated with clouds, great power and glory (see 8.38–9.1). For Mark, as for Daniel, the power and glory belong to God and his kingdom, and their association with the Son of Man signals that he is the emissary of God. In Daniel the Son of Man is a heavenly figure associated with God and opposed to the beastly powers that arise from the sea and plunder the earth. This imagery of the beastly powers, derived from the ancient creation myths, has come to represent the demonic powers in apocalyptic writings. That the demonic powers are at work in the great affliction is implied by 13.14, and this is the way the tradition was understood by Paul (see 1 Thessalonians 4.13–5.11; 2 Thessalonians 2.1–11) and Revelation.

## Learn a parable from the fig tree and other sayings, 13.28–31

This parable and its associated sayings do not fit easily at this point. On the reading of Mark 13 set out above the request for a clear sign has not been satisfied. Rather, Jesus has called for watchfulness. Now there is a parable which seems to imply that a series of signs has been given. The parable is based on the fig tree. It is not likely that there is any connection with the 'cursing of the fig tree' of 11.12–14, 20–25. The fig tree was one of the most common trees in Palestine. It is notable too because, unlike many other trees in the area, it loses its leaves in winter. Thus the growth of leaves heralds the approaching summer. The parable involves recognising that when 'these things' happen 'he is near' or 'it is near', 13.29. The Greek only implies the subject of the verb, which could be 'he' or 'it'. If 'he', it would seem to refer to the Son of Man; if 'it', the end. In terms of the flow of the chapter, given that 13.7 has stated 'the end is not yet', it would make sense if it is the end that is imminent. But what are 'these things' that constitute the sign that the end is near? If Jesus asserts that the end is not yet in 13.5–23, can this mean that 'these things' refer to 13.24–27? But this is the description of the end itself.

A way around this problem is to allow that, while Mark 13.5–23 teaches that the end is not yet, this does not exclude a sense that the end is imminent. Difficulties remain with this view in that the gospel must first be preached to all the nations. But Mark, with Paul in his sights, might well have thought that this task was well advanced. Certainly it is unlikely that Mark would have included 13.30 had he not thought that the fulfilment of all things was imminent. It is despairing exegesis to argue that 'this generation' which will not pass away until 'all these things' have come to pass is anything but those alive at the time. The earlier part of the discourse was directed to a situation in which the followers of Jesus must struggle with persecution and calamity, in which false prophets and false Messiahs offer false hopes. Now, in this parable, the problem is complacency in a situation where nothing seems to be happening, providing early evidence of problems caused by 'the delay of the *parousia*'. As with apocalyptic writing, Mark adds a saying affirming the binding nature of these words (compare Revelation 22.19).

A parable and sayings about watchfulness, 13.32–37

This group of sayings emphatically denies that any except the Father knows the day or the hour of the end and was designed specifically to deny signs warning of the end. Because of this the call to watchfulness and alertness is redoubled, 13.33. 'Watch out, be alert, for you do not know when the time is.' The parable concerns a householder going on a journey, giving authority and tasks to each of his servants and the command to the doorkeeper to be watchful. No indication of when the householder might return is given. The lesson is, 'be alert and ready because you do not know when the lord of the house comes'. This is the call to constant vigilance, being always ready. The warning, 'lest coming he finds you sleeping', sets up a resonance for the reader coming to the narrative of Jesus' prayer in Gethsemane where, having told Peter, James and John to be watchful (14.34), three times Jesus came only to find them sleeping (14.37–42). The whole section concludes, 'What I say to you I say to all, be watchful'.

## PASSION AND RESURRECTION, 14.1–16.8

### Betrayal and arrest, 14.1–52

**The Passover plot, 14.1–2*

The passion story begins with the announcement of the approach of Passover and Unleavened Bread, both of which commenced on the 15th of the Jewish month Nisan and the latter continued until Nisan 21. The scene of this incident is set two days before Passover. The Jewish day runs from sunset to sunset. Given that 15th Nisan commenced Thursday evening, two days before is probably the Wednesday, being 13th Nisan. If Mark was using a Roman calendar, it might have been Tuesday. The first scene of the passion is set on this day, which is the first firm date that Mark has given. Only on one occasion (11.12) has it been made clear that Mark intends a sequence of two successive days. Thus Mark does not provide an outline of Jesus' last week in Jerusalem. Given the sequence of the narrative of Jesus' Galilean mission, it seems likely that Mark intends a somewhat longer period in Jerusalem. Now, as the passion approaches, Mark provides a calendar of events which highlights the importance of the events of these days.

The plot was initiated by the chief priests and scribes (see 8.31; 11.27 where the elders are also mentioned). They *sought* to arrest Jesus and put him to death. Mark evaluates this as an act of treachery, probably anticipating the betrayal by Judas (14.10–11, 18–20), though the chief priests and scribes initiated the treachery so that it might be implied that Judas acted in response to their initiative. Their plan was to avoid an arrest on the feast because of the popularity of Jesus with the crowds of pilgrims at the festival. Yet Jesus was arrested on the evening the Passover commenced. What might have changed their plans was the treachery of Judas, which offered a soft arrest away from the crowds, averting any threat of riots, at least at the arrest.

The announcement of the plot (14.1–2) forms an *inclusio* with the description of the treachery of Judas (14.10–11). We could say that the anointing is sandwiched between the two sides of the plot to arrest Jesus. Given this perspective, it seems that those who plotted against Jesus unwittingly co-operated with Jesus in the mission for which he was being prepared in the anointing.

### +*The anointing of Jesus for burial: 'in memory of her', 14.3–9*

Mark sets the next scene in the house of Simon the leper in Bethany where, it is probably implied, Jesus was staying with his disciples during this visit to Jerusalem. All four Gospels have anointing stories. Only Matthew follows Mark closely, putting the story (in a slightly abbreviated form, as was his custom) in the same context. The only significant difference is that Matthew (26.8) names the disciples as those who objected to the waste, whereas Mark indicates only that the objection was made by unspecified people at the dinner (14.4). Given that Matthew often softens Mark's criticism of the disciples, this is a strange reversal. Matthew may be making clear what is implied by Mark because the narrative implies that the disciples were with Jesus. Matthew follows Mark's saying that what the woman did will be spoken of, in memory of her, wherever the gospel is preached. Paradoxically, her name is not mentioned.

John also sets his anointing story in Bethany. There are some notable agreements with Mark, in the description of the perfumed oil, its value, and the sayings about anointing his body for burial and about always having the poor. Most of the rest of the story differs from Mark. In John, Jesus was in Bethany *prior* to his entry to Jerusalem. He was at the house of Mary, Martha and Lazarus.

Objection to the waste was made by one of the disciples, Judas Iscariot. Mary anointed Jesus' feet, not his head.

Luke (7.36–50) sets his story somewhere in Galilee in the house of Simon, a *Pharisee*. The person anointing Jesus is described as a sinner and Simon objected, not over waste but to the fact that Jesus permitted such an action by a sinful woman. While the hospitality of Simon implies some relation to the Jesus movement, Jesus contrasted his grudging gratitude with the overflowing gratitude of the woman who had been forgiven much. There is no reference to the anointing as a preparation for burial and no saying about the poor. The woman is not named and there is absolutely no reason to identify her with Mary Magdalene, although this was done in the fourth century and is commonly assumed by readers of the Gospels today.

The Markan story is set in Bethany, in the house of Simon *the leper*. This as another instance of the Jesus mission operating by household hospitality. The mission charge to the twelve (6.10) lays down the principle of using a single household in each town or place. Hence it is likely that Jesus and the disciples were guests in the house of Simon for the duration of their stay. Given the laws of uncleanness it is likely that Simon was a leper cleansed by Jesus, whose gratitude was expressed in hospitality to the Jesus mission. But this story is not about Simon. His hospitality is the context for the story of the anointing of Jesus. It is an objection /correction /commendation story but in the context of the passion story the focus is on the anointing of Jesus for burial. Both facets are important in the context of Mark. Indeed, it is through the objection that Jesus clarifies the purpose of the anointing.

Anointing the head of an honoured guest with oil was customary amongst the well to do. But the failure of Simon to do this, a deficiency made up for by the woman, is not Mark's point (contrast Luke). The Markan story stresses the precious quality of the oil. The description of the jar or vase indicates that it was of spherical shape, not necessarily that it was made of alabaster. Reference to the breaking of the jar makes clear that all of the oil was expended on the anointing. Like the widow who gave her two coins (12.41–44), this woman gave all. Mark has enclosed chapter 13, with its warning of doom and destruction for the temple and the nation, with these two stories about 'true devotion', 'true religion' of two women, two stories of hope in the midst of despair.

The anonymous *objection* lays stress on the substance rather than the objectors. The objection brings to light the value of the oil, more than three hundred *denarii*, that is, the earnings of a day labourer for almost a year. The purpose of the objection was to assert that the proceeds from the sale of the oil should have been used for the poor. This criticism comes from the ethos of the Jesus mission with its concern for the poor. For this reason it is likely that Matthew has rightly read Mark in attributing this objection to the disciples. Mark has not used anonymity to shield the disciples but to focus totally on the objection rather than the objectors.

Jesus' response is a *correction* of those who made the *objection* and a *commendation* of the woman. He defended the woman on several grounds: (1) 'She has done a good thing for me'; (2) 'You always have the poor . . . but you do not always have me'; (3) 'She has anointed my body for burial in advance'. In this way the woman's action is made a prophetic action, pointing to Jesus' imminent death and burial. It is notable that in Mark Jesus' body was not properly prepared for burial after the crucifixion (contrast John 19.38–42) and the women who later came to perform that duty found an empty tomb (16.1). While Jesus' mission was committed to the poor it was these special circumstances that justified the exceptional behaviour of the woman. The saying about the poor is the crux pronouncement, 'You always have the poor with you and you are able to do good for them whenever you will, but you do not always have me [with you]'. By making the action done to himself exceptional, justified in the context of his impending death, Jesus' saying in this story has become a manifesto flying a policy of commitment to the poor.

The final saying (14.9) further brings out the significance of the woman's action in the context of the passion narrative. So integral is it to the story of what happens to Jesus in the passion that wherever the gospel is preached, what she did will be spoken of. Mark, followed by Matthew, has ensured that this is so. 'Crucified, dead, buried' have become statements of the creeds and this story elaborates the details of the burial of Jesus. Yet, while the story is told in memory of her, her name is lost in the mists of time. Perhaps that is because, for Mark, what she did as a prophetic sign was more important than her identity as the one who performed the act. Mark had no interest in elevating the woman's status to that of a saint. His intention was to make her action prophetic of the coming death and burial of Jesus.

*+Judas, one of the twelve: betrayal for silver, 14.10–11*

The plot, announced in 14.1–2, is now formulated. By placing the initiative with the chief priests and scribes (14.1–2), Mark implies that Judas was corrupted by them. The enormity of what he was about to do is brought out by the stark opening. 'And Judas Iscariot who was one of the twelve went to the chief priests to betray him to them.' If the virtuous act of the woman in anointing Jesus has remained anonymous, this diabolical act has not. Mark concisely makes three points about the consequence of this action: (1) The chief priests rejoiced. This suggests a scenario even better than they had hoped for. (2) They offered to give Judas silver (money), though no sum is named. Was this the inducement? Though Mark has noted the offer subsequent to the treacherous visit of Judas, this could be understood as the explanation (after the fact) for the treachery of Judas. (3) Judas sought how to betray Jesus 'conveniently/easily'. It is this final point that suggests that it was the co-operation of Judas that made possible the arrest of Jesus at the Passover festival.

*+Preparation for Passover, 14.12–16*

Mark announced a new scene with the arrival of the first day of Unleavened Bread, when the Passover was sacrificed. The problem with this scenario is that the lambs for Passover were sacrificed on the afternoon of 14th Nisan. The suggestion that Jesus was using a different Jewish calendar is of no help with this problem. If Mark were not using a Jewish calendar but a Roman one, this would be on the same day. Whatever the problems we have with Mark's method of dating, there is no doubt that the Gospel portrays Jesus with his disciples preparing to celebrate the Passover. Preparation began with a question from the disciples to Jesus. 'Where do you wish us to go to prepare for you to eat the Passover?' Whereas Jesus had enjoyed hospitality in Bethany, travelling by day up to Jerusalem, pilgrims celebrated the Passover in Jerusalem. Jesus' response was to instruct two disciples to go into the city, where they would see a man carrying a water jar, to follow him and, where he entered, to inquire of the householder, 'The teacher says, "where is my room where I may eat the Passover with my disciples?"' He told them that the householder would show them a large upper room prepared and ready; 'and there you will prepare for us'. From this we can see that the idiom of the disciples' question to Jesus, which referred only to him eating the Passover, presupposed that they would be eating it *with him*. Mark tells us that they went out [from Bethany?] and came into the city [Jerusalem] and found everything as Jesus had said. There they prepared the Passover. The description of the sending out of the two disciples foretelling exactly what they would find closely echoes the sending out of the two disciples to prepare for Jesus' initial entry to Jerusalem (11.1–7). The point of both of these prophetic fulfilments is to stress the divine purpose in these events.

*+Passover and the sign of betrayal, 14.17–21*

Mark again indicates a new scene by noting a time change. Evening had come. Mark did not, in this instance divide the days at evening, perhaps adapting his idiom to suit his readers. At evening Jesus came with the twelve. It is possible to read this as meaning Jesus and the twelve plus the two disciples sent earlier. Almost certainly Mark includes the two sent earlier with the twelve. Perhaps he supposes that the two, having prepared the Passover, rejoined Jesus and returned with him and the other disciples in the evening.

The meal scene depicts the group reclining and eating. This is the setting for an astonishing revelation by Jesus as the warning of a correction story. It is introduced with one of only two solemn 'Amen I say to you' sayings in the meal setting (for the other see 14.25). Jesus told them solemnly, 'One of you who eats with me will betray me'. The *reader* already knows that Judas, one of the twelve, has made a commitment to betray Jesus (14.10–11) and now learns that Jesus knows this also. But the disciples did not know (apart from Judas), and their grief and uncertainty is colourfully depicted with each one saying, 'Is it I?' Jesus answered that the betrayer was the one of the twelve who dipped with him in the dish. Because Judas knows and the reader knows the identity of the betrayer, Mark does not narrate the enactment of the sign. More important for Mark is the continuing warning of Jesus in the form of a passion prediction concerning the Son of Man. The saying makes a number of complementary points. (1) What happens to the Son of Man is 'as it is written', that is, according to the scriptures which reveal the plan and purpose of God. (2) Yet the Son of Man is to be betrayed by a man. The divine plan does not rule out the reality of human agency. (3) Nor does the divine plan remove from that man the responsibility for his action. Jesus pronounced, 'Woe to that man. It would be good [we would say 'better'] for that man if he had not been born.'

Neither the fulfilment of the sign Jesus had indicated, nor the exit of Judas to betray Jesus, is narrated. The warning hangs in the air so that the reader is like the disciples at this point, not knowing whether the sign was fulfilled, not knowing whether Judas responded to the warning. But that is to suppose that the reader knows no more than the narrative has made known. No doubt there have been 'first-time readers' who have known nothing of this story but what their reading of Mark has taught them. Most of Mark's readers have known of Jesus' fate before reading of this in Mark. The purpose of Mark was not to inform the readers of this but to deal with it in such a way that it did not become a scandal tripping up potential believers. His contribution was to show that betrayal did not catch Jesus by surprise. The plan and purpose of God finds expression here without exonerating the betrayer.

*+The supper and the sign of Jesus' death, 14.22–26*

The actual meal is now introduced, marking a new scene. Jesus had given a sign of his betrayal (14.17–21). Now in the midst of the meal he gave a sign of his death. Mark has made quite clear that these actions took place in the context of the Passover meal (14.12–16), while they were eating.

Other accounts of this event are given by Matthew (26.26–29) and Luke (22.15–20) and Paul (1 Corinthians 11.23–26). All are influenced by the subsequent death of Jesus and the early Christian practice of observing this meal in worship. No attempt can be made here to recover the meal on the last night free from subsequent interpretations. Mark's Gospel is a document of faith from the period following the death of Jesus. Because this aspect of the last meal of Jesus with his disciples became a central feature of the worship of the early church there is need to remind the reader that we are dealing with Mark's interpretation. Yet, because there are common features in all of the accounts, it is certain that the liturgical practice of the early church is rooted in something distinctive that Jesus did at the last meal. Many of these features were common in a Jewish meal and this can be noted in a comparison of Jesus' actions in the two feeding miracles (6.41; 8.6–7). With the bread Jesus *takes* (also 6.41; 8.6), *blessed* [to God] (also 6.41, while 8.6 uses *gave thanks* but uses *blessed* of the fish), *breaks* (also 8.6 and 6.41), and *gave* ( 6.41 and 8.6). Interestingly, Mark 14.22–23, having used *blessed* of the thanksgiving in relation to the bread, then uses *gave thanks* of the thanksgiving in relation to the cup. In other words, these are interchangeable terms for Mark. The thanksgiving in relation to the bread may well have been given in the words, 'Blessed are you, Lord our God, who brings forth bread from the earth'. The thanksgiving in relation to the cup echoes the Passover liturgy, giving thanks to God, who creates the fruit of the vine.

Mark mentions none of the distinctive elements of the Passover meal, though the presence of the cup of wine is consistent with Passover. What is distinctive is Jesus' words in relation to the bread: 'Take, this is my body.' This is both more than anything that was said in a normal meal (or the feeding miracles) and less than what is said in other accounts of the Last Supper. Understood as a prophetic sign (see Ezekiel 5.5, in which the prophet pronounces 'This is Jerusalem', referring to his preceding symbolic actions signifying the destruction of the city), Jesus predicts his death in terms of the broken bread signifying his broken body. The prophetic sign goes further because the disciples were instructed 'Take', which, as Matthew correctly interprets, also implies 'eat'. Participation in the symbolic action of Jesus implies that discipleship involves following Jesus in his death, which is precisely the way Mark interprets the response of discipleship to the passion predictions (8.31–38; 9.31–37; 10.32–45).

Distinctive and more fully elaborated are Jesus' words in relation to the cup. 'This is my blood of the covenant'. Some texts, following Luke 22.20 and 1 Corinthians 11.25, read 'new covenant', but this is a harmonisation even if not against the Markan meaning. Given the context of the Passover, reference to the covenant now sets Jesus' death in the context of the Exodus liberation. The covenant was ratified with the *sprinkling* of blood (Exodus 24.8), but here the wine is to be drunk. While there was no command to 'eat', the command for all to 'drink' is explicit. Because of the Jewish belief that the life was in the blood and that it belonged to God, even the symbolism of drinking blood was shocking and it is surprising that none of the texts reveals any trace of the impact of this shock.

Naturally the words 'This is my blood' are no more to be taken as straightforward fact than 'This is my body'. These are expressions of prophetic symbolism in which Jesus predicts his death and the participation of the disciples in it. The language concerning his blood 'being shed/poured out for many' suggests a sacrificial context, though this is unclarified. The notion of the one for the many echoes the language concerning the suffering servant (Isaiah 53.11,12) whose work makes *many* righteous, who *pours out* his life (*nephesh*) to death and bears the sins of *many*.

Jesus' words of prophetic symbolism conclude by recalling the thanksgiving in relation to the cup. These are introduced by a solemn 'Amen I say to you'. The words make clear that Jesus knew this was his last supper with the disciples until the kingdom of God had become a pervasive reality, which Mark probably associated with the coming of the Son of Man. It is here that Mark introduces the word 'new'. Then Jesus would drink the fruit of the vine 'new' in the kingdom of God. Here we have an image of the messianic banquet which grows out of the Jewish scriptures.

They concluded by singing a hymn (14.26). The Egyptian Hallel (praise) Psalms (113–118) were customarily sung at Passover, 113–114 before and 115–118 after. No mention is made of the opening hymns, but reference to the closing hymn is a formal closure of this scene. Here the closure is also the setting for the next scene. They went out from the room to the Mount of Olives. The Mount of Olives was considered to be part of Jerusalem as far as the requirements of celebrating Passover in Jerusalem were concerned. Perhaps the reason for this was the need to provide space for the great crowds of pilgrims who arrived for the festival. This was of no interest for Mark but provided the opportunity for the next scene, which appears to take place on the way there, and ultimately for the betrayal of Jesus.

### +*Jesus predicts the flight of the disciples and the denial of Peter, 14.27–31*

It is a Markan characteristic to narrate a journey from one place to another as in 14.26 (6.45; 8.27; 9.33) and then to describe an event or conversations 'on the way'. Thus 14.26 is a bridge passage, providing closure to the supper and the context for the present dialogue between Jesus and his disciples.

The Passover supper Jesus celebrated with his disciples is sandwiched between the account of Judas' agreement to betray Jesus (14.10–11) and the prediction of the flight of the disciples and the denial of Peter (14.27–31). In the Passover supper itself Jesus had specified a sign to reveal the betrayer (14.18–21). All of this hardly bodes well for the continuation of Jesus' mission. Of the twelve he had chosen, one would betray him, another would deny him and the rest would be put to flight.

The present narrative can be seen as a correction story. Jesus, by predicting what will happen, warns the disciples and offers opportunity for correction. 'You will all be scandalised', that is, caused to stumble and fall away. The warning is justified by the scripture Jesus quotes (Zechariah 13.7). But the quotation in Mark has been changed. It is not 'Strike the shepherd' but 'I will strike the shepherd'. This only makes clearer that God initiates the strike, not by commanding it, as in Zechariah, but by himself striking, and affirms the plan and purpose of God in the events that overtake Jesus (14.43–50). 'The sheep will be scattered.' 'And leaving him they all fled' (14.50). Thus, although warnings offer the opportunity of correction, Mark was writing well on this side of the predicted events. He knew that the warnings had failed. Correction stories are told for the benefit of the readers, in this case warning of the dangers of defection.

Beyond the warning there was the promise that after he was risen Jesus would go before them into Galilee. This is a promise that remained unfulfilled at the conclusion of the Gospel (16.7). Peter is again spokesman (14.29 and see 8.29, 32; 11.21), affirming that he at least would not stumble and fall. This led Jesus to a second warning, specifically to Peter. Now, using a solemn 'Amen I say to you' saying, Jesus warned Peter that 'Today, this night before the cock crows twice, you will deny me thrice'. Mark also reports that this warning failed and narrates the denials of Peter as Jesus had predicted (14.66–72).

The warnings serve four purposes. In the narrative they offer opportunity for correction, although that opportunity had passed by the time Mark was written. From this perspective the warnings look like fixed predictions. Nevertheless, the warnings make the disciples look even worse than they otherwise would have looked when they fail. Most importantly, they show that the events that overtook Jesus did not take him by surprise, that they were indeed part of the plan and purpose of God. Further, they remain as warnings to the readers.

In the face of this second warning Peter asserted the more strongly that he would not deny Jesus even if he had to die with him, indeed all the disciples claimed this. Ensuing events show that words are cheap.

*+Gethsemane: first failure: failure to 'Watch', 14.32–42*

The warning complete, Mark introduces the new scene by indicating their arrival on the slopes of the Mount of Olives at the place called Gethsemane, a name meaning 'oil press'. There Jesus told them to sit while he prayed. He moved away from the disciples, taking with him Peter, James and John, that is, three of the four brothers whose call is narrated in 1.16–20 (see the discussion of 3.13–19 above), the three who had accompanied Jesus on the mountain of transfiguration (9.2). The scene is now set.

Mark then uses two verbs powerfully to reinforce the sense that Jesus began to be deeply troubled and distressed. Now alone with the three he allowed his deep distress to become evident. Further, his words to them reinforce what they should have seen. 'I am overwhelmed with grief unto death; wait here and *watch.*' This was the watchword of the closing part of the apocalyptic discourse (13.34, 35, 36). There the call was to *watch* lest the absent master should come and find them sleeping. That motif resonates with this story.

The narrative then portrays Jesus moving a little way and throwing himself on the ground, a description that emphasises a desperate and exhausted state. The desperation is confirmed by the double report of Jesus' prayer, first summarised by the narrator and then reported. He prayed that if it were possible, that the hour should pass from him. In the report of the actual words of the prayer we should probably understand '*Abba*' as the actual address of Jesus, for which Mark has given the Greek translation which is rendered 'Father'. *Abba* is the Aramaic form of the intimate address of a father by his child. Mark makes Jesus' characteristic use clear to his Greek readers. Thus the prayer begins from the basis of Jesus' intimate relationship with God as father. He acknowledges, 'All things are possible to you'. Again, in this incident, full of foreboding of the future, Jesus stresses that God is in control of all things. Against this background he asks, 'let this cup pass from me'. It has become clear already (10.38–39) that the cup which God has given Jesus to drink is one full of suffering (Psalm 75.8; Jeremiah 25.15) and that those who follow him would drink it also. Now, at the moment of impending crisis, Jesus asks that God, for whom all things are possible, would allow this cup to pass from him. Given that Jesus had foretold the necessity of his suffering and death, this apparent moment of wavering reinforces the stress and strain borne by Jesus. The moment is portrayed in terms of an heroic struggle in which

Jesus wrests himself from overwhelming grief in the agonising cry, 'Not what I will but what you will'. In this way Mark reinforces the reader's awareness of the plan and purpose of God in the events about to be narrated, but without diminishing awareness of the human stress and strain involved in the fulfilment. Thus Jesus emerges from this heroic struggle with a cry of commitment to the purpose of God.

When Jesus came back to the three disciples he found them sleeping (see 13.36) and said to *Peter*, '*Simon*, do you sleep? Were you not able to *watch* one hour? *Watch* and pray that you do not enter the *testing*; the spirit is willing but the flesh is weak.' The scene of Jesus praying and returning to find the disciples sleeping is repeated three times in all. On each occasion Jesus prayed the same desperate prayer, ending with commitment to his father's will. Each time he returned to find the disciples sleeping. The use of the old name 'Simon' implies a falling back and the repetition forcefully demonstrates the failure of the disciples to watch with Jesus in his hour of need, *and theirs*. After his time of prayer Jesus was prepared for all that was to follow. He had prayed for deliverance but when the time came he was ready to submit to his father's will. They had not prayed and they were not ready when the crisis came. Jesus had prayed that the cup might pass from him. They had not. Nor had they had prayed to be delivered from the time of testing. When it came they fled (14.50) and Peter, facing his own peculiar test, of which he had been warned, failed miserably (14.66–72). The threefold failure here is matched by the threefold denial there.

The scene concludes when, after prayer, Jesus came a third time and found them sleeping. Jesus' words are unclear. Because in 14.42 Jesus tells the disciples to 'Arise' or 'Get up', it seems best to take his opening words in 14.41 as a question, 'Are you still sleeping and taking your rest? Enough.' The opportunity for watching and prayer had passed. The *moment* for the *betrayal* of the Son of Man had arrived. That betrayal is the intended meaning in 14.41 is confirmed by reference to the betrayer in 14.42. Reference to the betrayal of the Son of Man into the hands of 'sinners' foreshadows the handing over of Jesus to the Romans (15.1). There is no evidence of Roman participation in the arrest of Jesus in the Markan narrative (14.43). Because the betrayer was near, Jesus called on the three disciples to wake up and to get up. The moment of crisis had arrived, there was now no time for preparation. Jesus called on them to go with him to meet that crisis. Mark does not portray Jesus passively awaiting his fate, but courageously going out to meet it, perhaps even to make it.

*+Treachery: betrayal with a kiss and a second failure, 14.43–52*

Betrayal, 14.43–49

The urgency of the previous scene is now made clear: 'And immediately, while they were speaking' the betrayer arrived. To emphasise the treachery involved he is named 'Judas, one of the twelve'. Each time Judas is named he is identified as the one who *betrayed* Jesus. To make clear the enormity of his action the reader is reminded that he was one of the twelve (see 3.19 and 14.10, 43). Judas came with a crowd armed with swords and clubs. There is no mention of soldiers, neither temple guards nor Roman soldiers. Yet something more than a rabble is implied because they came from the chief priests, scribes and elders (see also 11.27), the groups that constituted the Sanhedrin. Mention of the three groups again here makes it surprising that the elders were absent from the description of the plot to arrest and kill Jesus (14.1–2).

It is sometimes thought that Mark implies that Jesus was not known to the arresting body because Judas had to identify him with a sign. This does not seem to be Mark's meaning. He reports Jesus' claim to have been 'with them daily teaching in the temple' (14.49). The public notoriety of Jesus is not questioned by Mark. What then was the role of Judas? First, he knew where to find Jesus at a time and place where a 'soft arrest' was possible away from tumultuous crowds of supporters. Second, at night on the slopes of the Mount of Olives, amongst the trees and with a group of men all dressed alike, even with flaming torches positive identification would not have been easy. Judas provided positive identification so that there was no confusion with the arrest.

For Mark the role of Judas was all this, and more. His treachery is emphasised whenever he is named. Here it is further stressed by noting the manner of the betrayal, 'with a kiss'. This is reiterated in the narrative by Judas, telling those with him what the sign would be and by the narrator reporting the kiss (14.44–45). The arrest is reported in matter-of-fact fashion immediately after the sign. Judas, having betrayed Jesus, vanished. Nothing more is said of him, not by Jesus nor the narrative of the Gospel.

Two responses to the arrest of Jesus are reported. A bystander drew a sword and cut off the ear of the servant of the high priest. Mark does not name the 'bystander'. This would be a very strange way to describe one of the disciples. Mark might imply that the armed crowd was not a tightly organised arresting force but had gathered a curious following along the way and that one of these offered some resistance to the arrest of Jesus. Or it may be implied that the bystander was a pilgrim also on the slopes of the Mount of Olives that evening. Either way, the resistance of the bystander sets the disciples in a bad light. We will shortly learn that at the arrest of Jesus they fled. In Mark Jesus makes no critical remark concerning the bystander who acted in his defence. Jesus' criticism was aimed at the arresting crowd. 'As if to arrest a *robber* you have come out with swords and clubs to arrest me.' If Jesus, drawing on Jeremiah 7.11, had likened the business of the temple to a den of robbers (11.17), the arresting crowd was now treating him as a robber. But was this justified? Jesus was to raise this question by reminding them, 'I was daily with you in the temple teaching and you did not arrest me'. The night arrest out on the slopes of the mount of Olives is thus contrasted with Jesus openly, freely and daily teaching in the temple. This description implies a longer period of teaching in the temple than is often assumed. It should be remembered that Mark only once gives a clear two-day sequence (11.12) and for the most part we must conclude that he has depicted typical scenes rather than sequential days.

### Second failure: flight, 14.50–52

If Jesus contrasted his open behaviour with the surreptitious and violent behaviour of those who arrested him, he also affirmed the will and purpose of God being worked out through it all, 'that the scriptures may be fulfilled' (14.49). The scene ends with the note, 'And they all left him and fled' (14.50). Who 'they' are is not specified. It is not a reference to the arresting crowd, because they took Jesus to the high priest (14.53). And there was a young man who had not yet fled (14.51–52). Those who fled can only be the disciples and, in the light of 14.27, Mark has made this clear to the reader.

What, then, is the point of the narrative about the young man who *followed* but fled when an attempt was made to arrest him? Describing him as *following* after the disciples had fled shows them up badly. Yet the young man does not fare much better. When they attempted to arrest him he fled naked, leaving them grasping his garment. Mark's purpose with this narrative is not altogether clear. There is certainly a comparison with the disciples because 14.50 concludes with reference to their flight, although there is no evidence that they were threatened. At least the young man continued to follow until he was threatened and then he had to flee away naked, escaping, as it were, only with his life. If this is intended to echo Amos 2.16 then the young man is commended as being stout-hearted among the mighty. There is no reason to think that the scene is the author's signature, like the fleeting appearance of Alfred Hitchcock in his films.

## Trial, denial, sentencing and mocking, 14.53–15.15

*+Trial: Jesus before the Sanhedrin, 14.53–65*

The new scene commences, 'And they brought Jesus to the high priest'. The high priest is not named in Mark, though Caiaphas may be presupposed (see Matthew 26.3, 57). Mark then describes a gathering of all the chief priests, the elders and the scribes, who constituted the Sanhedrin (14.53, 55). This word for the Jewish council came as a loan word from Greek into Hebrew. What follows is presented as a trial in which a verdict is brought down (14.63–64). Problems with Mark's account of the trial arise from a reading of the Mishnaic Tractate *Sanhedrin*. Understanding the historical situation in Jerusalem around 30 CE is complex. The Mishnah was formulated to deal with the conditions pertaining to Jewish life after the Jewish war and in its finished form reflects the early third century CE. Many of the historical questions concerning the trial of Jesus are beyond the scope of this study. But Mark presupposes some understanding of the Jerusalem Sanhedrin. Only sketchy details of its constituency are given (14.53, 55). More detailed knowledge must be drawn cautiously from the Mishnah. Seventy-one members were drawn from the chief priests, scribes and elders representing the seventy elders plus Moses of Numbers 11.16–25. Here we have to decide whether Mark intends to implicate only the Sanhedrin, and has been careless with his language, or has intentionally implicated the three classes of Jerusalem society that made up the Sanhedrin. It seems more likely, in the light of the weight of blame for the crucifixion of Jesus, that Mark aims at what seems to be a wider group than the Sanhedrin. On the Sanhedrin see Schürer, *The History of the Jewish People in the Age of Jesus Christ*, Volume 2, pp. 199–226.

Mark has another unfinished story to tell in the context of the trial of Jesus. The prophecy of the flight of the disciples has been fulfilled. The denials by Peter are yet to come. Having set up the context of the trial, Mark notes that Peter 'followed' Jesus. This is the proper disposition of a disciple and for that reason Mark has added, 'from afar', from a distance. Peter is presented as a person with a conflict of interests, as a disciple of Jesus and yet concerned ultimately for his own safety. Even so he followed right into the court of the house of the high priest, an inner courtyard where Peter sat with the servants warming himself by the fire. By breaking his account of the trial at this point Mark has cleverly provided an anticipation of what is to take place in the next scene (14.66–71).

Returning to the trial, presumably in the house of the high priest, Mark indicates that 'the chief priests and the whole Sanhedrin sought *evidence* against Jesus in order to put him to death' (14.55). This is an alternative description to 'chief priests, the elders and the scribes' of 14.53 and 'the chief priests with the elders and the scribes and the whole Sanhedrin' of 15.1. As the chief priests were part of the Sanhedrin, specific reference to them in 14.55 indicates their leading role in this process, which is dramatically demonstrated in the high priest. This is a little less clear in 15.1, but they are singled out even when saying 'with the elders and scribes'. Even so, the whole Sanhedrin was involved, none were to be exonerated, even if the high priest and chief priests are shown to be leaders in this process. Having stated the objective of the Sanhedrin, Mark then describes the process. There were many conflicting false witnesses against Jesus. Mark has narrated Jesus' prediction of the destruction of the temple (13.2). That is not in dispute here. The charge is that he said, '*I will destroy* this temple', that after three days he would replace the temple made with hands with a temple not made with hands (see John 2.19). Mark's account of the charges against Jesus seems to have combined evidence that Jesus predicted the destruction of the temple with the early Christian teaching about the resurrection on the third day. Mark's central interest in these accusations is to show that the evidence was false and the witnesses could not agree, invalidating their testimony (Numbers 33.30; Deuteronomy 17.6).

Because the witnesses had failed to produce valid evidence Mark portrays the intervention of the high priest. He stood up in the middle of the gathering and called on Jesus to answer the accusations brought against him. Jesus was silent. Mark intends the reader to perceive in Jesus' silence in the face of conflicting false witness the silence of the righteous sufferer (Psalm 38.13; 39.9; Isaiah 53.7). The high priest sought to lead Jesus to incriminate himself. Whether or not this process was legally proper is not relevant to an understanding of Mark. This reading is confirmed by the follow-up question to the silence of Jesus. 'Are you the Christ, the Son of the Blessed?' Did Jesus claim to be the Messiah? The term 'Son of the Blessed' is a typical Jewish periphrasis or circumlocution, a way around *naming* God when speaking of him. Used of the Messiah, Son of God carried the sense of divine appointment (see Psalm 2.7). If the aim of the high priest was to get Jesus to incriminate himself he achieved some success. Jesus did not remain silent. To the specific question he replied, 'I am'. There is no reason to take these words to mean anything but 'I am the Christ, the Son of the Blessed'. What is surprising is that Jesus here admits this to the hostile high priest when the Gospel resonates with the secrecy motif, which finds its clearest expression in 8.29–30. On trial with his passion imminent, Jesus was prepared to acknowledge his messiahship. Mark makes no specific comment on this point and we can thus only seek for a narrative confirmation. In terms of the trial it is hard to see what such an admission would achieve. It is not clear what offence would have been committed by the claim to be the Messiah, though some traditions would have taken such a claim as evidence that the person was not the Messiah.

The Markan Jesus was not content simply to give an affirmative answer. Messiahship must be redefined. Part of that redefinition takes place in the Markan narrative as the reader follows the passion of the Messiah. Redefinition is also given by the continuing words of Jesus, which connect his affirmation to a complex of scripture quotations from Daniel 7.13–14 and Psalm 110.1. 'You will see the Son of Man.' There is no reference to the time this will happen. The initial point to be made is that Jesus' answer redefines messiahship in terms of the Danielic Son of Man as understood by a first-century CE person who believed Jesus to be Messiah, Son of Man. The conflation of ideas and figures is clear in this combination of texts in which Mark at least (perhaps Jesus and other Jews also) identified the Son of Man with the Messiah and used a messianic text intercalated with the text from Daniel. What this has done is to combine two seemingly contradictory images: the Son of Man sitting at the right hand of *power*, another periphrasis for God; and coming on the clouds of heaven. The question to be asked is, for Mark, what is the destination of the Son of Man? In Daniel the Son of Man is coming to *the Ancient of Days* (another periphrasis for God). If this is Mark's sense then the two statements seem to be out of order. Should the Son of Man not first come and then sit? Rather, Mark gives expression to the view that the risen Jesus (Son of Man) was exalted to the right hand of God from whence, on the last day, he would come (return) on the clouds of heaven. The coming Son of Man is thus spoken of in terms of the threat of judgement.

The response of the high priest was to tear his own clothes, a symbolic action signifying the end of a blasphemy trial. The action implies that Jesus was the chief witness and that he has been convicted on the basis of his own words. This is confirmed by the question 'What further need do we have of witnesses? You have heard the blasphemy.' But there seems to be no blasphemy in anything that Jesus has said. His own words, quoting scripture, avoid using the name of God, using the periphrasis 'the power'. His words can only be considered blasphemy if: (1) it is understood that Jesus claimed to be the Son of Man; and (2) the Son of Man was understood to be a heavenly figure, indeed a divine figure. Alternatively, 'blasphemy' may be understood in a more general sense of insulting talk (see 15.29).

The high priest then called for a verdict and pronounced Jesus *guilty* (see 3.29) and they unanimously condemned him to death. What followed then was a mocking where some (of the Sanhedrin?) began to spit on him and they blindfolded him and hit him, calling on him to prophesy, that is, probably say who had hit him. The irony was that while they called on Jesus to prophesy, Mark depicts the parallel scene of Peter outside (14.66–72) fulfilling Jesus' prophecy of 14.30–31. The attendants slapped Jesus' face. Compare the mocking of Jesus by the soldiers, 15.16–20; by the passers-by, chief priests and scribes and those crucified with him (15.27–32). This careful juxtapositioning of trial and mocking, sentencing and mocking, crucifixion and mocking, is evidence of Mark's crafted narrative. Ironically, Jesus' opponents recognised his kingship only in their mockery of him.

*+Peter's denials, 14.66–72*

This episode begins 'And while Peter was below in the court'. The denials by Peter were predicted by Jesus (14.30–31) and foreshadowed by Peter's arrival in the court of the high priest (14.54). Now the action returns to Peter in the court. The resumption of the story of Peter picks it up precisely where it had left him, warming himself at the fire (14.54, 66–67). With some dramatic artistry Mark tells of Peter's threefold denial of Jesus. There is a correlation between Peter's threefold failure to watch with Jesus and the threefold denial. Jesus was active in prayer and he overcame the test of his arrest and trial. Peter slept, fled in the crisis and now . . .

In three brief scenes Peter denies any association with Jesus. There is a progression. In the first Peter was recognised by one of the servant girls of the high priest as a disciple of 'Jesus the Nazarene' (see 1.9, 24; 10.47; 14.67; 16.6). But he denied this, saying 'I neither know nor understand what you say'. He then withdrew to the forecourt and the cock crew. Peter ignored this warning but the reader has been alerted by it. In the second the same girl identified Peter to *bystanders* and again Peter denied this. A little later the *bystanders* said to Peter, '"Truly you are one of them, for you are also a Galilean." But he began to curse and to swear that he did not know the man of whom they spoke.' There is an intensifying of Peter's denial as his identification became a more public affair. At the end Mark announced, 'Immediately a cock crowed a second time'. Nothing is left to chance. Mark reminds the reader, through Peter's memory of Jesus' saying, 'Before the cock crows twice, you will deny me thrice'. The scandal of betrayal and denial by his own disciples has been reported. By predicting these events Jesus shows that they have been caught up into the plan and purpose of God. But for Peter, remembering Jesus' warning brought home the horror of his failure. His response is unclear. Certainly Mark says that he wept, but it is unclear whether 'He broke down and wept' or 'He threw himself down and wept'. Mark depicts Peter's grief, his deep remorse at his dismal failure and the failure brought home by memory of the warning.

*+Sentencing: Jesus before Pilate, 15.1–15*

+Interrogation, 15.1–5

1 Time: in the morning, 15.1. Beginning with 'And immediately early in the morning', Mark indicates that the cock's crow not only signalled Peter's dismal failure but also heralded the approach of morning and the next stage in the drama of the passion of Jesus. This, the first of five specific time references dividing the day of crucifixion into three-hour periods from morning to evening (15.1, 25, 33, 34, 42), emphasises the gravity of that day. Just what happened early in the morning according to Mark is unclear because of textual variants. A second gathering of the Sanhedrin with a wider constituency can be implied from 15.1. The inclination to read Mark this way is encouraged by the Mishnaic regulation that a trial should not be completed on a single day. This does not help Mark's account because the evening and following morning constitute a single day by Jewish calculation. The best way to read Mark 15.1 is as a resumption after the interruption of the narrative of Peter's denial. Thus 15.1 resumes with a restatement of 14.63–64 where a verdict is given declaring Jesus to be guilty and condemning him to death. This is the basis from which the new action takes place.

What happened early in the morning was that Jesus was sent bound and *handed over* (betrayed) to Pilate. The use of the same term to describe the *transaction* between the Sanhedrin and Pilate and of the transaction between Judas and the chief priests (14.10–11) which, in practice, was a conspiracy with the three groups making up the Sanhedrin (14.43), suggests that Mark wishes to portray these groups as treacherously *betraying* Jesus to Pilate. Mark 15.10 confirms this reading. In the last act of handing over Jesus, Pilate himself reluctantly becomes a party to the treachery, handing him over to be flogged and crucified (15.15). In Mark, Pilate is largely freed from any blame. Mark's picture of Pilate, who was prefect of Judaea from 26 to 36 CE (see the inscription at Caesarea Maritima), is contrary to what we know of him from other sources (see Philo, *De Legatione ad Gaium*, 38; Josephus, *War*, 2.9.2–4; *Antiquities*, 18.3.1–2). In fact, Pilate seems to have been unscrupulous and merciless. Mark's favourable picture of Pilate must therefore be read as an attempt to throw the blame for Jesus' death as exclusively as possible on the Jewish *authorities*, especially the chief priests (15.10–11). Mark's reasons for doing this are fairly clear. First, Mark already reflects the reality of the struggle of the early Christian movement with Jewish authorities (13.9), a problem that was accentuated by the mission to the nations (13.10). Mark's account of Jesus' conflict is to be read in the light of the early Christian struggle. Perhaps more important for Mark was the church's increasing orientation to the mission to the nations. For this the good-will of Rome was crucial.

2 The charge and its significance, 15.2. Mark's account gives no hint of a formal trial before Pilate. Rather, the trial had already taken place and a verdict had been given. The hearing before Pilate seems to have been to decide what is now to be done. The hearing took the form of two questions by Pilate, interspersed by a report that the chief priests made many accusations against Jesus. The first question, 'Are you the king of the *Jews*?' (15.2, cf. 15.9, 12, 18, 26), should be considered the basic charge that had been brought against Jesus. It could be considered a fair summary of Jesus' admission (14.61–62) in terms a Roman would understand. When the same point was made by the scribes they referred to 'Christ the king of *Israel*'. The use of 'Jews' reflects a Roman, non-Palestinian perspective. But where Jesus had answered the question of 14.61 first with the affirmative 'I am', and only then qualifying and elaborating, here his answer was, 'So you say!' or, that is the charge. Throughout the rest of the passion narrative, while Jesus does not, others do, whether sincerely or not, refer to him as the king of the Jews (15.9, 12, 18, 26, 32). Perhaps Jesus would not answer because the title 'king of the Jews', in the mouth of the Roman prefect, meant something more overtly political and military than the reality of his messiahship. But for Mark the title, king of the Jews, legitimately reveals the crucified one.

3 Reported accusations, 15.3–5. Jesus' refusal to answer the question was the opportunity to report the many accusations brought by the chief priests. This report has two functions. It again stresses the leading role of the chief priests in the betrayal and crucifixion of Jesus (see 14.10 and 14.1, 43, 53, 55; 15.1). It provides the basis of Pilate's second question. Given the many accusations, will Jesus offer no answer? Mark then reports that the silence of Jesus made Pilate marvel. Perhaps Mark also expects his readers to recall Isaiah 53.7–9.

> He was oppressed and he was afflicted,
> yet he did not open his mouth;

like a lamb that is led to the slaughter,
and like a sheep that before its shearers is silent,
so he did not open his mouth.
By a perversion of justice he was taken away.
Who could have imagined his future?
For he was cut off from the land of the living,
stricken for the transgression of my people.
They made his grave with the wicked and his tomb with
the rich,
although he had done no violence,
and there was no deceit in his mouth.

Isaiah goes on, as Mark does, to interpret what happens to the servant as a consequence of human wickedness and God's will and purpose,

yet it was the will of the Lord to crush him with pain. . . .
The righteous one, my servant, shall make many righteous,
and he shall bear their iniquities. . . .
he poured himself out to death,
and was numbered with the transgressors;
yet he bore the sins of many,
and made intercession for the transgressors.

(Isaiah 53.11–12)

Indeed, it is difficult to think that Mark's treatment here and elsewhere has not made use of this tradition in Isaiah in an attempt to make sense of the death of Jesus the Messiah.

*Jesus or Barabbas?, 15.6–15

Mark sets the scene by mentioning a custom of releasing a prisoner as an act of clemency at the feast (Passover). We have no evidence of this practice outside the Gospels. There were two notable prisoners, Barabbas, a brigand and murderer, and Jesus. The crowd gathered and asked Pilate to release a prisoner. Pilate, knowing of Jesus' innocence (15.10, 14), asked if he should release 'the king of the *Jews*'. But the chief priests had prompted the crowd to ask for Barabbas. So Pilate asked, 'What shall I do with the king of the *Jews*?' (15.12). Mark says that they *again* (?) cried out 'Crucify him!' (15.13). To this Pilate responded, 'Why, what evil has he done?' But they cried out all the more, 'Crucify him!' So Pilate gave way to the crowd, released Barabbas, had Jesus flogged and delivered him to be crucified. The point of the flogging is unclear. There is no suggestion that it was to arouse sympathy for Jesus because there were no more attempts to release him. Perhaps we can say no more than that, for Mark, this was part of the way of the cross. Notably, there is no stress on physical brutality, only a summary note to the effect, first flogging and then delivered to be crucified.

In this scene, just as Pilate is a foil for the chief priests, so Barabbas is a foil for Jesus. We know nothing of Barabbas other than what we find in the Gospels. We seem to have the second part of his name because *bar* is Aramaic for 'son' and his name means 'son of the father'. Some manuscripts of Matthew 27.16 read Jesus Barabbas. It is not his name that is important but his manifest guilt of capital crimes and Jesus' innocence. Mark shows that the chief priests now act alone in their conspiracy against Jesus (15.10–11). The crowd, like Pilate himself, are pawns manipulated by the chief priests. Mark is not concerned with whether this is the crowd of pilgrims that heralded Jesus' entry to Jerusalem (11.8–10).

Mark makes a number of points. Jesus was innocent of any crime. Pilate, well intentioned, wished to release Jesus (15.9) but was unable to resist the unreasonable ill will towards Jesus by the chief priests that had led to his arrest (15.10). Frustrated, he chose provocatively to use of Jesus the Roman title, 'king of the Jews', which had been given to Herod. This was an affront to the Jewish authorities. For Mark, it meant that Jesus' messiahship was revealed ironically by Pilate and that Jesus was crucified as if this charge had been sustained, the charge being attached to the cross, 'The king of the Jews' (15.26). Mark also portrays a Roman centurion confessing, 'Truly this man was [a] son of God' (15.39) at the moment of Jesus' death. There is no coincidence that the kingship of Jesus and his status as son of God should be bound up with his crucifixion, his death. Barabbas was guilty but he went free. Jesus was innocent but was crucified. 'The righteous one, my servant, shall make many righteous, and he shall bear their iniquities.'

## Crucifixion and mocking, 15.16–41

### **The mocking of Jesus: a parody of the truth, 15.16–20*

The proceedings so far had taken place outside Pilate's residence in Jerusalem (his main residence was in Caesarea). Mark now notes that the soldiers led Jesus into the court which is the Praetorium, that is, the residence of the prefect. The next scene took place in that inner court. In the previous inner court scene Peter had played the buffoon (14.54, 66–72). It was now the turn of the soldiers. When the prisoner had been brought in the whole *cohort* was called together. Jesus had been handed over to the soldiers (15.15). Now they were to do their job. Outside there had been only a representative guard. Who called them together is unimportant. Probably a full cohort (600 soldiers) is not implied, but the term may have been used of the full complement of the procurator's force in Jerusalem.

The mocking took its cue from Pilate's reference to Jesus as 'the king of the Jews'. He was dressed like the emperor in royal purple. Purple was a colour for royalty, if for no other reason than that purple dye was very expensive, being an extract from a shellfish. Complete with a crown of thorns which, contrary to popular art, probably had the thorns radiating outwards like the rays of the sun, suggesting the association of the divine emperor with the divine sun, the soldiers hailed Jesus as 'king of the Jews'. They beat him on the head with a reed, spat on him and mockingly knelt before him. Mark concludes this 'act' by noting succinctly, 'And when they had *mocked* [him]' (15.20), thus leaving no doubt about what the soldiers had done to Jesus. Unlike subsequent Christian art, Mark does not feature any brutal torture of Jesus but the *mocking*, which the reader is expected to recognise as a parody of the truth. Jesus was indeed the king of the Jews and the soldiers did well to kneel before him. But they mocked him. The mocking complete, they removed the purple and dressed Jesus again in his own clothes. Mocking over, the scene moves from a pretence that reveals truth to a reality which ends with the note, 'They led him out to crucify him'.

*+On the way to crucifixion, 15.21–24a*

They compelled Simon of Cyrene to bear his cross. Cyrene was a city in North Africa in what is now Libya. Yet he seems to have been settled in Judaea because Mark says he was coming in from a field or from the country. Apparently he was passing by. Yet he appears to have been known to Mark and his readers because he is also identified as the father of Alexander and Rufus. Perhaps Mark implies that this chance happening resulted in Alexander and Rufus joining the ongoing Jesus movement. Simon was compelled to bear the cross, no doubt by the soldiers. Usually this was borne by the convicted 'criminal'. No reason is given for drafting Simon into service. What was carried to the place of execution was the cross piece.

The journey was from the Praetorium to Golgotha, an Aramaic word meaning 'skull' and interpreted as the place of the skull. Probably the name relates to the appearance of a hill and not the later legend that the skull of Adam was buried there. The location is not known but would have been outside the city walls of the time. There *they* offered Jesus wine mingled with myrrh as a drug to dull the pain. It is unlikely that Mark attributes this action to the soldiers because crucifixion was intended to be as brutal and as painful a form of execution as possible. It may be an allusion to Psalm 69.21. Widely practised in the ancient world, crucifixion was adopted by the Romans as capital punishment for slaves and non-Romans. The victim was fixed naked to the cross by nails or some other means, and, exposed to the elements, was left to die, sometimes taking days to do so. In the end the cause of death was generally asphyxiation. While the Babylonian Talmud is too late to be directly relevant, it (B. Sanhedrin 43a) mentions a custom of giving a pain-killing drink to those facing the death penalty, making more likely that this humanitarian offer came from a Jewish source rather than Roman. But this is not important for Mark, who is more intent on making clear that Jesus refused the offer. That is, Jesus not only accepted his fate but did not seek to avoid the pain and suffering it involved. Mark ends this matter-of-fact account with the understated 'And they crucified him' (15.24a). One would not guess the physical torment involved from this statement. Evidently Mark was more concerned with other factors than the sheer physical torture that Jesus underwent. What these factors were we will discover by attending to what Mark actually tells us.

*+An interruption for the fulfilment of scripture, 15.24b*

Between the first statement, 'And they crucified him' (15.24a) and the second (15.25), Mark has placed a reference to the casting of lots for Jesus' clothes. The incident was important enough for Mark to interrupt his account of the crucifixion to make clear the echo to Psalm 22.18, associating the death of Jesus with the fulfilment of prophecy. Psalm 22 concerns the righteous sufferer. Mark records the opening words of this Psalm as the great cry of Jesus from the cross before he died (15.34). Consequently, this small detail concerning Jesus' clothes is part of a larger picture Mark has painted of Jesus.

**Crucifixion and mocking, 15.25–32*

Interruption over, Mark resumes his account of the crucifixion by noting that it took place at the third hour, that is, 9 a.m. by our calculations (15.25). This second of five time references on the day of crucifixion emphasises the significance of the day by time-referencing the passing events.

The inscription of the charge for which Jesus was crucified, which was probably nailed to the cross, read 'The king of the Jews'. This is a variation on a theme, which began with Peter's 'you are the Christ' (8.29); continued with the question of the high priest, 'Are you the Christ, the Son of the Blessed?', which Jesus answered in the affirmative (14.61–62); and Pilate's, 'Are you the king of the Jews?'. Although Jesus did not answer (15.2), Pilate persisted in his reference to Jesus as the king of the Jews (15.9, 12); and the solders mocked Jesus, dressing him like a king, kneeling before him, saluted him, saying, 'Hail, king of the Jews' (15.18). Now Jesus was publicly executed as the king of the Jews (15.26).

Although Barabbas had been released, Jesus was crucified between two robbers, one on his right and one on his left. This imagery is reminiscent of the request of James and John to sit one on the right and the other on the left of Jesus in his glory (10.37). Jesus answered that this position was not his to give because it was for those for whom it had been prepared (10.40). It is tempting to think that Mark has planned this resonance. Two things might put this in question. A different word has been used for 'left' in each place and Mark later notes that those crucified with Jesus *insulted* him (15.32). Mark may well have wished the readers to remember Isaiah 53.12 also, 'he was numbered with the transgressors'.

Mark's portrayal of the crucifixion concentrates on the mocking of Jesus. This began with the soldiers, without using any term to describe what they did to Jesus. They performed a pantomime in which Jesus was the central figure and the butt of their ridiculing play. This was followed by the threefold mocking of Jesus at the cross, by the passers-by (15.29–30), the chief priests with the scribes (15.31), and those who were crucified with him (15.32). Three different terms are used for this threefold mocking.

1 The 'passers-by', 15.29. Roman practice was to crucify criminals in prominent places, by the roadside, where travellers would see. Mark's description implies this situation. Those passing by *abused* him. The term cannot mean 'blasphemed' here. Shaking their heads they were saying, 'Ha! You who would destroy the temple and build it in three days, save yourself and come down from the cross.' The passers-by reiterated the charge that Mark has shown to be false (14.56). The implication of this statement is that if he can destroy the temple, surely he can come down from the cross. Interestingly, early Christian tradition recorded by Eusebius and Origen asserts that it was precisely because of the crucifixion of Jesus that Jerusalem and the temple were destroyed (Eusebius, *History*, 3.7.7; Origen, *Contra Celsum* 1.47). Contrary to this mocking, Jesus' kingship or messiahship involved the cross so that he would have invalidated his vocation by coming down.

2 The chief priests with the scribes, 15.31. The coalition against Jesus has systematically placed the chief priests first with the leading role of the high priest at the trial (14.53–65). Before Pilate it was the chief priests who accused him (15.3). At the cross the chief priests, along with the scribes, *ridiculed* him to one another *in the same way* as the passers-by (15.31). Thus what these two groups did is not distinguished by content but by address. The passers-by addressed their words to Jesus, *abusing* him. The chief priests *ridiculed* Jesus amongst themselves and with the scribes. Taking account of the differing audiences, their words were similar but not identical to those of the passers-by. New is the admission, 'He saved others'. This may be an acknowledgement of the healing ministry of Jesus. Alternatively, we might understand this to mean 'He *claimed to* save others'. Also explicit is Jesus' admission that he was the Christ (14.61), which was translated in Roman terms as 'king of the Jews' (15.2, 9, 12, 18) and here is expressed in more nationalistic terms as 'king of Israel' (15.32). Coming down from the cross is presented as a challenge to provide a sign which would lead them to believe that he is the Christ. In Mark's terms, however, coming down from the cross could only prove that Jesus was not the Christ (8.35 and see 11.27–33).

3 Those crucified with him, 15.27, 32. They *insulted* him. Mark provides no clues to what form the insults took. If even those crucified with him insulted him, his position was desperate indeed.

*+Crucifixion and death, 15.33–41*

Mark tells of the coming of darkness over the whole land from *the sixth to the ninth hour* (15.33), that is, from 12 noon until 3 p.m. Did Mark see this as a foreshadowing of the moment when the sun would be darkened (13.24)? Certainly the darkness is perceived as a sign of judgement (Amos 8.9). The time of the end of the darkness is mentioned *twice* (15.33–34). Important events happened at this point.

1 Jesus cried out with a *loud* (great) voice. Reference to the *loud* voice suggests that not only the content of what was said is important. The loud voice implies that Jesus was not exhausted, was not at the point of death. This has implications for the interpretation of the manner of Jesus' death. His words are a transliteration of the Aramaic of the opening of Psalm 22, which Mark has also translated. Yet the misunderstanding by some of the bystanders is only possible in Hebrew (*Eli* rather than *Eloi*). Psalm 22 gives expression to the experience of the desolation of the righteous sufferer and is the climax of betrayal, desertion, denial and mocking.

2 Some of the bystanders thought that Jesus had called for Elijah. This no doubt has some connection with the expectation that Elijah would come before the day of the Lord (Malachi 4.5–6). Mark gave expression to this expectation but identified John the Baptist with the returning Elijah. One of those who thought Jesus had called for Elijah ran and offered Jesus a drink of sour wine (vinegar) in a saturated sponge on a cane and called on the bystanders to wait and see if Elijah would come and take Jesus down. This can be understood as a compassionate act or, when the echoes of Psalm 69.21 (LXX) are noted, the suggestion, 'Let us wait to see if Elijah will come' can also be understood as mockery, as if Elijah would come to take him down! Nothing is said about whether Jesus accepted the drink or not.

3 Jesus died. He died when he had given a loud cry. Was this a second loud cry? Or are we to understand this as another Markan resumption? For example, the verdict on Jesus having been given in 14.64 is repeated at the resumption in 15.1 following the account of the denials of Peter (14.66–72); and the crucifixion of Jesus noted *before* (15.24a) and again at the resumption at 15.25 *after* the quotation of Psalm 22.18 to indicate the disposal of Jesus' clothes. What Mark has done is to show the response to the loud cry of Jesus before noting that, having given the loud cry, Jesus breathed his last, he died.

4 The curtain in the temple was torn in two from the top to the bottom. The entrance to the holy place and the entrance separating the holy place from the holy of holies, entered by the high priest on the day of atonement, were each covered by a 'curtain' (see Exodus 26.33, 37 and Josephus, *Antiquities*, 8.3.5). The latter was probably in mind. That it was torn from the top to the bottom implies divine action. The rending of this curtain is a sign of the destruction of the temple, leaving access to God open after the death of Jesus. For Mark it seems to be a symbol of the rejection of the special place of Israel in the purposes of God, leaving open the mission to the nations. The beginning of Jesus' mission was marked by the tearing apart of the heavens revealing the Spirit descending like a dove upon Jesus. At his death the veil of the temple was torn apart from top to bottom. Thus Jesus' mission is framed by these events.

5 The centurion, seeing *the way* Jesus breathed his last, said, 'Truly this man was [a] son of God' (15.39). The manner of Jesus' death places weight on the great cry. Was it the *strength* of the cry with which Jesus *gave up* his life, the words he uttered, or a combination of the strength and the meaning? The strength of the cry indicated that Jesus' life had not been squeezed out of him and just drained away. Rather, he gave his life in full strength. He gave his life hanging alone on the cross, abandoned by his supporters, mocked by passers-by, chief priests and scribes and even by those crucified with him, and in a sense of abandonment even by God. Whatever the centurion might have meant, for Mark this is the climax of the recognition of Jesus. At the depth of his passion a centurion made what for Mark was the most perceptive confession (see 1.1, 11; 9.7; [14.61] 15.39). The centurion then represents the mission to the nations (13.10), where the true confession of faith first finds expression in association with the mystery of the crucified Messiah.

At his baptism the heavenly voice proclaimed 'You are my son', and at his death a Roman centurion confessed 'Truly this man was [a] son of God'. Jesus' mission is framed by the two voices which reveal his relation to God. Recognition of this framing heightens the significance of the role of the centurion, raising the question of his symbolic function in relation to Markan Christianity.

6 There were also women watching *from a distance* (15.40). The reader is somewhat caught by surprise as Mark reveals that Jesus was not abandoned by all of his followers. A group of followers from Galilee not previously mentioned is now revealed, a large

group of supporters who had come up to Jerusalem with Jesus. They had not only come to Jerusalem, but also to the scene of the cross, not to the foot of the cross amongst the mockers but watching *from afar* (cf. 14.54). Mark refers to a large group of women amongst whom were those who *ministered* to Jesus on his journey to Jerusalem. Mark provides another hint concerning the way Jesus' itinerant mission operated. The use of the hospitality of houses has been noted frequently. Here only, Mark notes that Jesus was also served by a group of women who travelled with his mission, they followed him and ministered to him. Of these, Mary Magdalene (from Magdala on the western shores of the sea of Galilee) and another Mary are named. The latter Mary might be identified as the mother of James the small and Joses, or the wife or daughter of James the small and mother of Joses. There are no good grounds for identifying this Mary as the mother of Jesus or of those known as the brothers of Jesus. A coincidence of the names of James and Joses with two of those named as the brother of Jesus (6.3) is hardly convincing, as these are amongst the most popular Jewish names of the time. A third woman, Salome, is also mentioned. Textual variants for this verse probably arose when the women named were no longer known to the readers. Mark mentions these women also because of the role they have yet to play in the story (see 15.47; 16.1–8). The irony of the absence of the disciples and the presence of the women has been carefully constructed and is heightened by the call to the women to be the first witnesses to the risen Jesus (16.7).

### +Burial, 15.42–47

Mark's account of the burial of Jesus makes a number of important points. (1) It confirms beyond doubt that Jesus was dead. (2) It introduces another 'stranger' whose role implies that the burial of Jesus had been neglected by his family and friends. (3) Though the women waited on the sideline they had not abandoned the burial duties. (4) There is no mention of the disciples. Here, as in the account of the crucifixion, their absence reverberates through the narrative.

Mark announces the arrival of evening on the preparation of the sabbath. The reader knows that Jesus has been dead since 3 p.m. The centurion and those at the cross also knew this. Now we learn that Joseph of Arimathea also knew this. He is introduced as a stranger to the reader and to the Jesus movement. Arimathea may be identified with Ramathaim, about twenty miles from Jerusalem. Joseph is said to be a respected member of the *council*, which is perhaps to be understood as the Sanhedrin, though this is not Mark's usual term. If a member of the Sanhedrin, this might indicate Joseph's continuing legal concern with a person previously condemned.

Mark's time references lead to a puzzle at this point. Given that evening had come, it was no longer the preparation but the sabbath itself and requirements for the Passover and sabbath were much the same. If we allow a rather loose meaning, implying the approach of evening, Mark makes sense. Deuteronomy 21.23 demanded that the body of a criminal should be removed for burial before sundown on the day of execution. The Roman practice of crucifixion did not comply with this requirement. Victims often took days to die and were left hanging as a warning to others. The action of Joseph is to be understood against the background of Deuteronomy 21. It is true that *The Mishnah* and Talmudim give more detailed requirements concerning burial, but we cannot be confident that these were in force in the time of Jesus or even when Mark wrote. On this reading Mark's reference to it being evening already should be taken as an inexact reference to the approach of evening. Joseph was concerned that Jesus should be buried before evening, hence the haste.

Joseph is also described as one awaiting the kingdom of God. Although many pious Jews were waiting for the rule of God, the language of 'the kingdom of God' is characteristic of Jesus and implies a positive relation to Jesus. The burial of Jesus by this 'stranger' is nevertheless a reflection on family and friends who were under obligation to perform this duty.

The context of the story has prepared for a brief quest story. Joseph was concerned to bury Jesus. That was the task at hand. Obstacles to the success of the quest were: (1) fear of Pilate and the need to gain his agreement; (2) the practice of the Romans to make a spectacle of victims. Mark, in matter-of-fact fashion, reports that Joseph dared to come to Pilate and request the *body* of Jesus, thus overcoming the first obstacle. Pilate had then to be convinced that Jesus was already dead. This was done by calling for evidence from the centurion. This provided, Pilate gave the *corpse* to Joseph. The second obstacle was thus overcome. Yet the burial process remained to be done. The basic requirements were performed. A linen cloth was bought and the body wrapped in it was laid in a tomb hewn out of rock and sealed by a stone at the door. Such rock-hewn tombs with rolling stone doors were common in Jerusalem at this time. While there is no reference to anointing the body for burial, Joseph had undertaken a difficult and expensive task because Jesus seemed to be abandoned by his supporters.

Yet this was not so. Mark notes that two of the women who had watched the crucifixion *from afar* now saw where Jesus was buried. They were Mary Magdalene and the other Mary, now described simply as the one of Joses, which we know means mother of Joses from 15.40. Reference to them here prepares for their role as witnesses to the risen Jesus.

### +Resurrection, 16.1–8

This final scene is portrayed as a failed quest story. The women came *seeking* (see 16.6, 'You *seek* Jesus of Nazareth who was crucified') to anoint the crucified body of Jesus of Nazareth. The obstacle they expected to find (the great stone blocking the door) was not there. Nevertheless, their quest failed. The body was gone. Jesus was not there. The report given to them by the heavenly messenger was, 'He is risen'. The message given to them for the disciples and Peter implies a *correction* to their quest. Not the body but the risen Jesus would be found in Galilee. The quest *could be fulfilled* in an unexpected way. Yet it should not have been unexpected because, the messenger said, 'You will see him there just *as he told you*' (16.7 and see 14.28). Nevertheless, Mark explicitly reports the failure of the quest because the women were afraid and told nobody anything (16.8). Yet the existence of the Gospel *implies* a positive fulfilment beyond failure.

Mark announces the end of the sabbath, the purchase of scented ointment by the three women mentioned in 15.40, two of whom appeared also in 15.47, and their coming to the tomb of Jesus very early in the morning of the first day of the week, to anoint the body of Jesus. 'Very early' indicates before sunrise but Mark also indicates after sunrise. Perhaps he meant that they set out in the dark but arrived after sunrise. Reference to the second Mary is a shortened form of the reference in 15.40. In 15.47 Mark has used one part of the identification of that Mary from 15.40, and here in 16.1 he has used the other. It remains unclear whether this Mary was the mother, wife or daughter of James. What is important is the continuity of these women as witnesses of the crucifixion, burial, empty tomb and the message of the resurrection.

As is common in Mark the journey to the tomb is narrated (16.1–2) before the report of the conversation that took place on the way (16.3). They questioned who would roll away the great stone to enable them to enter the tomb to anoint the body. But on arrival they found the great stone rolled away and entering they found no 'body' but a young man on the right side clothed in a long white robe, understood to be a heavenly messenger (or angel, see 2 Maccabees 3.26, 33). Mark reports that the women were *afraid* (16.5 and see 9.15; 14.33). Picking up the same language the messenger tells the women 'Do not be afraid' (16.6 and compare Jesus' words to his disciples, 6.50). The messenger recognised that they sought the *body* of Jesus the Nazarene (16.6, compare 1.9, 24; 10.47; 14.67). That it was the body is confirmed by the words 'See the place where they laid it'. This conversation is to make dramatically clear that Jesus was not in the tomb but *risen*. The messenger makes the great concluding pronouncement of the resurrection, instructing the women to go and tell the disciples and Peter. Peter is singled out because, not only did he flee with the others, he denied Jesus three times. What the women were to tell them includes, 'He is risen' and 'He goes before [leads] you into Galilee, there *you will see him*, even as he told you' (16.7). In 14.27–28 Jesus had told the disciples that they would be scattered, but after he was risen, 'I will go before you into Galilee'. The messenger makes the connection, indicating that the disciples should have expected this.

But what is the significance of Galilee for the reunion of Jesus with the disciples? Is this a new beginning for them after failure, back where they started with Jesus? Or does Galilee represent the place of mission for Mark, is it Galilee amongst the nations, Galilee as the symbol of Gentile mission? See Isaiah 9.1 and Matthew 4.15. That does not seem to be the way Mark understands Galilee. Rather, geographically the focus on Gentiles was outside Galilee (see 5.1–20; 7.24–8.10). Or was Galilee the location of the original readers of Mark? The suggestion that Galilee signifies a new beginning has much to commend it. Perhaps from this perspective the new beginning signals *mission* and in this way the nations are not lost from view.

Mark indicates that the women went out and fled from the tomb, overtaken by fear and trembling, and said nothing to anyone. This seemed so extraordinary as an ending that others have added to Mark. Scholars are agreed that the textual evidence is clear. All that follows 16.8 has been added by other and later editors and should not be considered a part of Mark. Yet 16.8 was very early thought to be an inappropriate ending. *Once the other Gospels were written*, with their accounts of resurrection appearances, it has seemed to many readers that Mark must also have included such accounts. Given that Mark was written first, it was written without the knowledge of what the later Gospel writers would do. Nevertheless, now that the later additions have been recognised, it has often been suggested that Mark was prevented from finishing his Gospel or that the original ending has been lost. There is no evidence for either of these views except the sense that the present ending is abrupt. There are precedents for such endings as 'For they were afraid' (see R.H. Lightfoot, *The Gospel Message of St Mark*, pp. 80–97), which is a little more abrupt in Greek (ἐφοβοῦντο γάϱ) than in English. More important than grammatical objections is the suggestion that some fulfilment of 'you will see him' is needed. This is what the alternative endings supply, but not as 16.7–8 implies.

Mark's mysterious ending is in keeping with the mystery that runs through the Gospel where, even when Jesus is revealed, he remains a mystery. Part of the mystery is the *reported* silence of the women. That Mark was written at all is evidence of the effective reception of the witness to the risen one *somewhere* in the Markan community. What then is the function of the report of the silence of the women? Does it have anything to say beyond emphasising the *mystery* of the resurrection? The women were to report to the disciples and Peter the implied *instruction*, 'He goes before you into Galilee, there you will see him, even as he told you' (16.7 and see 14.28). This clearly implies that they should go into Galilee. It signals that the restoration of the disciples lies in the future and is dependent on them going to Galilee where Jesus had gone before them. When they follow him they will see him and their discipleship will be renewed. This concluding scene casts a shadow over the Jerusalem church because they were called to go into Galilee. For the reader it sets the realisation of discipleship out in the future as a challenge to be fulfilled.

The Markan account is contrary to the instruction of Jesus according to Acts 1.4, where Jesus ordered the disciples 'not to leave Jerusalem but to wait for the promise of the Father'. The view of the centrality of Jerusalem in the universal mission is heavily dependent on Acts. It is not seriously doubted that the Jerusalem church played a leading role until the Jewish war of 66 CE. Even Paul, who struggled with the leadership of Jerusalem, does not put in question but actually confirms that leading role (see Galatians 1.1–2.14). He did, however, put in question Jerusalem's control of the mission to the nations.

Mark's focus on Galilee challenges the central authority of Jerusalem. In many ways Mark is the Gospel which best represents the Pauline point of view. Its critique of the disciples (the twelve) and the family of Jesus is pointed. This is important when it is remembered that James, the brother of Jesus, and Peter were the two leading figures of the Jerusalem church. Mark also interprets Jesus as having declared all foods clean (7.19), has Jesus himself declare that the sabbath was made for man, not man for the sabbath, that the Son of Man was Lord of the sabbath (2.27–28), in other words, Mark broke down the walls of ritual discrimination that separated Jews from Gentiles. This seems to be one aspect of Mark's interpretation of Jesus' prediction of the destruction of the temple also. It should have been a house of prayer *for all the nations* (Mark 11.17; Isaiah 56.7), and now the curtain in the temple had been torn from top to bottom, opening up access to God (15.38). Thus the ending of Mark reveals another aspect of the worlds in conflict.

Mark challenged the central authority of the Jerusalem church and tradition with an account of the resurrection that commissioned the disciples to return to Galilee. The commission was rooted in an earlier prediction of Jesus, which grew out of the warning of the apostasy *of the disciples* (14.27–28) and Peter's denial (14.30–31). The warnings did not enable the disciples or Peter to avert the predicted failures. When Jesus was arrested they all fled (14.50), and soon after this Peter denied Jesus three times (14.66–72). Now, although Jesus had told them that after he was risen he would go before them into Galilee and the heavenly messenger had sent a reminder via the women, 'He goes before you into Galilee, you will see him there, even as he told you', it is implied that the disciples failed to go to Galilee. This is the force of the final words of the Gospel, 'They said nothing to anyone; for they were afraid'. Mark implies another failure to be prepared by the disciples and Peter even when Jesus had told them in advance. The fact that the women told no one anything about this does leave a loophole or an excuse for the disciples. But they should have known anyway because Jesus had foretold them of this. Nevertheless, the failure of the women, which Mark has carefully reported, does soften the account of the failure of the disciples to go into Galilee.

Another outcome concerns the women who had emerged in a strongly positive light from 15.40 on. Now their fear and silence rather pulls them back to the level of the rest. At least they did not flee, did not deny Jesus and were present at his crucifixion and burial as well as attending the tomb at the earliest reasonable opportunity. Although this presents them in a comparatively strong light, they ultimately share the failure with the disciples, the failure to return to Galilee with the consequences for the Jesus mission flowing from its centralisation in Jerusalem.

Chapter 7

# Addenda: endings

## SHORTER

The shorter ending was not added before the fourth century. Most manuscripts that adopt this go on with the longer ending as well. Even the shorter ending was not enough. The shorter ending indicates that the women 'told everything they were commanded to those around Peter and that afterwards Jesus himself sent out through them, from east to west, the *sacred* and *imperishable proclamation* of eternal salvation'. Not only is this short piece full of non-Markan language; it overlooks the fact that 16.8 says the women told no one anything, and it says nothing about the disciples obeying the command to go to Galilee. It is evidence that some scribe could not be content with the mystery of the silence of the women. But his solution satisfied no one so that it had to be combined with the longer ending.

## LONGER

While the longer ending (Mark 16.9–20) is clearly secondary, being absent from major early manuscripts, appearing after the shorter ending in others, it is earlier than the shorter ending, being known to Tatian (*c.*140 CE) and Irenaeus (180 CE). The high concentration of non-Markan language confirms the manuscript evidence that this ending is also non-Markan. No more than the shorter ending does the longer tie up the loose ends of 16.1–8. Rather, it is a summary of a number of traditions known to us mainly in the Gospels of Matthew, John and Luke as well as Acts. Whoever compiled this ending does not display Mark's dramatic skills.

The ending presents a series of three appearances, the *first* to Mary Magdalene, already mentioned in 16.1. It identifies her as the one from whom Jesus had driven seven demons, which is mentioned in Luke 8.2, but not by Mark. John 20.11–18 deals with an appearance to Mary Magdalene and Luke 24.11 tells of the failure to believe her report from the empty tomb. Thus this summary might be a compilation from Luke and John.

In the second appearance scene Jesus appeared in another form to two disciples while they were walking. This aspect of the Markan ending is a brief summary of Luke 24.13–35. There is a difference. In the Markan ending the other disciples would not believe the two, whereas in Luke the two find that in their absence the Lord had appeared to Simon. Hence there is no hint of unbelief in response to their story.

As in Luke (24.36–49), an appearance to the whole group of disciples follows (Mark 16.14–20). Thus Luke 24 provides the plan of three appearances, to Mary Magdalene, the two, and the group of the disciples, specifically numbered as eleven in Mark (16.14). The commission of 16.15–16 owes most to Matthew 28.19, but there is also the influence of Acts 1.8. The indication that those sent by Jesus would cast out demons and heal the sick is consistent with Jesus' mission charge to the twelve (6.7, 13) but reference to speaking in strange tongues is dependent on Acts (2.4), as is the idea that they would be immune to the poison of snakes (Acts 28.3–6) and the idea of the ascension to the right hand of God and the confirmation of their mission by signs and wonders.

## CONCLUDING REMARKS

Neither the shorter nor the longer ending does anything to illuminate Mark. The modern reader will not be misled by the call (16.7) to follow Jesus who has gone before. Discipleship is following in the way of Jesus so that, for Mark, it is inevitable that the disciple will need to learn the way of the cross. The way of the cross involved Jesus in a conflict with the world dominated by the powers of evil, and the disciple who follows in the way in which Jesus has gone before will also find himself or herself immersed in conflict. One of the surprises of Mark is to discover that the women followers of Jesus, of whom only a few escape anonymity, fare much better than the men, including the twelve. But the challenge remains unfulfilled for all. Jesus goes before (16.7), and the disciple must follow after him if there is to be the opportunity to see him. Mark has so often turned out to be a chronicle of failed opportunity, largely because the followers of Jesus have continued to share the values of the world (9.33–38; 10.35–45) even though Jesus had told them 'It shall not be like this amongst you'. Worlds in conflict involve a clash of values. But it turns out that it is not a clash confined to Jesus and the kingdom of God on the one side, and the prince of this world and the world on the other. It is also a clash of values between Jesus and those who should follow where he leads. Mark reveals severe reservations about the values of the mission that remained centred on Jerusalem. There, it seemed to Mark, many of the values with which Jesus himself struggled, re-emerged amongst his followers. Mark stands on the side of the law-free mission to the nations (the uncircumcision mission), which was in conflict with a mission based on sabbath observance, purity and food law observance and is encapsulated in the slogan 'the circumcision mission'. In this Mark stands on the side of the Pauline understanding of the Gospel, while Matthew represents a mission based on law observance, which was the expression of the Jerusalem church best represented by James the brother of Jesus and Peter (see Galatians 2.1–14).

# Bibliography

Achtemeier, P.J., 'Person and Deed. Jesus and the Storm-Tossed Sea', *Interpretation* 16 (1962), 169–76.
—— 'Towards the Isolation of Pre-Markan Miracle Catanae', *JBL* 89 (1970), 265–91.
—— 'The Origin and Function of the Pre-Markan Miracle Catanae', *JBL* 91 (1972), 198–221.
—— '"And He followed Him": Miracles and Discipleship in Mark 10.46–52', *Semeia* 11 (1978), 115–45.
—— 'Mark as an Interpreter of the Jesus Tradition', in J.L. Mays (ed.), *Interpreting the Gospels*, Philadelphia: Fortress Press, 1981, 115–29.
—— *Mark*, Proclamation Commentaries, Philadelphia: Fortress Press, 1975; 2nd edn 1986.
—— 'Mark, Gospel of', *ABD* 4 (1992), 541–57.
Anderson, J.C. and Moore, S.D. (eds), *Mark & Method: New Approaches in Biblical Studies*, Minneapolis: Fortress, 1992.
Aune, D.E., *The New Testament in its Literary Environment*, Philadelphia: Westminster Press, 1987.
Barton, S., *Discipleship and Family Ties in Mark and Matthew*, SNTSMS 80, Cambridge: Cambridge University Press, 1994.
Bauer, Walter, *A Greek-English Lexicon of the New Testament and Other Early Christian Literature*, 2nd edn revised and augmented by W.F. Arndt, F.W. Gingrich, F.W. Danker, Chicago and London: Chicago University Press, 1979.
Beasley-Murray, G.R., *Jesus and the Kingdom of God*, Grand Rapids, MI: Eerdmans/Paternoster, 1986.
Best, Ernest, *Disciples and Discipleship: Studies in the Gospel according to Mark*, Edinburgh: T & T Clark, 1986.
—— *Following Jesus: Discipleship in the Gospel of Mark*, JSNTMS 4, Sheffield: JSOT, 1981.
—— *Mark The Gospel as Story*, Edinburgh: T & T Clark, 1983.
—— 'The Role of the Disciples in Mark', *NTS* 23 (1977), 377–401.
—— 'The Use of the Twelve', *ZNW* 69 (1978), 11–35.
Black, C. Clifton, *Mark: Images of an Apostolic Interpreter*, Columbia: University of South Carolina Press, 1994.

Black, C. Clifton, *The Disciples according to Mark: Markan Redaction in Current Debate*, Sheffield: JSOT Press, 1989.
Borg, Marcus J., *Jesus in Contemporary Scholarship*, Valley Forge: Trinity Press International, 1994.
Bultmann, R., *The History of the Synoptic Tradition*, translated by John Marsh, New York: Harper and Row, 1963.
Bultmann, R. and Kundsin, K., *Form Criticism: Two Essays on New Testament Research*, translated by F.C. Grant, New York: Harper and Bros, 1962.
Burridge, Richard A., *Four Gospels, One Jesus?* , Melbourne: Collins Dove, 1994.
—— *What are the Gospels? A Comparison of Graeco-Roman Biography*, Cambridge: SNTSMS 70, Cambridge University Press, 1992.
Collins, A.Y., *The Beginning of the Gospel: Probings of Mark in Context*, Minneapolis: Fortress, 1992.
Cook, M.J., *Mark's Treatment of the Jewish Leaders*, SNovT 51, Leiden: Brill, 1978.
Cranfield, C.E.B., *The Gospel According to Saint Mark*, Cambridge: Cambridge University Press, 1959.
Crossan, J.D., 'Mark and the Relatives of Jesus', *NovT* 15 (1973), 81–113.
Daube, D., *The New Testament and Rabbinic Judaism*, London: The Athlone Press, 1956.
Dewey, J., *Markan Public Debate: Literary Technique, Concentric Structure, and Theology in Mark 2.1–3.6*, SBLDS 48, Chico, CA: Scholars Press, 1980.
Donahue, J.R., 'A Neglected Factor in the Theology of Mark', *JBL* 101 (1982), 563–94.
Eusebius, *The Ecclesiastical History*, 2 vols, Translated by Kirsopp Lake, J.E.L. Oulton, H.J. Lawlor, Loeb Classical Library, Cambridge, MA and London: Harvard University Press/William Heinemann, 1926, 1932. Also translated as *The History of the Church* by G. A. Williamson, Harmondsworth: Penguin, 1965, 1989.
Fowler, R.M., *Let the Reader Understand: Reader–Response Criticism and the Gospel of Mark*, Minneapolis: Fortress, 1991.
Furnish, Victor Paul, *Jesus according to Paul*, Cambridge: Cambridge University Press, 1993.
Gundry, R.A., *Mark 1–8:26*, WBC 34a, Dallas, Texas: Word Books, 1989.
Haenchen, E., *Der Weg Jesu. Eine Erklärung des Markus-Evangeliums und der kanonischen Parappepin*, Berlin: A. Topelman, 1966.
Hengel, M., *Studies in the Gospel of Mark*, London: SCM, 1985.
Holladay, C. H., *Theios Aner in Hellenistic Judaism: A Critique of the Use of this Category in New Testament Christology*, SBLDS 40, Missoula, MT: Scholars Press, 1972.
Hooker, M.D, *The Message of Mark*, London: Epworth, 1983.
—— *The Gospel according to Saint Mark*, London: A & C Black, 1991.
Hultgren, A.J., *Jesus and his Adversaries. The Form and Function of the Conflict Stories in the Synoptic Tradition*, Minneapolis: Augsburg, 1979.
Josephus, *Works*, 9 vols, translated by H. St J. Thackeray, R. Marcus, A. Wikgren, Loeb Classical Library, London: William Heinemann, 1927–65.

Juel, D.H., *Messiah and Temple. The Trial of Jesus in the Gospel of Mark*, SBLDS, Missoula, MT: Scholars Press, 1977.
— *A Master of Surprise: Mark Interpreted*, Minneapolis: Fortress, 1994.
Kee, H.C., *The Community of the New Age. Studies in Mark's Gospel*, London: SCM, 1977.
Kelber, W., *Mark's Story of Jesus*, Philadelphia: Fortress Press, 1979.
Kingsbury, J.D., *The Christology of Mark's Gospel*, Philadelphia: Fortress Press, 1983.
— *Conflict in Mark: Jesus, Authorities, Disciples*, Minneapolis: Fortress, 1989.
Lightfoot, R.H., *The Gospel Message of St Mark*, Oxford: Oxford University Press, 1980.
McCowen, Alec, *Personal Mark: An Actor's Proclamation of St Mark's Gospel*, New York: Crossroad, 1985.
Malbon, E.S., 'Disciples/Crowds/Whoever: Markan Characters and Readers', *NovT* 28 (1986), 104–30.
— 'Fallible Follower: Women and Men in the Gospel of Mark', *Semeia* 28 (1983), 29–49.
Marcus, J., *The Mystery of the Kingdom of God*, SBLDS 90, Atlanta: Scholars, 1986.
Marshall, Christopher D., *Faith as a Theme in Mark's Narrative*, Cambridge: Cambridge University Press, 1989.
Marxsen, W., *Mark the Evangelist: Studies on the Redaction History of the Gospel*, translated by James Boyce *et al.*, Nashville: Abingdon, 1979.
Matera, F.J., *The Kingship of Jesus: Composition and Theology in Mark 15*, SBLDS 66, Chico, CA: Scholars Press, 1988.
Morgenthaler, R., *Statistik des Neutestamentlichen Wortschatzes*, Zürich: Gotthelf, 1958.
Neusner, J., *The Idea of Purity in Ancient Judaism*, Leiden: Brill, 1973.
Nineham, D.E., *The Gospel of St. Mark*, Pelican New Testament Commentaries, London: Pelican, 1963.
Perrin, N., *What is Redaction Criticism?* , Guides to Biblical Scholarship, New Testament Series, Philadelphia: Fortress Press, 1976.
— *The New Testament: An Introduction*, New York: Harcourt Brace Jovanovich, 2nd edn, 1982.
Rhoads, D. and Michie, D., *Mark as Story: An Introduction to the Narrative of a Gospel*, Philadelphia: Fortress Press, 1982.
Robbins, V.K., *Jesus the Teacher: A Socio-Rhetorical Interpretation of Mark*, Philadelphia: Fortress Press, 1984.
Schürer, E., *The History of the Jewish People in the Age of Jesus Christ*, Volume 2, revised and edited by G. Vermes, F. Millar and M. Black, Edinburgh: T&T Clark, 1979.
Schweizer, E., *The Good News According to Mark*, translated by D.H. Madvig, Richmond, VA: John Knox, 1970.
Stock, A., *Call to Discipleship: A Literary Study of Mark's Gospel*, Good News Studies 1, Wilmington, DE: Michael Glazier, 1982.
Streeter, B.H., *The Four Gospels: A Study of Origins*, New York: Macmillan, 1925.
Stuhlmacher, Peter (ed.), *The Gospel and the Gospels*, Michigan: Eerdmans, 1991.

Talbert, C.H., *What is a Gospel? The Genre of the Canonical Gospels*, Philadelphia: Fortress Press, 1977.
Taylor, Vincent, *The Formation of the Gospel Tradition*, New York: Macmillan, 1933.
—— *The Gospel According to St Mark*, London: Macmillan, 1957.
Telford, W.R. (ed.), *The Interpretation of Mark*, Issues in Religion and Theology 7, Philadelphia and London: Fortress Press/SPCK, 1985.
*The Mishnah*, translated with introduction and notes by Herbert Danby, Oxford: Oxford University Press, 1933.
Theissen, G., *The Miracle Stories of the Early Christian Tradition*, translated by F. McDonagh, Edited by John Riches, Philadelphia: Fortress Press, 1983.
Tiede, D. L., *The Charismatic Figure as Miracle Worker*, Missoula, MT: Scholars Press, 1972.
Tolbert, M.A., *Sowing the Gospel: Mark's World in Literary-Historical Perspective*, Minneapolis: Fortress, 1989.
Tuckett, C. (ed.), *The Messianic Secret*, Issues in Religion and Theology 1, Philadelphia and London: Fortress Press/SPCK, 1983.
Via, D.O., Jr., *The Ethics of Mark's Gospel – The Middle of Time*, Philadelphia: Fortress Press, 1985.
Votaw, C.W., *The Gospels and Contemporary Biographies in the Greco-Roman World*, Facet Books, Biblical Series, Philadelphia: Fortress Press, 1970.
Weeden, T.J., *Mark – Traditions in Conflict*, Philadelphia: Fortress Press, 1971.
Wink, Walter, *Naming the Powers: The Language of Power in the New Testament* (volume 1 of *The Powers*), Philadelphia: Fortress Press, 1984.
Wrede, W., *The Messianic Secret*, translated by J.C.G. Greig, Greenwood, SC: Attic, 1971.
Wuellner, W., *The Meaning of 'Fishers of Men'*, New Testament Library, Philadelphia: Westminster, 1967.

# Biblical index

## 1. Hebrew scriptures

## 2. Deuterocanonical works



## 3. Pseudepigrapha 171



## 4. New Testament

# Ancient authors

## Early Jewish sources



## Rabbinic sources



## Early Christian sources

# General index